TRANSFORMING TRAINING

A Guide to Creating a Flexible Learning Environment: The Rise of the Learning Architects

David Mackey
Siân Livsey

KOGAN PAGE

London and Philadelphia

First published in Great Britain and the United States in 2006 by Kogan Page Limited

120 Pentonville Road   525 South 4th St, #241
London N1 9JN   Philadelphia PA 19147
United Kingdom   USA
www.kogan-page.co.uk

© David Mackey and Siân Livsey, 2006

The right of David Mackey and Siân Livsey to be identified as the authors of this work has been asserted by them in accordance with the Copyright, Designs and Patents Act 1988.

ISBN 0 7494 4171 2

British Library Cataloguing-in-Publication Data

A CIP record for this book is available from the British Library.

Library of Congress Cataloging-in-Publication Data

Mackey, David.
    Transforming training : a guide to creating a flexible learning environment : the rise of the learning architects / David Mackey, Siân Livsey.
        p. cm.
    ISBN 0-7494-4171-2
    1. Employees--Training of. 2. Organizational learning. I. Livsey, Siân. II. Title.
    HF5549.5.T7M223 2006
    658.3'124--dc22
                                                                    2005031003

Typeset by Digital Publishing Solutions
Printed and bound in the United States by Thomson-Shore, Inc

Contents

Acknowledgements

The researching and writing of this book has allowed me to experience the generosity of many learning architects. People have given their valuable time to share experiences of what the world of learning has meant for them and in doing so they have contributed to my learning, a gift I am grateful for to the following: David Kinson, Simon Hazeldine, Nickie Gibbs, Sue Roberts, Alison Wibberley, Sarah McDermott, Caroline Mather, Ian Bennett, Jayne Dickenson, Brian Snowdon, Julie Steele and Darrel Biss. I wish to acknowledge the tutors, trainers and mentors who have enabled me to develop my skills and qualities as a learning architect. Special thanks go to Steve, my family and friends, for their continual support, friendship and inspiration.

Siân

This has been an exciting project, mostly made so by the many people who have been prepared to share their experiences and their views on learning and on the development of people in today's often challenging world. Particularly I would like to mention Rob McWilliam, Margaret Burnside, Chris Dunn, John Kilvington, Dermott Bradley, Matthew Guy, Brenda Myrans, Steve Burnett and Nick Alcock together with two people who provided early stimulus for this project, Sue Newton and Mark Woodhouse. The most special of thanks go to my wife, Sally, whose own studies continue to inspire my efforts.

David

Introduction

We are aware that readers have different outcomes for wanting to read an introduction to a book. It may be that you are the type of reader who starts at the beginning of a book and works his or her way methodically through until the end. You may have flicked through some of the chapters, and are now at the front of the book trying to make some sense of what you have scanned. It may be that you have a specific topic that you are searching for, and are hoping that the introduction will indicate the book's layout in a little more depth than the contents. You, like us, are attracted to books that will provide you with a valuable resource, a book that will stimulate thought and provide some comfort for the role you have in learning.

Whatever your reason for reading this we hope that the introduction and the rest of the book will provide you with the outcome you want.

WHY WE HAVE WRITTEN THE BOOK

You may well be familiar with organizations striving to continuously improve and become more competitive through a variety of structured approaches to learning. Identifying those approaches that will work within the modern, changing organization is at the heart of a debate travelling far and wide. We hope this book is a significant contribution to the debate, since we are deeply involved in that debate in our everyday work, and in particular we became more involved in it as we assembled this book. We have debated with an extensive range of colleagues, business partners and friends. There is raging agreement that the need to harness learning has never been so important and raging disagreement about the best approaches for success.

We have mused over our personal histories in the world of learning, training and people development. Can everything be really changing as quickly as it seems? Where did it all start, this journey to excellence in learning? For how long have people in organized societies been seeking to improve capabilities that will provide success in life? Were the first recognizable results of training the highly drilled Roman legionnaires? Or way before that, just how did the Egyptians learn how to organize a work force for such enormous projects? Is the most realistic reference point for us an acceptance that useful training and learning only began with the intense automation of the factories of the early 20th century? Whatever the true overall timescales, we need to recognize that little of that history has prepared us to succeed in a world where the fundamental role of learning is growing at an unprecedented rate. We recognize that little of our personal experience has prepared us for the current rate of change impacting organizations and impacting the management of organizational and personal learning. We strongly suspect that is true for almost all readers. Our belief is that in today's world of learning few organizations have yet found all of the best ways to do things, and much of the fine detail remains to be agreed.

In the preparation of this book, we have talked to people who have embarked on remarkable, innovative journeys to organizational and individual learning. Other journeys have already proven expensive and less than successful. There remain many opportunities for new travellers to embark in totally inappropriate directions. We humbly offer guidance as to geography and orienteering. This book shares with you ideas of best practice for your personal journeys to individual and organizational learning. In addition, this book sets out to assist you to recognize and prepare for the likely hurdles on those journeys. No two journeys to learning excellence are the same. Issues, concerns and frustrations differ between chosen journeys, though we hear a common theme. 'Because of my experience, because I've read the literature, because I've been to the conferences, I know what I need to do and why, but I am really struggling with how to do it and to make it all work.' This book is about how. Depending on the nature of your journey, the ideas we share with you may be revolution or evolution. If you have made a journey beyond the one we describe, we genuinely look forward to hearing about it. We know we have so much more to learn.

We searched for a title for all these people responsible in different ways for designing, building, implementing, evaluating and maintaining learning in changing organizations: people bringing learning to organizations, to teams, to individuals, both in traditional training and development functions and those elsewhere. We have chosen the term _learning architects_. We were taken by an image of people building structures for learning and then seeing their ideas grow and flourish, to be 'inhabited' by people absorbing benefit. Architecture is about providing solutions robust enough to handle the forces of change, solutions that are regarded as strong and resilient by those individuals who will benefit. The challenge for many learning architects is the provision of an organization-wide architecture for learning, an architecture capable of supporting proactive, focused learning solutions in today's environment of change.

As we have developed our ideas they have been shared and developed with a number of people occupying a range of roles in large, corporate organizations, and with people working in smaller organizations, as well as with individuals working alone. These people, for all their different designated roles, have an important shared interest – to provide effective learning for a range of people. In their different ways they all fully qualify for the title of learning architect.

WHAT THE BOOK IS ABOUT

This book is written mindful of our peers in training and development, corporate universities, learning functions, human resources (HR) and organization development (OD) – particularly those charged with an ever-growing list of new responsibilities. You may have a very modern title in a function with itself a modern title.

Your current focus may well be in one or more challenging directions. Your task may be to develop organizational learning, a learning organization or to align with a new knowledge management function. Your focus may be on the realignment of your function in a 'value-adding' business partnership with your parent organization while selecting appropriate learning interventions from an ever-increasing list of possibilities. You may well be faced with operational challenges connected with new governmental legislation, reskilling the learning function team, creating a new vision for the function and all these in organizations existing in states of constant, churning flux. As a networking colleague observed, 'We've become, as a company, pretty good at handling massive, continuous amounts of change. But it's proving difficult for anything to stay still long enough for us to provide training on it, or even, sometimes, deciding exactly what "it" is!'

We are very conscious that a growing number of our colleagues managing learning functions are facing highly significant change as they have become almost the only permanent resource assigned to learning and development. Departmental sizes have been reduced, and this might well be combined with a transfer of learning budgets from a central fund to the line. You may sit, splendidly alone, in a learning function or you may be the 'learning specialist' in an HR function. Being the sole learning professional in an organization requires new operational models and, indeed, a learning architect approach.

> I have 180 people reporting to me, 120 making highly sophisticated electronic components and the others interfacing into the remainder of the corporation. Now I'm told that the company is to stop having a central training department and I am to 'take responsibility for the development of my people', whatever that means! At least I have a training budget, so I have talked one of my brightest managers into making sure we get the right training with best use of that budget. She doesn't yet know a great deal about training, but I'm sure she'll make it happen.

We have also written our book for those many people charged with providing the benefits of effective learning interventions even though personally they are less familiar with the world of HR, training, learning, personal development or organizational development. Many of those who today manage, implement and motivate learning are not the familiar faces of old. As the number and size of traditional central learning functions reduce, there is a clear growth in the numbers of both internal and external people charged with the provision of organizational learning. Typically, these new people include functional trainers in line departments, training consultants, coaches and mentors, as well as line managers charged with the direct development of their teams and team members.

I know that I have always unofficially coached people in the organizations I have worked for. To have the role of workplace coach formalized is a real step forward for both the company and for me, an opportunity to make change happen in a way that will really work. I know that I have been able to coach managers through significant change projects by helping them to understand where their personal beliefs are helping and hindering them. Now, my real challenge is to ensure that coaching is used throughout the organization, and I have to start with the board.

Should you be somebody seeking to harness the benefits of learning in today's fast-moving world, this book has been written for you. You may be bringing the benefits of learning to whole organizations, or to individuals, including yourself. In every case there will be significant, practical assistance in this book for you.

KEY AREAS OF INSPIRATION

In compiling the practical book that we were seeking, we looked for expertise and experience from outside the traditional areas of training and learning. Who else has experienced, or is experiencing, the impact of change, particularly in what are traditionally regarded as service functions?

We examined the manner in which information systems (IS) functions have handled years of pressure as a service function, often maligned while struggling to explain their vision and prove their worth. They, like us, are faced with the challenges of partnering and proactively leading the organization into new directions and new opportunities. IS functions have often been perceived to fail in the provision of an appropriate service to the organization, while being recognized as a service without which an organization cannot survive! Often their professionals have struggled to form relationships with business leaders and struggled to find common language. They indeed have many things in common with a learning function, particularly the need to be highly responsive while keeping within the bounds of agreed costs and return of investment.

We learned from those IS functions that were perceived as being successful business partners to organizations, helping to provide the organization with a competitive business advantage. Not surprisingly, there was a lot in common with the operational approaches of learning functions perceived as successful within their organizations. A concept that has obviously been vital to the success of many IS functions is the implementation of IS architectures that support the organization's needs; frameworks from which can be consistently 'hung' the information systems deliverables for the organization. These architectures are sufficiently robust to support integration and reintegration of information systems involving complex mixtures of networks, computer hardware and programs. These system architectures, able to cope with constant change, ensure the function is regarded as responsive to the continually flexing organizational needs.

IS functions were also an interesting area to examine the potential of outsourcing, a familiar part of life over many years in the realms of IS. Many organizations, large and small, have outsourced much, if not all of their IS work. This has often included the switching of the ownership of staff to the outsourcing organization. Success has been at the best patchy. The experience has resulted in a steep and sometimes painful learning curve for IS functions, which can provide interesting insights for learning functions seeking new commercial models.

We also took notice of the considerable work that is being conducted in the fields of client relationships, client account management and customer focus across many types of organization. We have considered how, through recognition of the organization and the learner as customers of the 'learning architect', it is possible to apply well-proven customer-focused initiatives in working with learners, at both an organizational and an individual level.

We have very deliberately considered a selection of these successful approaches in other worlds in building mechanisms for success in our world of learning. There are many parallel needs and a range of parallel solutions. In our world challenges include making the appropriate selection of exciting new learning technologies and the need to bring business-focused learning effectively and efficiently to our workforce. We may be charged with having the front line empowered and equipped to deliver first-rate customer care, with their capabilities centred on learning associated with an organization-wide customer care initiative. Learning has to be available in different learning delivery formats and in a variety of languages across the organization. And the learning deliverables change rapidly as the organization works with and learns from its customers and consumers. We need control and flexibility, consistency and an ability to change rapidly. Just like our colleagues in IS we need an architecture. And we need account management processes to manage the expectations of our learning clients.

OUTLINE OF CHAPTERS

The first section of the book, up to Chapter 5, concentrates on the processes of creating a learning environment from the view of both the organization and the people in the learning function. The second section looks at the skills and qualities required by learning architects.

Chapter 1 explores the role of learning in modern organizations, particularly in relation to change and organizations that require instant solutions. Organizations and individuals have to reappraise what learning is all about. The learning architect is the key person to build the architecture for the organization of today. This chapter describes the four types of learning architect that we have identified. We urge you to read Chapter 1 in order to find the type of learning architect that best fits with your role.

Chapters 2 and 3 have high relevance for the corporate learning architect but will provide essential information for the other three types too. Chapter 2 introduces the concept of the continuum that a learning architect, working in an organization with a learning function, seeks to move along. It focuses on the 'establishing' phase, and provides guidance on establishing learning strategies, plans and policies: activities that are more suited to an organization that has some degree of stability, or where the learning function has time and resources.

Chapter 3 continues with the journey of learning excellence through the remaining stages of the continuum: 'positioning' and 'guiding'. It provides relevant sources of inspiration and practical guidance for those learning architects who are seeking to move the learning function from reactive to proactive, or are providing learning in an organization where the speed of change or lack of resources requires learning to be done in a very different way.

Chapter 4 recognizes the role of the learning architects who do not have a learning function to manage. The role of tactical, functional and individual learning architect will resonate with many of you. This chapter provides valuable signposts for you to recognize, position, develop and enhance the vital role you have in building a learning architecture in a less than traditional way.

Chapter 5 has significance for all learning architects, as we identify and provide suggestions for some of the tools and techniques available to the learning architect working in a modern way: designing and building the learning architecture, evaluation, commercial models and branding.

Chapters 6 and 7 indicate a shift from the broader scope of learning in the organization to the role of the learning architect as an individual. We are aware that learning architects of all types need skills and qualities that will enable them to create the learning architecture.

In Chapter 6 we highlight some of the key skills that successful learning architects are using, and provide some examples and case studies of coaching, facilitating, influencing, mentoring, negotiating, marketing and project managing. Chapter 7 seeks to capture the unique qualities that learning architects are displaying in their roles: qualities such as creating a network, knowing what you want, remaining motivated and building rapport. We provide some top tips and actions that you can take to develop those qualities for yourself.

Chapter 8 is a useful resource for all learning architects who seek to discuss or confirm the various methods of delivering learning in an organization. We highlight methods that provide a more reactive training approach and those that move the activity towards proactive learning. Advice is offered about selecting and managing the provider of learning.

Chapter 9 is a collection of topics that we found were most frequently being discussed by learning architects. We highlight those frequently asked questions by providing a summary of current thinking and a signpost for those who may seek reassurance from knowing what other people are interested in. We are sure that some of you will have a topic that you believe should be in this chapter. If so, share it with us and other learning architects.

STIMULATE LEARNING

We have worked to write this book in the style we advocate for our learning architects, one of consultancy. It provides not so much definitive answers as a methodology, a toolbox of processes to identify and manage your own 'journey to learning excellence'.

We trust we have built an essentially practical book based on practical experience and research. We cannot provide every answer for your own organization. Only you can do that, and we are sure that is exactly how you wish things to be. What we have done is to allow you to identify your particular starting point, evaluate the possibilities and then make your own choices as to direction. Once you have made your choices we have provided further mechanisms to move you to success, evaluating and checking as you move.

There will be sections of this book with which some readers are familiar. We know that some learning architects have made tremendous strides in implementing the learning strategies and concepts we discuss in the book. Seasoned training and development professionals may well be familiar with parts of the earlier chapters, and for those readers the book is designed primarily as a 'dip in'. We hope that the book will provide some ideas for the next steps on your vital journey. For people new to many of the principles of organizational learning, we suggest that you read it as a developing story from front to back.

Throughout the book reference is made to four types of learning architect. A full description of each type is given in Chapter 1. While we believe that all chapters in the book will be of interest, specific chapters will have particular interest for each type of learning architect.

Learning architect type one

The corporate learning architect. Responsible for learning within an organization. Senior position managing a team of learning professionals.

Learning architect type two

The tactical learning architect. Responsible for learning within an organization. Senior position with a learning and development background and no directly reporting team.

Learning architect type three

The functional learning architect. Responsible for learning in one area of an organization. Probably with no learning and development background.

Learning architect type four

The individual learning architect. Mainly responsible for learning for individuals.

Chapter	Title	Level of interest for:			
		L A Type 1	L A Type 2	L A Type 3	L A Type 4
1	Organizations, learning and change	H	H	H	H
2	Establishing the learning function	H	U	U	G
3	A journey to learning excellence	H	U	U	G
4	Managing learning without a team	U	H	H	H
5	The business of learning	H	H	H	U
6	Skills of a learning architect	H	H	H	H
7	Qualities of a learning architect	H	H	H	H
8	Delivering learning	U	H	H	U
9	Current learning issues	G	G	G	G

Key: H = high interest, U = useful ideas, G = general interest

Figure 0.1   Using the book

Part I

Creating a learning environment

1

Organizations, learning and change

The purpose of this chapter is to introduce themes that are explored throughout this book:

▌ the transforming aspects of learning, particularly in support of rapidly changing organizations working in a rapidly changing world;
▌ the developing role of the learning architect; moving from being the reactive 'head of learning delivery' to a proactive, organizational performance-focused position;
▌ the manner in which a learning architect is to work: his or her personal development, use of teams and interaction with the organization.

INTRODUCTION: THE TRANSFORMATION OF LEARNING

Change and a need for learning

This book is about a transition in the provision of learning, particularly in times of significant change. It is about journeys and roadmaps to better places – better in terms of being more useful, more rewarding and more engaging. It is about employing learning as a critical weapon in the fight for an organization's success. It is about strategies, tactics and people. It is particularly about special individuals who make things happen and the tools and techniques they employ. These special people are our learning architects, handling a proactive, organizational performance-focused role to deliver the benefits of learning to today's organizations and today's individuals. Figure 1.1 illustrates the topics that are introduced in this chapter and discussed throughout the book.

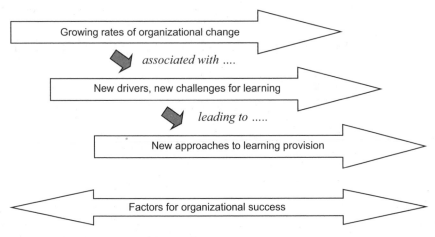

Figure 1.1 Change and learning

An irresistible growth of change flows throughout the world of business, government and commerce. There is impact on organizations and their people from change generated externally, as well as by change generated within the organization as it pursues its performance objectives. The need for capabilities to both handle the impact of change and take advantage of the capabilities of change underpin an ever-growing need for learning for individuals, teams and organizations.

Organizations implement learning initiatives for their staff and for other stakeholders in many different ways. Those same organizations use many different titles for the functions that provide learning, as well as for the people who work for and with these functions. We wrote this book for everybody and every function involved with learning. The book's real benefit lies with those who are seeking proactively to transform the contribution of learning in organizations with which they are connected.

In researching this book we have met many fellow travellers on exciting journeys designed around those concepts of meaningful learning that we hold dear and which form the heart of this book. We have often learnt from these fellow travellers; many have learnt from us. We built much of the basis for this book on the wisdom that resulted from these meetings.

A journey to learning excellence

Transformation is about journeys. This book is about transforming the processes in providing learning as well as the people involved. It is about a 'journey to learning excellence'. In order to navigate the journey, to generate new ideas and new approaches to the successful implementation of learning, we needed to be sure of our starting point. As the book developed we continually examined a series of fundamental questions about the role of learning and its positioning as an organizational investment. What will prompt organizations to allocate hard-won revenues and precious resources to the development of their people and to educating the whole organization and its stakeholders, often in tight economic times when any discretionary spend will be seriously examined? Do such organizations take comfort from results of the vast amounts previously invested in learning? What guarantees are there for success with current and future initiatives? We wanted to investigate these questions before we started to describe our journey to somewhere better. We questioned and we debated long and hard with others who are planning journeys to excellence in learning. 'Money', 'resource', commitment', 'a coaching culture', 'readiness to learn' and a host more were among the more obvious items that were constantly included in the discussions. We are certain we have only some of the answers to our questions.

What our questioning did was to increase our certainty that there is one key factor for success in the provision of learning in today's rapidly changing, time and results-focused world. Our critical success factor is the availability of a dedicated learning architect working in a style that is appropriate for a particular organization and its particular challenges and opportunities. This critical success factor, this learning architect, is the person who will lead the transformation of learning. This book is about these people: these learning architects.

FACTORS FOR ORGANIZATIONAL SUCCESS

Building appropriate knowledge and nurturing the wisdom to utilize that knowledge are among the fundamental building blocks of organizational success. The learning architect and the learning function are owners of the processes that discharge these responsibilities. However, learning excellence alone is obviously not enough. Our experience in business, and in particular in the provision of learning initiatives, has resulted in a model in which we consider learning as one of six keystones for organizational success. In any organization, learning entwines with leadership, an ability to handle and to use change, cultural awareness and an unrelenting eye on fulfilment through a client focus – making things happen. Altogether these are the six overlapping, interacting essentials for readiness in organizational survival and success as an organization 'goes to market' – irrespective of the nature of the enterprise.

Learning is the effective and efficient acquisition and skilled use of knowledge by the organization and its stakeholders – internally and externally. The challenges this book addresses are effectiveness and efficiency – providing the correct knowledge for the correct people at the correct place, and having them skilfully apply the knowledge in an appropriate timeframe.

Leadership is the skilful use of knowledge in motivating, levelling with and developing individuals and teams; the use of wisdom centred on knowledge of how individuals function, and of organizations, competition and marketplaces. A senior team, particularly, has to show leadership – shaping the objectives, strategies and processes for the organization's success. As one of these senior people a learning architect provides the opportunities of learning in support of the attainment of the organization's success, however that success is defined: heightened cost control, differentiation in marketplaces, flexibility to react to client and stakeholder demands and so on.

Fulfilment concerns having the correct processes, premises, promotions, products and services, and bringing them to focus on the organization's market in an efficient manner. It is also about fulfilment of the people resource for organizational success: recruitment, compensation, development and promotion.

Change needs to be understood and absorbed by organizations and by individuals, particularly in terms of how resistance to change is handled. Organizations and individuals need to be able to proactively apply the power of change in influencing markets, clients, buyers and all other stakeholders.

Cultural awareness is about knowing how the organization and all its stakeholders exist together and work towards success. It includes, for example, knowledge of the market and the competition in a commercial world, and an understanding of politics, with both large and small 'p's, in the public sector.

Client focus is about the client-centric behaviours of the organization and its people, which respond to the importance of a client's culture in providing the highest levels of service.

Each of these six elements – learning, leadership, fulfilment, change, cultural awareness and client focus – has reactive and proactive aspects. They are reactive in terms of being necessities in handling situations that occur in the quest for survival, and proactive in terms of availability for use as weapons for gaining momentum and performance success.

This book concentrates on learning, and particularly its interaction with change associated with an organization. However, it is impossible to forget the scope and contents of the other components, each interleaving with learning. Learning can only play its own key role in organizational survival and success when the other components are fully playing theirs. Without the presence of the other five components, learning will be at best poorly focused.

All these six fundamentals need to be effectively and efficiently in place for an organization to succeed. A key role for the learning function is to ensure the growth of the organization's competences in all six. In addition, the learning architect personally needs to have high levels of competence and wisdom in all six areas, not only for personal application, but also to be a role model, coach and mentor across the organization.

GROWING RATES OF CHANGE IMPACTING ORGANIZATIONS

The learning architect and his/her team have to recognize all aspects of change and be 'change masters'. In a world dominated by increasing change the learning architect and the learning function have to be able to master new approaches and new tools to provide the organization with the correct learning approaches – developing talent, the 'best' people for their organizations, potentially as a marketplace differentiator in an increasingly commoditized world.

Change and the new organization

There was a time when we were accustomed to change at a constant rate, and 'change' most often meant 'larger': mergers, acquisitions, globalization, all tending to produce ever larger, often monolithic organizations. In more recent years, things have become dramatically different. Change now is more rapid and often has a discontinuous nature. Marketplaces emerge, product and service lifetimes are shortened, differentiated 'uniques' are more difficult to prove.

New types of organization, leaner in structure and swifter to market, have swiftly grown to challenge old orders. Today's focus is external – on clients, customers, consumers and on other stakeholders – rather than internally on the organization's hierarchy. The expectations of stakeholders are constantly widening. This is particularly true of the expectations of clients, the original purchasers of our products and services, and of consumers, the eventual users of those products and services. There is a constant need to develop the competences of staff able to manage these expectations. Front line employees become empowered while sophisticated systems are built to help those front line staff access and manipulate information. Organizations are looking more and more to outsource nonessential functions. This may lead to the transfer out of the organization of some staff, but it demands increased competence of those remaining. Other organizations are globalizing. There is a vast difference between the competence set for a local purchasing department and that of a globalized category procurement function. The competences needed to discharge roles in these high-expectation situations are broad and deep, for both operational staff and their managers.

> We got to this strategy, in part, because we started to grow so fast that we couldn't hire people fast enough. So we moved one business function at a time away from people into networks, where customers and suppliers, managers... could all access information and each other directly. And then we turned off the paper.

This is Thomas L Friedman reporting on developments at Cisco in his book *The Lexus and the Olive Tree* (2000). It is an excellent example of fundamental change within an organization. It is highly interesting to consider the impact for a learning function considering the new competence of the staff involved.

Older organizations are adapting or they swiftly perish. Newer, 'virtual' organizations have become familiar, either because they were built that way, or because of outsourcing of many non-core functions. Virtual organizations have few recognizable traditional trappings: few direct employees, few corporate palaces, often no familiar components of training and development. These situations bring another set of challenges to the learning architect and the learning function team, particularly if they were schooled in traditional learning environments.

Change and the employee

Within a changed world and 'new' organizations there have emerged new relationships between an organization and its people. The traditional job for life has all but evaporated in many places. People are rarely now prepared to give a personal, partially unthinking, faith that they will be looked after, including their pensions, in exchange for unstinting, focused endeavours over many years. New psychological contracts between organizations and workers reverberate with conflicting approaches and issues. A new realization is growing that successful organizations are ones that are able to develop the talent of their staff more effectively than other organizations, and that are able to 'engage' their workforce (see Chapter 9). One organization declares that hiring already accomplished people is its 'brand' (potentially removing much of the traditional rationale for learning and development, and thus for a function to supply them). Another organization declares itself as an 'employer of choice' and promotes 'people development' as the prime reason for scarce resources to join them. The psychological contract between organization and staff will have a fundamental impact on the strategies and tactics of those with responsibility for learning and development.

The very nature of work has changed. Many people seek flexible working hours, and many contemplate the experience of working from home. Managers no longer simply manage; they almost invariably have their own operational tasks in addition to being 'field coaches' of their team members, a role that requires a sophisticated set of competences.

Change and the learning function

Our learning function, its staff and its programmes all need to recognize the impact of change, and to be fully committed to working with change as a resource. People, teams and organizations are changed by the learning programmes we build, and those programmes are built while much around is continually changing.

A wide and deep package of new abilities, new tools, and new approaches is required for the learning architect and his/her team: abilities, tools and approaches vastly different from those familiar in 'training and development'. Typical of such a new approach and new tools to be employed is the tool shown as Figure 1.2. This tool allows the plotting of the rate of organizational change – possibly internally, possibly externally, possibly both – against the stability of staffing for different parts of the organization. Staffing stability is low, perhaps, when the organization has a virtual team orientation, many contractors and outsourced departments.

Staff stability would be high for an organization with many fixed staff, low turnover and high hierarchical command and control. Such analysis allows the learning function to proactively provide guidance to the organization as to the appropriate learning initiatives – where monies and resources could be best applied towards organizational success.

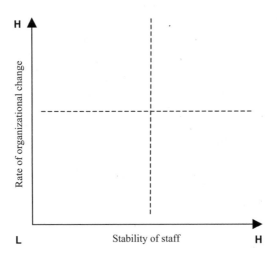

Figure 1.2 Analysing the situation

This style of analysis will assist the learning architect in deciding how, where and when learning can be implemented. What can a learning function offer in different circumstances? What is the best way of providing learning and of developing a learning environment? What is the role of individuals in the learning function and their leader, our learning architect?

This is typical of the new tools and techniques for learning function staff as they move towards a more consultative role, while often still having to be masters of more traditional tools and techniques associated with such items as learning needs analysis and classroom delivery.

DRIVERS AND OPPORTUNITIES FOR LEARNING

A number of drivers for learning are apparent in response to organizations' search for success aligned with their search to work with change. Some of these have been with us for many years, albeit today with modified focus. Others are new, in response to the 'new world'.

▌ **The organization itself as a driver for learning.** There is the much-quoted belief that well-skilled, well-motivated people are today's differentiator between competing organizations – the 'talent'. Indeed, many state that having the 'appropriate people' is now the only differentiator between organizations. Each of the six essentials for organizational success discussed earlier has connections to hiring, retaining, motivating and skilling the correct people. But simply having the correct people is not enough. It is as well to keep in mind the lessons of fine, skilled armies in history that have been annihilated by hordes of 'lesser' mortals who were wisely led, applied a creativity of approach and chose the battle ground with care. It is the ability to use learning wisely across and beyond the organization that is all-important – not the learning mechanisms themselves.

▌ **The organization as a whole as a focus of learning.** The many views on the 'learning organization' show how organizations, improving their readiness for success, are seeking to take advantage of all their available history, experience, current stimuli and predictions for the future. Vast amounts of effort, time, resource and money are being applied to building knowledge management and enterprise resource management systems as learning backbones for organizations. These learning backbones are built to effectively and efficiently absorb, reformat and make available information and learning throughout the organization. A role of the learning architect and the learning function is to manage the use of the collected knowledge in ways that can benefit the organization. The much quoted words of Jack Welch are so apposite: 'In the end, the desire and ability of an organization to continuously learn from any source anywhere and rapidly convert this learning into action, is the ultimate competitive advantage.'

▌ **A growing demand for learning generated by individual managers across the organization.** Functional managers require their staff to respond accurately and quickly in today's customer-focused, rapid-response work environment. These managers emphasize the need for readiness of their staff and, sometimes grudgingly, the need for the learning initiatives that develop that readiness. Not that those functional managers are always prepared to allow their teams to stop work while they learn! A galaxy of 'in-place learning methods' is becoming established in parallel to the classroom.

▌ **Individual staff themselves providing a 'pull' for learning.** New personal motivations, the new psychological contract between staff and employer, the search for an improved work/life balance, the need to be more qualified than other candidates at selection time, in the case of the older employer the wish to be qualified for a second career and/or a fulfilled retirement: all these and more provide stimuli for an organization to provide appropriate learning in an appropriate manner for its staff. This may be provided as 'traditional' learning through internal training workshops, or through a host of modern approaches ranging from partially funded MBA courses through to individuals being given laptop computers for self-study from the internet, or perhaps through a powerful focus on coaching and mentoring across the organization.

▍ **A general need for 'learning' and 'knowledge' for stakeholders.** As organizations change far more rapidly than in the past in response to market forces and to legislation, stakeholders have ever widening and deepening requirements. Typical of such requirements are:

- Shareholders in quoted companies: now that many people are personally dealing on the web they expect up-to-date, meaningful information about companies.
- Suppliers and customers, requiring knowledge and learning about products and services, enabling them to make rapid commercial decisions, and to be involved in true working partnerships and 'value adding' relationships.
- Commercial, governmental and public sector organizations all face swelling portfolios of legislation to be understood and implemented. Data protection and health and safety are typical of the areas growing in importance to which organizational stakeholders need to have accurate timely access – not just data, but information and knowledge as to their significance.

▍ **Technology providing a vast range of opportunities for those responsible for learning.** Both for the delivery of learning and its administration, improved communication networks, intranets and extranets, a range of mobile personal tools and much else present powerful tools for the learning architect and the team. Technology has brought challenge too. Lack of familiarity with technology, vast over-selling of technology capabilities and some naive judgements about people's willingness to work with new methods of learning are among the issues with which learning functions are learning to cope.

Every organization will present its learning architect and its learning function team with a selection of the drivers and opportunities for learning discussed in the paragraphs above. With so many possibilities, a key point for the learning architect will always be the recognition of the priorities for learning within a particular organization as one of the start points for the 'journey to learning excellence'. In parallel is the important need to implement monitoring and reviewing of priorities as time goes by, as learning plays its role and other factors ebb and flow.

TRADITIONAL CHALLENGES, NEW CHALLENGES FOR LEARNING

As learning programmes are implemented the challenges for those responsible for learning fall into two major groupings. Some are recognizable, traditional challenges that have been with us for some time. Other challenges are newer, often linked with the impacts of organizational change that we have discussed above.

Included in the traditional challenges to the successful implementation of learning are:

▌ There has been low investment in learning and development in many organizations. Research continually shows in some organizations that only tiny fractions of corporate revenues or public funding are invested in meaningful learning. There have been a number of reasons for this. Some organizations have adopted policies of hiring experienced people requiring little or no training. Elsewhere, throughout the last decade of the last century and into the current century, financial constraints have limited spend as many industries and public bodies experienced downturn and a lack of funds.

▌ Some functional units, for whatever reason, have little faith in 'corporate overheads' and will attempt to do their 'own thing' whenever possible. Even when the organizational learning budget is in the control of a centralized learning function, other functions will find the money to take on external learning initiatives with little or no involvement of the learning function. Senior management in operational units can be seduced by external learning suppliers approaching them directly with an attractive proposition. This can break the brand, the focus, and the learning culture and strategies being built by the learning function. A major issue is that these one-off learning initiatives can often be perceived as successful, as there will be a 'buzz' around anything sponsored by the senior management of the unit. What the professionals in the learning function recognize is the difficulty of maintaining that buzz once the learning initiative has been completed and the external organization has gone. There is a middle ground here, but it requires trust and understanding across the organization and a real belief in the 'value add' of the learning function.

▌ A failure to believe in the benefits of learning initiatives, often espoused from the senior areas of an organization, coupled with intense pressures on line management to perform and produce, has resulted in managers being reluctant to release delegates, and/or to cancel delegates from learning initiatives at very short notice. Compounding this failure to train their people through formal learning events is the situation that many managers are neither competent nor confident to coach and mentor their staff. This is poor role modelling indeed if there is to be a learning culture.

▌ The inability of the learning function to demonstrate its worth, its return on investment to the organization can be a problem. This has often been a result of the inability of the learning function to recognize and to work with metrics that satisfy senior management. Summaries of 'happiness sheets' are never the answer, but what else can we do?

In addition to all of the above, today's implementer of learning often faces an additional set of newer and different challenges:

▌ Amongst the casualties of 'delayering' and reduced function size is, quite frequently, the training and development function itself. Still responsible for a full portfolio of learning initiatives, the head of such functions is often now working with few staff – even, in some cases, none.

▌ The world in which we exist becomes more ambiguous and complex. The level of knowledge of 'business' required by people in the learning function, should they intend to work in a consultative style, is growing exponentially. New areas of knowledge are growing up, with issues such as organizational ethics and the environment. The staff in the learning function have a real opportunity to role model 'critical learning' as they keep themselves up to date and capable of using their knowledge in an appropriate manner.

▌ In common with the other 'enabling' functions such as finance, human resources (HR) and information systems (IS), the learning function is being continually quizzed about its 'value add' to the organization. How does it justify its existence? What does it really contribute to the organization and its success? In the commercial world the questions are about how the learning function contributes to increasing shareholder and consumer value. The function will need to demonstrate that it has considered which of its activities are appropriate, which are not, and what to do about those activities – discontinue, outsource, simplify?

▌ In direct response to the rate of change in the world, the rate of change of knowledge and the complexity of the skills to use that knowledge have escalated. Knowledge becomes obsolete very quickly; new deeper, broader forms of knowledge need to be used in more effective ways. Wisdom is more difficult to reach.

▌ The ever-increasing speed that is required to maintain commercial advantage or to control costs often minimizes the time that organizations are prepared to provide for learning initiatives. Activities that take people away from the workplace, revenue generation, client contact and satisfying client and customer demands are increasingly frowned upon. So time allocated to training by management is minimized, and this can be coupled with an unwillingness of individuals to attend learning initiatives since they are so personally continually busy.

▌ In some organizations there have been significant mistakes made with the implementation of new technologies in learning initiatives. Large amounts of money have been wasted in following over-optimistic claims for new approaches to learning. There has been a significant poor impact on the reputation of learning functions and learning professionals. These situations have often had highly detrimental impacts on learning budgets, already often much reduced.

▌ There is a growing cry from senior management about the lack of skilled people, in both 'traditional' and 'new' styles of organizations. Manufacturing companies complain about the lack of shop floor skills, literacy and numeracy. As such an organization transforms itself, in parallel with many other traditional organizations, towards a more service-oriented focus, the cry switches to the lack of service-centric staff. The complaints concerning 'the basics' also continue without pause. Somehow the blame for these situations is laid at the door of a learning function.

▌ Organizations have to change as they react to many forces: client and consumer expectations, legislation, global competition in the commercial world. Changes in strategies, structures, focus and their implementation all require changes in the competencies of the workforce. People need to be more entrepreneurial, more able to communicate effectively, more able to cope with a work/life balance. There may be recruiting to acquire the keenest of skills and the databases of contacts and knowledge, but the majority of new competencies will be provided through learning.

▌ There is a growing need for an acceptance in organizations and their management that not everything is 'trainable'. Learning functions need increasingly to have organizations recognize that aspects of competence cannot be developed in the classroom. We can assist with the development of skills, applied knowledge, the development of wisdom with creative techniques and an interest in 'learning to learn', but it is through leadership, coaching and a sound culture that motivation, willingness, attitudes, creativity and entrepreneurship will be developed.

I Learning initiatives have to be sufficiently flexible to cope with changing needs of the organization. And, at the same time, the choice of mechanisms to deliver learning is growing, wrapped in the fluffiest of terms, 'blended learning'. Choosing the appropriate tools and techniques, with all due consideration of budgets, and implementing them in the required 'flexible' manner is a key to success.

I The number of areas with which people responsible for learning have to interface, usually with no authority to control, continually increase. It has always been vital to have working relationships with delegates and their managers, as well as with those to whom the learning function report, quite often HR. Now, in addition, appropriate strategic and tactical alignment with groups responsible for talent management, governmental legislation, e-commerce strategies, IT strategies and knowledge management are critical to success.

I Many attempts at establishing learning organizations have proved to be less than totally successful, partially because of an inability to manage all the information required, partially because of the competence of the people involved.

I The traditional training and development function with its slower-paced environment and well-planned learning initiatives was an excellent place for learning professionals to learn their trade and benefit from any mistakes they made. Today's often frantic environment is unforgiving, and experience has to be developed quickly. There is a tremendous expectation on the learning architect and other senior learning function staff to coach their juniors.

As the learning architect builds the overall strategy for the 'journey to learning excellence' and its individual learning programmes these challenges need to be faced, together with any specific challenges with any particular organization.

NEW APPROACHES TO LEARNING PROVISION

So organizations change, and they will continue to change and evolve at least as quickly in the future. People are changing their views, their attitudes and their personal needs, and will continue to change. There continues to be, and will continue to be into the future, the need for learning initiatives aligned to that world of change – for organizations, real and virtual, for departments, for teams and for individuals.

Learning initiatives that match the needs of the modern organization in public and private sectors need to be, if they are to be acceptable to the new organization and to all of its stakeholders:

I cognizant of the impact of planned and unplanned change;
I cognizant of any new organizational learning needs, increasing staff productivity and improving the retention of new competences;
I cognizant of the expectations of the modern workforce;
I cognizant of the fact that much learning and development cannot take place in traditional ways at traditional speeds;
I quick to build and deliver;
I highly accessible to busy learners;
I built close to the point of operation rather than within the learning function;
I cognizant of the special learning needs of any key, high-impact staff members and other stakeholders;
I designed to make people more creative and innovative, more self-sufficient, more able to apply wisdom, more able to have people able 'to learn to learn';
I monitored and evaluated in innovative ways;
I whenever possible, planned to have some motivational 'quick wins';
I cost justified in innovative ways, often with a need to demonstrate 'quick wins' to rapidly justify costs;
I most probably, reducing overall learning costs;
I promoting continually improving best practice;
I inspiring and motivational;
I promoting organizational learning and a learning organization.

Across a range of organizations the chosen learning strategies and the plans for the 'organizational journey to learning excellence' will be different, though almost certainly with common themes for the organization, for the individual and for any team. See Table 1.1.

There are in place well-established mechanisms for planning, delivering and evaluating learning, which will help any learning professionals fulfil their responsibilities. These were built for those organizations where the rate of change is low and the head of learning's role is primarily charged with reactively serving the organization's learning needs. Such organizations do still exist, and Chapter 2 describes the appropriate learning tools and techniques. However, the more sophisticated challenges facing

Table 1.1   Aspirations

	From	To
The organization	Cost centre; central budgeting	Appropriate commercial model, possibly a profit centre
	Learning as something 'imposed', done in addition to working	Learning that is motivating, empowering, brand building
	Focused internally – training people for 'competitive edge'	Focus on all stakeholders for learning
	Job focus in training	Personal development focus
	Classroom delivery	Multiple sources of learning
Myself, a team manager	Using the training catalogue	Discussing and developing performance of the team
	Not personally fully trained	Interested in my own development, role model to the team
	Not understanding the potential of learning	
Myself; 'manager of learning'	Constrained, functional role	Strategic role
	'Doing', seen as reactive service supplier	Developing
	Low in the hierarchy	Key role; partnering the organization
My team	Part of a 'training machine'	Learning professionals
	Constrained, functional roles	Empowering, business developing
	Reactive	Consultative

today's head of learning in faster-moving organizations require the newer, more sophisticated mechanisms described elsewhere in this book.

Transforming for the revolution

We have been promised a revolution in learning, often voiced around the arrival of highly capable e-learning initiatives. Is this the world to which the learning architect must guide the organization? The revolution for which we need to prepare is more about information than learning. The revolution for which the learning architect needs to prepare aligns to SMS-type technology delivering current information anywhere, and massive search capabilities for all types of data, not just the written word. It is about growing organizational talent capable of accessing vast amounts of information from within our knowledge bases and elsewhere, and capable of making critical decisions. It is about moving the classroom teaching environment towards one where simulations and facilitated, action-oriented workshops are prime learning events. It is about developing competence in handling ambiguity, effective teamworking across cultural, language and organizational boundaries, conflict resolution, facilitating change, applying wisdom, critical analysis and critical communication. The learning initiatives that are classroom-based will be focused on 'toolbox' training on such topics as project management and problem solving.

Today's 'high performing' model

The development of organizational talent is fundamental for success. The model of work shown as Figure 1.3 encompasses the manner in which the modern knowledge worker performs, and where learning fits with this performance. Our knowledge workers need to be capable of turning available information, from a vast range of sources, into wisdom and into action. Such a capability in individual knowledge workers, in teams, in whole organizations, is developed in one or a combination of many possible ways – through workshops, through focused at-the-job events, through coaching and through a host of other available learning mechanisms (see Chapter 8).

As time moves on and organizational needs for success intensify, the performance model needs to be applied ever more effectively and efficiently by ever more capable people.

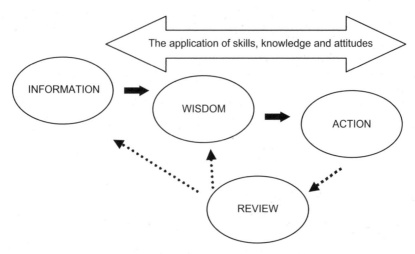

Figure 1.3   Knowledge worker performance model

TRANSFORMING LEARNING MANAGEMENT AND LEADERSHIP

In every organization seeking to be better placed for success and to be more robust against the impacts of change there will be key staff roles. When an organization plans for success these are the vital roles that must be filled with the most competent of candidates. Having these roles filled with people of the highest level of expertise is a real differentiator between organizations. In the provision of the correct learning solutions for these organizations it is imperative to have appropriate people in place, supported by the correct teams, together with the correct tools and techniques and the correct commercial models.

The individual empowered to build the organization's learning capabilities should be seen to have the opportunity of a key role of the highest importance. The role will, in fact, vary in many ways across different organizations. The exact nature of the role will be impacted by the size of the organization, by its 'marketplace', by its responsibilities to its stakeholders and by its culture and geographical spread. Discharging the responsibilities associated with a 'head of learning' role will be impacted by the form and availability of resources, together with the manner in which items such as budgets are managed within the organization. We have set out in this book to discuss such issues, and to provide criteria and arguments about the correct approach for an individual situation.

No two organizations are exactly the same. Each will be a unique amalgamation of individuals, goals, structure, culture and values. Each will be a unique grouping of individuals making up the workforce. Each will have unique sets of stakeholders and 'marketing' considerations. To fulfil his/her role the learning architect continuously monitors the organization, its environment, its culture and its operations to allow the implementation of appropriate strategies and tactics. To undertake these responsibilities the learning architect has to occupy an appropriately influential position.

The picture painted earlier in this chapter leaves no doubt that the list of challenges for senior learning professionals is ever increasing, as are the opportunities for getting the whole thing wrong: backing the wrong methodologies and/or the wrong suppliers, failing to effectively review and evaluate return on investment, failing to work towards motivating learners ('taking a horse to water...'), misreading the alignments between learning, the organization, its culture, its stakeholders. Any of these or any combination could be catastrophic, even fatal, in terms of the importance of the 'correct' learning to an organization. The organization has to have in place an appropriately capable head of learning.

So organizations urgently require individuals with the ability to accept and successfully discharge the responsibilities and accountabilities of leading and managing learning provision. We have conjured a name for these key people, these 'heads of learning'. We have called them *learning architects*, individuals managing the design and implementation of the appropriate learning for their organization. If we are going to take on these tough challenges, we are going to start with a resonant and appropriate title, a title that epitomizes a role that is responsible for designing, building, implementing, evaluating and maintaining learning in changing organizations. Learning architect implies strategists, planners, builders of direction and programmes for learning that are to be inhabited by people absorbing the benefits of learning: an unashamed derivative of the dictionary definition of 'architect'.

These are individuals, passionate about learning, who:

I have a keen understanding of their organization, its business and performance environment, its culture and its people;
I understand the importance of learning to all stakeholders;
I are passionate about the importance of learning, and share a joy with others in the implementation of learning that has a positive impact on individuals and organizations;
I manage the power of learning to provide the organization with the competitive differential of a workforce of knowledgeable, highly capable, highly motivated staff;

have a keen understanding of the importance of knowledge and behaviours, how they are developed and how they are skilfully applied in the pursuit of organizational and personal success;

are of growing importance to their current organization and are looked at with envy by competition.

These people are unlikely to see a reduction in their importance to successful organizations. Our belief is that their importance can only grow.

Roles and responsibilities

Our learning architect is the individual, fully understanding the organization's aspirations, strategies and plans, who delivers the capabilities of learning through and beyond the organization. This person leads a learning function that brings an 'intensity of learning' to the organization, learning that plays an irreplaceable role in the development of the organization's performance, culture and values. This 'intensity of learning' focuses on the development of individuals and teams at the place where learning has its real value – at the workplace with the manager operating as coach – and not always in the classroom. It is facilitated through a learning function that is itself a role model for the behaviours that are core to the implemented learning initiatives.

The learning architect balances the strategic and the tactical, the long term and the necessary immediate. The learning architect will fully understand the strategy of the organization, and particularly where the CEO and the senior team are focused. The major thrust of the learning initiatives must plainly be integrated into those strategies and focus. The organization will be expecting delivery of learning activities in the classroom and over the intranet; the senior management of the organization will be seeking to know that budgets are being used wisely in delivering increased abilities to key knowledge workers, that there is the development of organizational development, and that there is a long term plan – probably involving doing even more for less budget.

The learning architect will also be highly skilled in working with management across the organization. Our learning architect model, explored throughout this book, considers learning breaking away from its traditional home within HR. But the work of the learning function needs to interface to the work of HR and other units, as service is provided across and beyond the organization.

This is the individual capable of describing the art of the possible for senior management, vividly and with deep persuasion explaining how they can take advantage of the benefits of different learning initiatives, constantly articulating the role of learning and learning solutions within successful organizations – and doing this in the terms of the organization's 'business'. For example, he or she must be fully capable of debating the use of the internet for training with the most senior of people, and capable and willing to debate questions such as 'If the business is more and more using the internet in its business processes, what will be the impact on the learning architecture we require?', 'If this organization invested in internet-based training, what could be the impact and benefits for the organization's business strategies and processes?' and 'Would training our customer base using internet technologies assist in new ways of increasing our revenue from this customer base while reducing our costs?'

The learning architect will have a clear vision for learning in the organization in the current time and in the future. As a learning professional the learning architecture will have a personal '20-year view' of the direction of learning – the learning architect will be a real knowledge worker in his/her own field. He or she will appreciate what will have to be learned for organizational success, how it will be best learned and how resources will best be applied to the learning processes. This is interesting territory for our learning architect. For all the changes in learning process and technology in the past years there is a remarkable similarity in the themes that are being 'taught': leadership, teaming, performance management.

Overall, the learning architect will be the individual who considers a change in the role of the learning function from the provider of training and related activities to the key part of the organization that manages knowledge creation and transfer, and its conversion into wisdom by suitably competent people (see Figure 1.3). The learning architect will seek to establish an organizational culture of learning that:

- is embedded within, aligned with and linked to the organizational culture;
- interfaces to the human capital systems across the organization and reflects the appropriate competence frameworks;
- is responsive to change and itself is continually monitored to guarantee continuous improvement;
- is responsive to stakeholder feedback;
- promotes learner independence, a 'pull' on learning from stakeholders and a coaching culture.

Why the 'learning architect'?

Two primary concepts are at the heart of our reasoning for the adoption of the term 'learning architect'.

The first is truly pragmatic. We simply wanted a job title that truly summed up the importance of the role to be described. Although we know a number of people who are fulfilling the described responsibilities, there rarely was a suitable job title matching our belief of the importance of the role. We have met many people whose responsibility it is to drive learning as a keystone to the success of organizations. We have encountered as many different job titles as people. Some would consider 'head of learning' boring and academic, 'training and development director' in danger of appearing dated; 'chief learning officer' has gravitas but some would conceive of a 'me too' longing for the CEO role! Somehow the job titles seemed to fall short. Few reflected the proactive excitement of the role; fewer reflected the gravitas of a key role providing such a significant contribution to the success of the organization.

Our second reason for the title 'learning architect' is that we believe it provides a strong insight into the nature of the role. Managing learning as a tool for the modern organization requires leadership, craftsmanship, strategic thought and keen operational execution. Our concept was of somebody who planned and then saw something through to benefit. We could not resist the image of people building plans for learning and then seeing their ideas grow and flourish to be 'invaded' by people absorbing benefit. Architecture is about providing solutions robust enough to handle the forces of change, solutions that are regarded as strong and resilient by those individuals who will benefit.

In reality, the real consideration is the discharging of the learning architect role, not the name! All-important is the recognition of the vital importance of the role and its responsibilities, together with a level of empowerment to discharge the responsibilities, to really make things happen.

Four types of learning architect

We have clearly seen that fulfilment of the learning architect role is increasingly through a range of different people. We have used the name to include those working in 'conventional' senior roles in both commercial and public organizations. We have also used the name to include other people, a range of people that we will describe in this book. They include the growing numbers of those who, though not working in conventional training/learning roles, are taking more and more direct responsibility for learning for others and for themselves.

In different organizations, with different learning challenges, with different rates and impacts of change, different types of learning function and different resources, the learning architect role has to be different. What remains constant is the passion to use learning as an effective, motivating instrument in the effective development of organizations and individuals.

Our research and debate has identified a range of learning architects for different circumstances. For simplicity in building this book we have allowed our learning architects to fall into four broad types. Each type fits with the use of a set of strategies, tactics, tools and techniques, evaluation and metrics for evaluating success.

Type 1: the corporate learning architect

These people carry one of many titles, including head of learning and chief learning officer. Some continue to carry more traditional titles, including training and development manager. These are individuals charged with identifying, designing, implementing and evaluating learning initiatives across and beyond the organization with which they work – beyond to the organization's stakeholders, particularly customers and suppliers. They occupy, in a range of organizations, roles that report to a range of levels – from roles that are reporting deep within HR through to roles sitting on the major corporate board. Their individual background may have been in HR, possibly as a training specialist, or may have been more operational than learning oriented, having had a career progression through the line. The learning architect fulfils his/her goals through a team of learning professionals in functions whose names include learning function, corporate learning university and, more traditionally, the training and development department.

Our definition of corporate learning architect is broad. At one extreme it includes the traditional training and development manager role, reactive and steady in its approach to delivering learning. At the other extreme is a proactive master of change, using learning to move the organization towards its goals. This continuum might be labelled 'servant to architect'. Our belief is that the traditional role grew in a time of constant change and may well be a difficult implementation in today's world. Today our corporate learning architect is on a journey to learning excellence, strategizing, planning and implementing as he/she moves along the continuum.

Type 2: the tactical learning architect

There are a very large number of people who, while charged with many of the same responsibilities as the corporate learning architect, have to discharge those responsibilities with few or no staff. They do not have a team of learning professionals to help them discharge their responsibilities. What they do have is experience and expertise in the world of learning, and they use this experience and expertise to build virtual teams, to facilitate events themselves, to utilize third parties in making things happen. In larger organizations they may be the survivors of learning functions that have been reduced through cost cutting or strategic decisions.

Type 3: the functional learning architect

Today there are many organizations, large, medium and small, that have no central learning function. Delayering, restructuring, decentralization and cost cutting all may have contributed to the situation that has resulted in the lack of a recognizable learning function. Training budgets, where they are still in existence, may well have been devolved into line functions. Learning initiatives still need to be implemented, and this has resulted in there being people responsible for the implementation of learning initiatives without being part of a traditional learning structure.

Very differently from the tactical learning architect, the functional learning architect is often a person with little or no learning background. The type 3 architect will, very likely, have spent his/her time within a line function.

There are examples of people operating as a learning architect type 3 in medium-sized organizations that have grown up in such a way that a learning function has never been a feature. A middle manager, typically, has been asked to 'look after' training although he or she might well have no personal background in any of the appropriate areas. We have found such people, often also continuing to discharge their original 'non-learning' role in the organization, working with external providers, possibly in a very unstructured manner, to provide essential training workshops on such topics as customer care and workplace supervisory skills.

Type 4: the individual learning architect

These are individuals that are navigating a journey of self-development for people including, perhaps, themselves. They include individuals in corporate learning functions that are utilizing coaching and mentoring as part of an overall strategy, line managers who are using coaching as part of the development of their staff, together with individuals who are 'cherry picking' learning opportunities from within the organizations for which they work and other opportunities in their personal self-development.

In achieving their aims, a learning professional may adopt the techniques of different learning architect styles at different times, and implement the different techniques associated with the style. Styles may be used in parallel. A training and development director in a conventional organization may clearly be a learning architect type 1, a corporate learning architect, in discharging his/her duties – close to the left-hand extreme of the continuum, provider to architect. When providing coaching to a senior line manager from within the organization, the training and development director, in parallel, adopts the approach and techniques of learning architect type 4.

The major features of the different types of learning architect are shown in Table 1.2 and are described in detail in Chapters 2 and 3 for corporate learning architects and in Chapter 4 for the other types.

Table 1.2   The learning architects

	LA1 – traditional head of learning	LA1 – proactive change master	LA2	LA3	LA4
Team shape	Traditional T&D structure	New learning architect structure	No direct team	No direct team	Working alone
Role and responsibilities	Head of learning for major organization. All learning programmes through HR – soft skills and interpersonal skills.	Head of learning for major organization. All learning programmes including those aimed at job-related skills.	Head of learning for organization. All learning programmes including those aimed at work-related skills.	Provide learning into division of a large organization, or a small organization. All learning programmes including those aimed at job-related skills.	Provide coaching or 'local learning' to individuals or small teams.
Reporting	To head of HR	To most senior management of the organization	To most senior management of the organization	To management of division or small organization	Varied
Challenges	Difficult to react to changing organization, changing organizational needs.	New skills needed within team, almost always too much work to do.	No team to exercise aspects of managing learning. Limited time for proactive initiatives.	No learning background. Limited resources., Priority clashes, managing learning and other responsibilities.	Acceptance of this type of learning.

Table 1.2   The learning architects (contd.)

	LA1 – traditional head of learning	LA1 – proactive change master	LA2	LA3	LA4
Ways of working	Through training and development team. Classroom training courses are the most common form of learning activity.	Through learning function team, relationships with other players including performers. Interactive, facilitated events, coaching.	Through relationships with other players including performers, mostly external. Interactive, facilitated events, coaching.	Through relationships with other players including performers, mostly external. Interactive, facilitated events, coaching.	Personal skills
Measures of success likely to be employed.	Wise budget and resource use, training numbers met, happiness sheets. Kirkpatrick level up to 3.	Wise budget and resource use, ROI of learning initiatives, impact on success of organization, training numbers met, Kirkpatrick level up to 4.	Wise budget and resource use, training numbers met, happiness sheets. Kirkpatrick level up to 3.	Wise budget and resource use, training numbers met, happiness sheets. Kirkpatrick level up to 3.	Investigation of what has changed, Kirkpatrick level up to 3.

FRAMEWORKS FOR LEARNING SOLUTIONS

The learning architecture

A prime responsibility for the learning architect is the establishment of the organizational learning architecture. Architecture – again paralleling the dictionary – is about providing a framework for learning approaches and solutions that is robust against the forces of change. It calls for learning approaches and solutions that can be fully managed by the learning function, and that are regarded as robust and meaningful by those individuals who will benefit.

This learning architecture will be unique to the organization, providing a design, a framework for the implementation of learning across the whole organization. Performance in learning will be delivered across and beyond an organization through processes 'supported' on the learning architecture.

The development of a learning architecture is focused initially on the organization's performance needs, then on the resulting learning needs, and finally on how a technical architecture can be focused to best supply the solutions to the needs. As time goes by components of delivery mechanisms may change – we have to close a training block, we inherit tons of CBTs as the results of a merger. When changing situations in learning are acceptable within the architecture, when there is a 'fit' to the architecture, they are made available to learners in the organization; otherwise they are probably disposed of.

In the face of change throughout and beyond the organization the build of the architecture must reflect a high level of flexibility. As the developing performance goals of the organization demand an increasing range of learning solutions, the solutions must sit comfortably with the learning architecture, in terms of technical design, delivery mechanisms, return on investment calculations and fit with the other characteristics of the architecture.

An essential element in a learning strategy supported on a learning architecture is the identification of methods of assessment and evaluation. Short-term and focused on individual learning initiatives, the language is of 'assessment', 'tests of learning' and validation of materials. Longer-term, 'bigger picture' evaluation looks to the impact of whole learning programmes, of the learning strategy itself and mechanisms for feedback and change see Chapter 5.

A learning architecture for traditional times

Traditionally, an organization's learning architecture has been based on the training and development framework implemented in almost every organization. The building and implementing of this architecture is described fully in Chapter 2 of this book. In low-change, traditional organizations this will be sufficient to provide a learning architecture. The flow of strategy and information through the organization, the manner in which power and control are devolved and the manner the training and development framework is built up are shown in Figure 1.4.

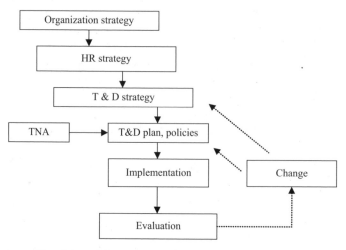

Figure 1.4   Traditional framework for learning

The strategy and the implementation plan will include details of how learning initiatives are sourced and how any financial justification is arrived at.

The learning plan is the documented list of events and activities across a period of time – typically a year – with the opportunity of regular updates. The style of operation tends to put responsibility on line management and on individuals to book themselves onto learning events. The whole process is reactive to the organization's performance needs and is highly structured. It is highly appropriate when there is only a low rate of continuous change across the organization and in the associated learning needs. Individuals 'know where they are' and there is every opportunity for implementing high-value learning events. Maxims such as 'world-class training' abound!

A learning architecture for newer times and situations

In Chapter 5 a learning architecture is introduced for more rapidly changing times. It very much acknowledges the fact that our traditional frameworks for designing, implementing and evaluating learning may well be too slow to react, too ponderous for today's rapidly flexing organization. It allows for the learning architect and any other staff associated with learning to act in a more proactive manner into the organization. The newer architecture will support a move from the traditional methods of building learning which were often training/classroom focused towards newer methods that are highly organizational-result focused.

As a key portion of the architecture there will be a technical infrastructure describing the delivery of learning. This promotes facilitation of learning through a variety of means, appropriate to the organization and what it seeks to achieve. The allowable delivery mechanisms may include books, learning rooms, information databases, internal and external facilitators, learning coaches, the internet, an intranet and many more. The architecture will include mechanisms to assist decisions about what methods of learning initiative are applicable to particular learning needs, considering, among other things, the reach and the richness of the method. *Reach* concerns where a particular method can be implemented: is the intranet stable? Does the company that facilitates that classroom workshop have viable facilitators in those places? Richness is more about level of content and usefulness; does it provide sufficient assessment of learning? Does that facilitator have the pedigree to work with such senior managers?

WORKING RELATIONSHIPS

With a need to make things happen quickly, to be proving worth, to be flexible, the learning architect needs to be highly conscious of those with whom relationships are to be built. Particularly when the learning architect staff team is limited in size, an ability to relate, to influence, to coach are increasingly the competences of the learning architect. Figure 1.5 will be used throughout the book as we discuss the role of the learning architect working with other people.

Figure 1.5 illustrates the 'players', the people with whom the learning architect must interface successfully to discharge the duties we have discussed in this chapter. *Performers* are all those people who 'put on a performance', 'deliver a performance' in facilitating learning to others: classroom trainers, facilitators, coaches, mentors, storytellers used in creative workshops, actors employed in role plays and so on.

Service suppliers are organizations and people who supply facilities, materials and the like that are fundamental in the provision of a correct environment and brand for the learning organization.

Each player relationship needs to be handled professionally and sensitively in helping to achieve the goals of the learning architect.

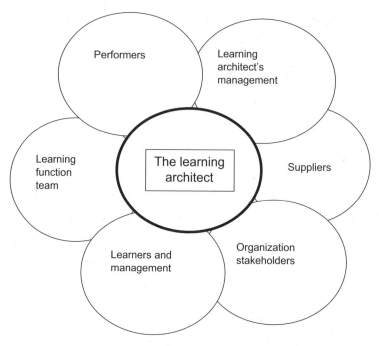

Figure 1.5   The players

The fundamentals: personal competence, team competence

Whichever style of learning architect best suits your role in the organization with which you work, your personal competencies need to be both
broad and deep. The modern role is likely to be a performance-based one,
requiring a high level of competence in business fundamentals as well as
a keen understanding of how learning can support an organization's success. The role will involve focused relationships with senior management,
and probably with other key internal and external stakeholders. The
competencies needed are those of influencing, mentoring, coaching and
the like (see Chapter 6).

The nature of the team will vary widely. As a corporate learning architect
you are likely to have a team of learning professionals. Working in the style
of other learning architects the team may well be very different; you may
well be building virtual teams, project teams brought together to respond
to a specific learning need.

THE COMMERCIAL MODELS

For the learning function, its programmes and its people to be capable of maximizing its contribution to the organization, the underpinning commercial models need to be correct. Existing control and reporting structures together with the financial models associated with a learning function have normally built up over time. They have been shaped and impacted by business success or failure, management fads, mergers and acquisitions and a host of other factors. The entrepreneurial learning architect needs to seize proactively any opportunity to implement models appropriate to the organization and its learning direction. He/she then has to work with senior management to implement those models.

There are choices to be made about reporting structures. Traditionally learning functions have reported into HR, and in many cases this has merit. (See Chapter 2 where we discuss traditional learning situations.) For organizations where a learning architect is leading learning into more powerful spheres, a different reporting structure may well be appropriate. (See Chapters 2 and 3 where the focus is on the corporate learning architect.)

There are choices to be made about financial models. There is a wide choice including central funding of a learning function operating as a cost centre, a function operating as a revenue centre, training budgets being with the line, and outsourcing models. These models and the appropriate occasions for their use are discussed in Chapter 5.

CHAPTER SUMMARY

▌ In modern organizations, having to deal with continuous change, there is a new urgency to the role of learning. It has to be designed rapidly, provide high impact and be delivered at the convenience of the learner. The role of people responsible for such learning is challenging and requires a broad and deep range of skills and knowledge.

▌ The managers of learning processes and learning functions have to build architectures of learning that support the current learning initiatives and are sufficiently flexible to absorb the new elements of learning associated with change across the organization.

▌ To be successful, learning aligns with the other drivers for success across the organization leadership, handling change, efficiently delivering solutions and culture awareness.

▌ The drivers for learning are growing in number and intensity. In addition to the traditional drivers from within the organization in having staff prepared for their roles, there is a growing pull for learning initiatives from individuals within the organization as well as from a range of external stakeholders.

▌ There are vital choices to be made in the manner that learning is managed, which include the correct funding model, the correct reporting structures and the correct learning architecture.

2

Establishing the learning function

Congratulations on your new role as head of the learning function. You can plainly see what is needed here. It is not yet the time for revolution. It is the time for solidification, and possibly controlled evolution. You need to put the function firmly under control, understand and exceed the needs of management in this steady, highly structured, focused organization. There will be time to move forward with your creative ideas in years to come. Just now it is all about ensuring the basics are in place, and there is a clear feeling within the organization that 'training' is in strong hands and is providing value for money.

The purpose of this chapter is to investigate strategic learning approaches for organizations with low rates of change and to give an introduction to learning strategies for learning architects.

INTRODUCTION TO THE CORPORATE LEARNING ARCHITECT

The corporate learning architect, our learning architect type 1, was introduced in Chapter 1. This person, working together with the team of learning professionals making up the learning function, is responsible for identifying, designing, implementing and evaluating learning initiatives for the organization for which he or she works.

In different organizations, in different circumstances, the corporate learning architect role will be very different. At one end of a continuum, at the 'beginning', is the role traditionally thought of as training and development management. Here the work is part of the human resources (HR) establishment and tends to be in a reactive mode, responding to the organization's learning needs. At the other extreme of the continuum is a role within a dynamic, flexible 'learning function' charged with proactively delivering learning initiatives in fluid, high intensity situations.

The majority of corporate learning architects are navigating their learning function along this continuum, seeking a position where the relationship with the organization and the function's processes provide the most appropriate learning initiatives for the organization. Table 2.1 shows some key aspects of the continuum.

Table 2.1   Corporate learning architect continuum

Status	Establishing	Repositioning	Guiding
Role	Establishing an efficient learning function.	Repositioning the learning function within the organization. Moving to a more proactive, performance-focused function.	Proactively guiding the organization into effective and efficient use of learning, potentially as a competitive force.
Operational focus	Cost control. Efficiency. Task.	Wise budgeting. Effectiveness. Projects.	Wise budgeting. Guiding the organization to maximum performance. Programmes.
Involvement in planning	Receives business plans; plans suitable learning activities.	Involved in functional business planning; ensuring that appropriate learning is fully included.	Proactively involved in business planning at top of the organization.

Table 2.1 Corporate learning architect continuum (Contd.)

Status	Establishing	Repositioning	Guiding
Brand	World-class training	Consultative. Performing.	Equal at senior management level. Partnering the organization. Learners will 'pull' the learning function.
Learner focus	Low interest. Training when necessary.	Learning directed towards current and future work; challenging, 'learning to learn', building wisdom.	
Evaluation focus	Budgets. Learner acceptance. Kirkpatrick Level 2.	Budgets. Impact on individuals. Kirkpatrick Level 3.	Return on investment. Impact on business. Kirkpatrick Level 4.
Processes	Traditional: strategy plan · fixed learning architecture.	Traditional processes no longer sufficiently responsive. Introduction of more consultative relationships with the organization. Emergence of a more flexible learning architecture.	
People	Delivery focus	Organizational performance focus	

The 'establishing' status provides a stable environment for the corporate learning architect and the learning function. Well planned, with an agreed budget, this situation allows the function to invest time in providing the much-discussed 'world-class learning solutions' in a highly responsive manner. As the function moves towards the 'positioning' status, a journey that often takes as long as two years, the focus moves more towards a business partnership as opposed to a master–servant relationship. Different sets of skills are required within the function as the role becomes ever more consultative. After another two or three years the function may well be able to move on to a 'guiding' status, using learning to 'guide' the organization to performance success.

THE ESTABLISHING STATUS

This chapter concentrates on the operation of the corporate learning architect and the learning function for the 'establishing' portion of the continuum. It describes the operational approach to 'grounding' a learning function. It is likely to be the most acceptable operational model when:

I A learning function is first being established, possibly with less experienced staff in the function.

I A learning function needs to be re-established, possibly after the appointment of a new learning architect, a 'grounding' in preparation for the function's development towards a position further to the right along the continuum.

I It is appropriate that the role of the learning function is a highly planned, highly structured one with high rigour in process design – probably in an environment of low rate of organizational change and/or when there is a widely distributed organization with diverse functions that respond well to a consistent 'corporate direction'. Time is available for the thorough planning and implementation of long-term learning strategies.

I There is a need to minimize costs associated with learning and the learning function. Priority and planning are the watchwords and there is highly limited scope for revolutionary, innovative approaches. Even evolutionary changes to the pattern of learning initiatives have to be strenuously cost-justified.

Characteristics of the 'establishing' approach to learning

In this 'establishing' status the most often seen characteristics of the corporate learning architect and the learning function include:

I The learning function reports into the HR function, with the majority of its learning programmes associated with 'soft skills' development. This results usually, though not exclusively, in other functions managing the training and development that is labelled with terms such as 'other', 'functional' and 'job related'. Sales force development is managed exclusively by the sales and marketing function, shop floor skill training by the production function.

I The majority of learning initiatives are focused through classroom delivery.

I A learning function mostly staffed by people from an HR background, each with a learning specialism. The team will typically include a small number of specialists in areas such as learning needs analysis, evaluation and e-learning.

I The function is often entitled 'training and development', managed by a 'training and development director'. Today, with a changing focus, more likely is 'learning and development'.

Head of learning: a reactive role

The typical major roles and responsibilities of a training and development director include:

I When starting out, analysing the organizational situation and placing the appropriate 'sticks in the ground' for developing and implementing training and development strategies together with the associated processes and deliverables. These take the form of learning strategies and plans.

I Once a journey towards the successful implementation of learning programmes has started, continually monitoring the performance of the learning function and its programmes. Consistently and continuously critiquing strategies and tactics in comparison with other organizations regarded as having applied elements of best practice including the usage of creative structures and innovative methods of operation. (See the discussion on benchmarking in Chapter 3.)

I Working with the 'owners' of the organizational factors for success discussed on page 15 of Chapter 1, understanding how each of these factors is brought into play within the organization. Also working with the owners within the organization of the important organizational processes and systems – people such as the head of information services. These people and their functional departments will be key in assisting learning architects in the implementation of learning initiatives.

I Making decisions and implementing plans about progressing current and future learning initiatives for enabling the organization and its people to be fully effective.

I Establishing criteria for absorbing new technologies and initiatives in learning.

I Managing personal development programmes for yourself and for other people engaged in learning programmes within your function and across the organization.

I Marketing the function capabilities and successes.

I Managing resources and budgets.

POSITIONING THE LEARNING FUNCTION IN THE ORGANIZATION

For the 'establishing' role of a corporate learning architect, the traditional positioning of a learning function within HR, discussed above, is as Figure 2.1.

Organizational structures here locate a learning function within HR alongside other functions with 'people' responsibilities – functions such as recruitment, appraisal, compensation and benefits. This structure, learning as a function within a function, has held true in many organizations even as the structure, role and responsibilities of HR itself has evolved over the years. An HR function may have taken a 'strategic', proactive stance in the organization, implemented organizational development approaches and devolved part of its role into functional HR appointments. Even with these and other fundamental changes, learning often will have remained as a department within the HR function.

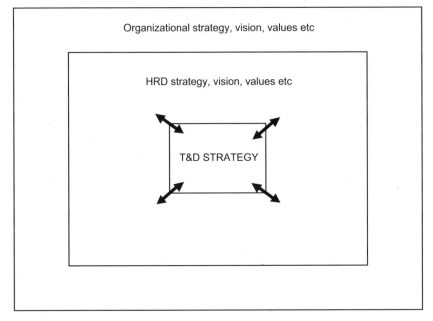

Figure 2.1   Traditional flows

The logic for this 'traditional' positioning of the learning function within HR includes:

▌ The learning function's strategies, vision, mission and operational ethos are easily aligned to those of HR, ensuring a direct link through to the strategic directions of the organization. A 'one source', consistent 'people' brand is promoted as learning strategies and tactics are developed within the overall framework of HR for the organization and its staff.

▌ It carries significant benefits for learning professionals, being close to a prime source of knowledge and direction about the people across the organization.

▌ Learning activities, when learning is regarded as an integral part of HR, are planned with an HR 'people development' focus. The learning initiatives that are planned are directly tied into the people development requirements established through the HR direction.

▌ People's 'learning entitlement' in terms of a 'learning policy' sits comfortably within an employee handbook published by an HR function.

▌ Staff within a traditional learning function, including its management, often will have developed careers through an HR route, choosing, for whatever reason, learning as their personal speciality field. The manager of the learning function, whatever the title he or she carries, simply sits as a direct report to the HR director.

Such is the acceptance of this HR–learning function relationship that it is not unknown for there to be instances of 'role reversal'. In global and distributed organizations, at locations lacking a local HR presence, a learning function may well be requested to 'spread its wings' and encompass much of the typical HR functionality as adjuncts to its own work.

IMPLEMENTING LEARNING

With the learning function embedded within HR, the traditional process of designing and implementing learning comprises these key components:

▌ the development of a learning strategy reflecting the strategies of the organization and the HR function;

▌ learning needs analyses at a number of levels, across the organization, for functional teams and groups, and for individuals;

▌ a learning policy that includes statements of the learning entitlement of individuals within the organization;

▌ an implementation plan for the agreed learning;

▌ learning design and facilitation;

▌ assessment of learning initiatives against the agreed objectives;
▌ evaluation and continuous improvement of all aspects of learning;
▌ reporting on progress up through HR to the senior management of the organization.

The flow through the organization of such processes is shown in Table 1.2 on page 37.

A LEARNING STRATEGY

Introduction

Learning strategies are generally written for use by members of the HR and learning functions. For staff in, and closely connected with, the learning function the learning strategy provides overall direction. It provides a framework in which decisions about learning can be made and implementation plans can be developed. For senior and line management it provides an overview of direction, and it should clearly demonstrate learning's contribution and value to the organization.

The learning strategy aligns with the organization's values, beliefs, behaviours and ways of working. The style and culture of the organization, or the culture that the organization is aiming to achieve, will be reflected in the structure, wording and presentation of the learning strategy.

A strategy's presentation and implementation need to meet the expectations of senior management. Should a learning strategy fail to align with senior management's vision of the current and future organization, the learning function is in danger of always operating at odds with the most influential people. Ensuring the 'fit' of a learning strategy with the requirements of senior management may need to be handled with political empathy. With the traditional organizational structure defined in this chapter, senior management in the learning function may well be dependent on advice from HR senior management for political guidance.

Building a learning strategy

The next section describes a 'best practice' approach to the design, development and implementation of a learning strategy. Using the organizational structure model with the learning function as part of HR, the learning strategy should become a subset of the HR strategy. This is certainly not the only model for the learning strategy, but it remains the most common and is certainly the one in which we personally first worked. There is also an assumption that appropriate strategy and direction are generally in place both for the whole organization and for HR.

In (past) times of true, consistent and predictable change, learning strategies were built with a five-year view. With current fast-moving changes in private and governmental organizations, even a 'traditional' learning strategy is unlikely to be sustained for longer than three years without significant modifications. Strategies will need to be reviewed annually at a minimum.

Structure and content of a learning strategy

A learning strategy document will include the overall direction, shape and approach of the learning function within the organization. It also must define the character of a learning function's operation within the organization.

The business strategies and directions of the organization must be fully supported by the operations of a learning function. Learning initiatives need, therefore, to be designed as an integral part of a business programme. A business programme to increase factory productivity may well involve reskilling of machine operatives. An improvement in the market sensitivity of the whole organization may well include a change/learning programme of workshops. The learning strategy outlines how business programmes are supported by appropriate learning initiatives and the joint responsibilities of 'learning staff' and 'business function staff'.

Our goal should be to present the learning strategy in a straightforward document that fully underlines the professional nature of the learning function. A typical learning strategy is from three to five pages in length. Written for the eyes of senior management, line management, HR and the learning function, the strategy is an internal document. 'Fit for purpose', it is a concise, descriptive document written in business language without learning jargon. Accepting this, as authors, never forget that there is always an element of selling involved with the strategy and the strategy document. It needs to reflect well on the learning function, which will use the strategy document as a key support to its *raison d'etre*. Throughout its life, perhaps against changes in personnel of organizational senior and line management, the strategy document and its content stand as a plain reminder of the use and usefulness of the learning function.

A typical learning strategy document structure includes paragraphs describing:

▍ the learning function's vision, mission, values, working philosophies and structure;

- the strategic directions, targets, objectives and priorities of the function;
- the overall 'learning journey' for the function; where it is now and where it needs to be;
- target performance objectives, achievements, metrics and the target levels of competence, attitude, belief, motivation and commitment that are to be aimed for across the organization;
- the manner in which the strategy will be integrated into the overall business strategy of the organization, the clear link between organizational needs and the 'deliverables' that are outlined in the strategy;
- without detailed description, learning and learning methodologies that will be employed;
- without detailed description, types and styles of learning initiative that will be implemented in fulfilling the strategy;
- outline charging strategies, resourcing plans for learning implementation and cost plans;
- the critical success factors for performance by the learning function.

Accept the fact that some of the target audience, particularly senior management, may not be familiar with the mechanisms of learning and development, and therefore preface any strategy document with a number of statements covering:

- the benefits to the organization of creating and implementing the strategy;
- the business environment into which the strategy must fit and assumptions you have made;
- the purpose of the strategy and how it should be used.

Levels of detail

The levels of detail included in learning strategies vary enormously between organizations. A highly detailed strategy, representing an attempt to establish the total framework in which the learning function is to operate, obviously provides a welcome focus. It can, however, result in the possibility of inflexibility when change is necessary following organizational alterations. Strategies produced in recent years are often limited to a set of high-level guidelines. Operational requirements of the organization may change rapidly, and an outline framework should ensure that the learning function may react in its need to be 'responsive', 'proactive', 'fast' and 'flexible'. However, authors need to avoid temptation to reduce the content to a level where it has little or no value. Keep in mind that a strategy is vital in providing a clear, long-term direction for everybody involved in learning and development. Clear, signposted directions encourage an environment where the skills, knowledge, behaviours and beliefs of the employees are built in line with the needs of the organization. Keep in mind that with a high rate of operational change, the learning strategy we describe here may be so flexed as to be of limited use; there may be the need for a different approach to the 'framework' with the use of a learning architecture (see Chapter 5).

Learning strategies do not concern learning needs for individuals, but recognize and make reference to the impact of strategic changes on the organization's overall staff or groups of staff. The proposed introduction of a new appraisal system or the provision of distance learning facilities could have a profound impact on the nature of the learning provided. Equally, learning strategies recognize results of current and planned changes in organizational business and performance objectives such as new levels of staff turnover and the implementation of staff succession plans.

CREATING AND IMPLEMENTING A LEARNING STRATEGY

Introduction: using a project approach

Our advice is to build an initial draft model of the strategy and obtain senior management's buy-in before completing the full process. This is an ideal opportunity to 'projectize' a major piece of work, an ideal task for the application of sound project management principles (see Chapter 6). In good project management style, fully research and analyse information before creating documentation. Examine any likely risks in the process, particularly possible sources of time delay. Be aware of the availability of people you wish to interview; consider the timing of any significant task you may have to include in your project such as a widespread set of interviews.

Especially if this is the first time your organization has built a learning strategy, be very clear about the purpose and format of the strategy, what you are trying to achieve. Clear definition will assist in building and selling the whole concept of a strategy as you work with people across the organization.

Overall, building a learning strategy will be a time-consuming activity, particularly in an organization without experience. Other considerations allowing, choose a quieter time for the learning function. This will vary between organizations, perhaps at the time of general holidays or when learning activities are at a lower intensity because the remainder of the organization is focused on the financial year-end.

Review existing strategies

Review a range of existing strategies:

▌ Benchmark any existing learning strategy within the organization against published local standards (CIPD in the UK).
▌ Discuss the history of different types of business strategies in other parts of the organization. What have been the critical factors for success in the development of financial, marketing and general business strategies? What were the key points in building and implementing strategies that are deemed to have been successful, useful to the function and also acceptable to senior management?
▌ Talk to key management and staff throughout the organization. If there is an existing learning strategy, question their knowledge of it, its use and its usefulness. Discuss any ideas they have for improvement.
▌ If at all possible, benchmark the existing learning strategy against similar strategies from similar organizations. Should you work within a large organization there may be other learning functions in other business units. With an active network you will find peers who will discuss the process of compiling a strategy, though be conscious that they may well regard learning strategies as fundamental to their organization's own future and therefore commercially sensitive. Discuss topics including:

  - What acknowledged meaning and use does the learning strategy have across the organization?
  - Why and how were specific elements of the strategy formed?
  - Why and how were learning budgets organized?
  - What was the impact of any budgetary decisions on the number of people attending courses?
  - Given the chance, would they change any of the approach to developing and implementing the strategy process?

Critically examine and analyse all this information, both internal and external. What factors lead to success and how easy are strategies turned into practical implementation plans? What form of budgetary and resourcing arrangements seems to be most appropriate?

Review materials and key information

▌ Become familiar with the organization's business and performance strategies as well as any key individual initiatives. Understand brand, vision, mission and values. Supplement what you know about the organization by reading appropriate documentation and by interviewing members of management.

▌ Become familiar with the strategies of other functions within the organization, particularly the HR strategy. A learning strategy must interface with other functions' strategies as well as being consistent with those of the whole organization.

▌ Review current learning initiatives across the organization. How well do they fit with any current learning strategy? Decisions will need to be made about non-concurrent learning initiatives. Will they have to be halted or be reduced? At what cost? At what motivation to those involved as learners and facilitators? This can be an enormous potential issue with large, multinational organizations where you may be writing a global strategy and where current learning initiatives across the world may challenge your work. This may be a major issue when selling ideas to senior management. There may be a need to explain why current initiatives, resourced and budgeted, are not within the proposed strategy. For example, should a new strategy be leading towards desk-based, e-learning approaches, what will be the impact on the buildings currently dedicated to 'training' and the staff involved?

▌ Examine HR planning information such as organizational development, performance management, reward and recruitment policies. Examine a selection of completed annual performance appraisal forms and similar materials. What personal development plans have been discussed for the people who are working to achieve the organization's success? These considerations will have a major impact on the learning strategies you propose.

Interviewing sources of information

Arrange interviews with a wide range of people: senior and line managers across the organization who have responsibility for the development of their staff together with people who have experienced or will experience learning initiatives. Ensure there is a true cross-functional input, with representative senior and line managers from all aspects of the organization, including operations, marketing, finance and HR. Particularly seek out those who are known to have strong views on learning and the learning function.

Interviews with senior management at this stage are particularly key to success. Before starting to build a learning strategy the organization's direction needs to be clearly understood. Be aware that a published 'direction' may not be the whole truth, and understanding potential future shifts in direction is vital. An organization structured around a centralized culture will have a significant impact on the infrastructure and the operation of the learning function, with strong vertical lines of control through to the delivery of learning. A management shift towards decentralization will impact on a learning strategy. As well as a change in any organizational 'message' provided within learning initiatives, there may need to be learning infrastructure changes: potentially, in this example, less reliance on 'training schools' and more on distance learning initiatives. Different, decentralized parts of the business may, through their management, prove to have different ideas about learning – with a significant impact on 'global' and 'local' learning strategies.

The issues outlined above need to be considered, discussed and confirmed before a usable learning strategy can be formatted. Countless hours of work in detailed implementation can be wasted if the baseline strategy is not consistent with the organizational direction. There has to be openness and trust in the discussions with senior management. Otherwise, a learning strategy faces the risk of being an embarrassing, costly white elephant. From our point of view, we need to use all our political skills. We need to consider who are the real power players, those whose vision of the future will be a major input to the direction of the organization.

Questions to which an answer is needed include:

I Where are we now as an organization and within its individual functions, and what internal and external factors cause these situations?

I Where do we want to be as an organization in three to five years' time, and how currently do we believe we are going to get there?

I What are the stated objectives for the organization and individual functions?

I What are the important external and internal challenges facing the organization/function over the next three years? Could they lead to a change in organizational objectives and provide significant learning requirements?

I What are the current important external and internal challenges facing the organization/function?

I Is it likely that there will be an evolution or revolution in our business in this timescale?

I Is it likely that the current people working within the organization will be the 'same' across the timescale? What are likely to be the impacts of retirements, redundancies, reskilling and graduate hire?

I What knowledge, skills, attitudes and beliefs will people need to have to help us to attain the organizational and functional strategy, in the short and long term?

I What impact will good/poor learning initiatives have on the results of the organization/function?

I What style(s) of learning initiative are appropriate across the organization? Do managers believe their teams are open to only classroom learning experiences? Is there a motivation for distance learning, particularly self-paced e-learning? Is there experience to support any views?

I How should the learning function interrelate with other parts of the organization in implementing learning strategies and plans?

I What should be the roles of managers and of staff during the design and implantation of learning initiatives?

As conversations unfold, check how your interviewees' comments compare with published organizational and functional strategies. If there seem to be discrepancies with published strategies, what is the impact for learning? Can you help; do you need to consider a different approach?

Interview a wide cross-section of staff about their views and experiences of learning within the organization. It is particularly important to interview people that have made more than 'tick box' comments on 'happiness sheets' at the conclusion of learning events. Talk to people who never seem to be involved in any learning initiatives. Do they believe something is missing? Or is there no support for learning in their working location?

What learning is needed?

Your interviews will have provided information about the learning initiatives you need to provide. This is matched with macro-level information from learning needs analyses. Outcomes of learning need analysis initiatives provide a clear view, at organizational, functional and individual levels, of the volumes of learning required and the associated urgencies. Outcomes also need to be considered against HR policies including appraisals, personal development plans, succession planning, recruitment policies and general staff planning.

Your research should have made you ready to formulate a draft strategy or modify an existing one. Once it is published, a reader of your strategy should see a clear flow of argument – from business and performance strategy, through the integration of learning into that strategy, to how (at summary level) the learning will be implemented. The reader will also clearly understand how all aspects of the planned learning initiatives will be monitored as they are implemented.

For each element of the strategies consider the resources needed. What is the best method of providing these types of learning initiative? Consider cost and quality. There are also some subtle things to consider. Consider long-term development plans for your learning function staff and their motivation if too much work involves outside agencies. Hotels cost money, but there are tremendous advantages in holding events away from the organization with overnight accommodation. If there are 'training schools' how are they budgeted? Must they be the preferred location?

One of the keenest decisions will be over the recommended methods of learning for each element of the strategy. What are the considerations? Internal or external courses? Formal learning courses or self-study material? Classroom based or on the job? What has worked in the past? What will need particular attention if it is implemented?

Risks and assumptions

For each element of the strategy consider the risks involved. What assumptions are you making? What could go wrong? What should you include in your strategy to minimize risk and to manage the effects of things going wrong once the plans associated with the strategy is being implemented? Be keenly aware of the risks that should be discussed with senior management early in the development of the learning strategy. Have these fully documented at the instigation of the strategy, and have them fully reviewed and recorded as the strategy is used, together with any other risks that emerge as time goes by. All this is a basis for upgrading the strategy and for 'best practice' considerations in the future.

Resources and budgets

As the strategy builds, the required resources, including budgets, will be identified. This will be a potential area for significant debate. Ensure there is a clear, convincing strategy for resources and finances before presentation to senior management. Consider resource and budget constraints, both current and those that future organizational directions may impose. Consider the best use of resources:

I People who will be directly involved in the facilitation of learning. What are the required competences for people who will implement the plans that flow from the agreed strategies? Where will suitable people be located? Will they all be located in a learning function within HR? Will they be permanently members of the learning function, seconded from other functions, or primarily from external consultancies?

I Will premises and equipment support the possible new initiatives? Are rooms large enough, correctly networked for computers and so on? Do enough people have their own equipment for remote learning initiatives?

I With large, distributed organizations the availability of suitably skilled external facilitators can be key to the success of 'global' learning initiatives. What is their availability and expertise, and what is their willingness to fit with the culture of learning that your strategy will propose?

I Internal relations with other functions. Will there be significant support for learning initiatives? What are the overall levels of coaching and mentoring across the organization to follow through with the learning initiates provided?

I Finances of the function. Should budgets for learning sit centrally with a learning function, within the jurisdiction of line managers, or within a compromise between the two? (See Chapter 5.)

When you have considered all of the available options, you will be ready to propose resources and funding budgets to deliver the optimum results. Any subsequent request for increased resources is likely to be closely questioned. Prepare by identifying, specifically, the ways in which any increase in resources will yield a demonstrable benefit to the organization. The nature of the benefits will vary, and will need to be agreed with the managers who own the appropriate operational programmes and the associated staff. Areas where benefits should be seen include:

I Directly calculated links between resource utilization and achievement of the organization's short, medium and long-term strategy. For example, employing a further trainer of sales skills should result in many more new salespeople being available to sell the organization's new line.

I Quantifiable returns on specific investments. For example, telephone skills learning will improve customer complaint handling and lead to an accompanying decrease in telephone charges.

Budgeting models

How learning will be budgeted across the organization will be a key factor. How, exactly, will the charges for learning be accommodated within the financial budgeting of the organization? This part of the learning strategy will need to be consistent with the requirements of the organization's strategic accounting policies and structures. Should you be suggesting new approaches to funding there will be a need to demonstrate strong evidence, probably based on benchmarked examples from other organizations, of the advantages of whatever you are advocating. Any chosen charging method should allow for the accounting of the true and total cost against budget of all learning initiatives.

Chapter 5 includes a discussion of the possible financial models for a learning function.

Final considerations

Having realistic strategies is about balance through the individual function, the organization and the overall environment. When a learning strategy is clearly seen to recognize all these aspects, the learning function will establish a reputation with senior management for realism and reliability. Learning strategies and activities consistently in alignment with the organization's overall business planning cycle, while handling the truisms of the external environment, significantly enhance the chances of achieving support.

Checks to be made throughout the development of a learning strategy and certainly before its submission include:

▌ What is the external environment in which your organization operates and/or will be operating? Is it in expansion, steady-state or contraction? Do the organizational strategies reflect this? Do your learning strategies and your budget requirements reflect this?

▌ How well were previous learning strategy submissions received by senior management? Have you learnt lessons? Have you paid enough attention to building your case and winning support?

▌ Can the organization afford identified budgets? If not, in which areas should you reconsider the strategy and the budgets? Have you prioritized your individual strategies? What could realistically be achieved with a decrease in budget if that is what is appropriate?

▌ Have you tended to overestimate or to underestimate the requested resources and finances? Failing to stay within budget in any year will make it more difficult in bidding for the following year's requirements. Obvious overestimation will cause your future budgetary requests to be viewed with suspicion.

▌ How will the strategy be monitored and evaluated as it is implemented? What are the risks associated with new types of learning initiative included in the learning strategy? Have you clearly explained these risks and the plans to handle them? What guarantees are provided for senior management and for line management of the staff involved?

I Have you included commitments to launch and implementation dates together with timescales as to when the benefits of the strategy will be forthcoming?

I Have you fully detailed the business assumptions you have made in compiling the strategy, particularly about the future business environment and the resources to be available (including finance)?

I Your submission will be a 'selling' presentation, verbal and/or documented. Think it through. For all your careful negotiations, what may be objections, from whom? What have you prepared to answer all the likely questions?

I What should be the appropriate level of detail in the final document? What types of documents are appropriate for the culture of the organization? What style of document will provide the correct image for the learning function? What styles of document do other functions use? Does the learning strategy have to look similar to, or even be part of, the HR strategy document?

Formulate the initial draft

With all the materials and the elements of the strategy in place, the initial draft model can be built. This will be presented to senior management in gaining agreement to finalize the published strategy document.

Consider that a large proportion of the audience that will receive and use the strategy when it is completed may not have a learning background. Appropriate language and focus are key, and ensure there is no inappropriate jargon. Discuss this initial draft model with a number of people, including management at all levels of the organization as well as fellow learning professionals.

Once you are comfortable with the initial draft model, present it to senior management, stressing the need for their visible, active support of the final strategy when it is implemented.

The final document

Taking heed of any comments from the draft senior management presentation, complete the strategy at a level of detail appropriate to its purpose within the organization.

Launch the strategy, with an appropriate level of publicity, to all levels of management across the organization and within the HR and learning functions. The document should be stand-alone and self-explanatory, but a covering letter always helps.

Monitoring, reviewing, refreshing

Staff of the learning function have a prime role to monitor the use and usefulness of the strategy:

▌ in meetings with line management, testing line managers' knowledge, understanding, agreement with and use of the strategy;
▌ by benchmarking the organization's strategy with those of other organizations;
▌ across the organization, and particularly within the learning function, analysing all planned and implemented learning initiatives and checking their consistency with the strategy.

The intention is to provide a consistent framework for learning through a strategy that will accommodate changes within the organization. Modifying an in-place learning strategy needs to be handled with sensitivity. A learning strategy normally requires an annual review and a complete overhaul after three years. With rapid changes in organizational activity a learning strategy is unlikely to be sustained for long without significant modifications – in fact, a totally different approach may be appropriate (see Chapter 3). The strategy has a prime role in guiding learning and development, and it is advisable to minimize modifications as rapid changes may produce misunderstandings.

Senior managers need to be involved in agreement to all modifications as the strategy is fundamental in the achievement of the organization's overall strategy. They require regular briefings from the learning function, in conjunction with line management, as to whether the strategy:

▌ remains appropriate in terms of the business needs and direction of the organization;
▌ remains appropriate when compared with the strategies in use by like organizations;
▌ is being implemented successfully and is consistently achieving its aims;
▌ is in need of modification, and how modifications should be implemented.

THE LEARNING IMPLEMENTATION PLAN

Introduction

In turning our high-level guiding strategy into operational tactics it is normal to develop and publish a learning implementation plan. This is an organization-wide plan detailing the learning workshops and other learning activities to be provided within a specific timescale. By reading the plan any member of staff will be able to understand the learning development initiatives that the organization is making available and how to take advantage of them.

When the implementation plan is being compiled the following need to be considered:

I The relationship of the learning plan to the learning strategy, described in previous paragraphs, and a learning policy, introduced later in this chapter.

I Results of learning needs analyses across the organization.

I The availability of learning and development resources including budgets, facilitators, coaches, mentors, materials and so on.

I Availability of those staff that have been selected for attendance at the nominated learning and development activities.

I Any actions in the organization that may affect the results of learning initiatives. Rumours of redundancy programmes will be likely to produce a demotivational impact on staff attending learning and development activities.

I The urgency and priorities of the required learning and development initiatives.

The plan is published as a document (and in a web-based format when possible) for everybody in the organization, and will typically include:

I an overview of the learning policy (see below);

I brief details of the staff currently in the learning function;

I aims, objectives and contents of each learning initiative;

I details of how individuals can be allocated places on any learning initiative.

Creating a learning plan

For each piece of the overall business strategy that is being supported through learning initiatives:

▌ Work within the 'umbrella' of the learning strategy. Ensure everything that is planned holds true to the agreed direction for learning.
▌ Continue the discussions with the business sponsors initiated as you developed the strategy. Talk with senior business sponsors who see the importance of changing the competences of the workforce. Talk with line managers who may possibly see lower importance for learning against their priorities for 'production'. Reconfirm the business strategies and the potential benefits to the organization as well as to the individual learners of appropriate learning initiatives. Talk with HR staff charged with the implementation of a cross-functional leadership programme.
▌ Agree the aims and objectives of the learning initiatives within the organization's activities. Anybody reading the learning plan, once it is published, should clearly understand the expected changes in performance associated with any learning programme. This may be in simple terms of a training programme's objectives, or in more sophisticated environments, connected with changes in detailed competences recognized across the organization.
▌ Agree the critical success factors for the learning initiative and individual activities. Agree what evaluation processes will be used.
▌ Consider the background and motivation of the learners who are likely to attend the activities in the programme; these factors will have a significant impact on the chances of success of the programme.
▌ Within the general guidelines of the learning strategy, agree what learning processes are most likely to contribute to achieving the objectives of the programme. There will be a mixture of many possible approaches to learning, including self-paced written materials, computer-based packages and classroom workshops. With the knowledge of what you are trying to achieve, what is the best approach or combination of approaches?
▌ Consider the availability of the prospective learners, facilities and nominated facilitators.
▌ Document the details, and finally agree everything with the business programme sponsor and the potential learners' line managers.

The published learning plan for any programme will include:

I the rationale for the learning and development initiatives in supporting the organization's strategies and the specific business programme;

I the aims and objectives of the learning and development initiatives together with its potential benefits to the organization and to individual learners;

I details of the learning and development activities that will make up the initiative and the overall timescales; dates, locations, times; the responsibilities of line managers and potential learners, including the manner in which learners will be allocated places on the activities within the programme;

I details of the success criteria for the learning initiative and how it will be monitored and evaluated.

A LEARNING POLICY

Purpose and role

Learning policies consist of statements describing the organization's strategic commitment to learning for its staff and how that learning will be delivered. They generally include a clear statement of the role of the learning function within the organization. Whereas learning strategies tend to be 'internal' to management, HR and the learning function, a learning policy is a document aimed at the staff, potential staff, and in some cases people external to the organization.

The prime reasons for organizations to prepare a learning policy include explanations for:

I the organization's strategic belief in and commitment to learning and staff development as integral parts of the development of the organization;

I the role and importance of learning and development for the organization and its staff;

I the role of the learning function in conjunction with the role of line management;

I why and how specific roles and specific groups have eligibility for learning initiatives;

I how individuals are eligible for learning initiatives, how they gain access to those initiatives, and the overall possibilities of personal improvement;

I the organization's commitment to current government initiatives and schemes, for example Investors in People in the UK, or any trade-oriented schemes.

The learning policy aligns with the organization's current vision, values and styles of working, or with the vision, values and style that the organization is aiming to develop. It needs to be consistent with other policy documents in the organization and with legislation in the areas of the law, health and safety, equal opportunities and data management. A learning policy and a learning strategy together are the guiding documents for all of the organization's learning and development initiatives.

The policy document is key for the learning function, possibly being the one document that represents the function across the whole organization. Many people, managers and their staff, as well as prospective recruits, will form opinions and expectations about the function and the organization through reading the policy document.

Responsibilities with a learning policy

The learning function is responsible for the creation and maintenance of the policy, but there has to be involvement of both senior management and line management. Since the policy represents the organization's commitments to its staff in the areas of learning and personal development, senior management are involved in its creation and publication. Once a policy is implemented senior managers will expect regular briefings as to whether the policy:

I continues to be appropriate in terms of the business needs and direction of the organization;
I continues to be appropriate when compared with the policies in use by similar organizations;
I is being implemented successfully and is consistently achieving its aims;
I is in need of modifications and how such modifications will be implemented.

Line management should contribute to:

I all phases of creating and implementing the policy;
I ensuring its implementation with their own staff;
I continuous monitoring and review of the policy's use and usefulness.

This involvement should help to ensure line management's commitment to the benefits of learning and development.

Structure and contents of a learning policy

A typical learning and development policy is an official document of the organization. It is typically a few pages in length. Often it forms a section of the employee handbook or the personnel practice manual. It is available to every member of staff, to potential recruits, and in some cases to people external to the organization.

With rapid changes occurring in business requirements, a policy will be unlikely to be sustained for longer than three years without significant modifications. The policy will be reviewed annually to ensure it is still appropriate.

In organizations with the availability of strong technology infrastructures, the policy will be available in screen-based formats as well as in hard copy.

Learning policies are generally structured in this way:

▌ a statement of the benefits to the organization of having a learning policy;

▌ an overall description of the purpose of the policy and how it should be used;

▌ an explanation for the reasons why learning is made available within the organization, emphasizing the benefits to staff and to the organization;

▌ a general description of what the organization provides in learning initiatives;

▌ details of individual staff members' possibilities of attaining formal qualifications;

▌ details of the organization's commitment to current government initiatives and schemes, Investors in People in the UK, or any similar trade-based scheme;

▌ descriptions of the various responsibilities of staff members, line management, the learning function and the whole organization within learning programmes.

Policies may include quantifiable statements of the organization's commitment to learning and development. These could include:

▌ the number of days per year that an individual employee can expect to devote to learning and development;

I   the amount of money per head the organization will spend annually on the provision of learning and development;

I   the percentage of payroll costs across the organization that will be devoted to the provision of learning and development.

Generally, however, organizations are understandably loath to include these quantifiable statements in a document with the permanent nature of a policy document. The business world changes rapidly, and these tactical items may have to change. It is quite normal therefore to find them included in the shorter-term learning plans, as above.

Creating and implementing a learning policy

Prime considerations in building and publishing a learning policy include the production of a document that will:

I   provide guidelines, agreed with and supported by senior and line management, as to the operation of the learning function;

I   be accessible physically to all levels of staff and any other nominated people;

I   reflect well on the learning function and the organization, particularly in comparison with rival organizations if the policy should be seen as a potential aid to recruitment;

I   raise expectations that normally can and will be fulfilled within the operating frameworks of the organization and the learning function;

I   lend itself to monitoring and modification with relative ease when the business situation demands;

I   encourage the involvement of all levels of staff in the creation and publication of the policy document.

Steps in constructing a learning policy are often an extension to the creation of a learning strategy as described above.

1.   The exact purpose of the policy is decided. Discussions with senior management review the impact of developing a policy and its potential format.

2.   Answers are collected to key questions:
     What standards will the organization use for individual roles? Will external standards be applied or will there be the use of internal measures such as competence statements (perhaps NVQs in the UK)?

What HR and/or line management processes will be used for supporting and testing any standards the organization employs?

How does the organization view future development of its people? How do initiatives align with HR programmes such as succession planning?

3. Any existing policy is reviewed:

   Management and staff throughout the organization are questioned about their knowledge of a current policy and their views as to its use and usefulness together with any ideas for improvement. The existing policy is benchmarked against examples from similar organizations and against any recommended standards (CIPD in the UK).

4. A 'straw model' of the policy at an outline level is written and discussed with a number of people chosen from all levels of the organization, including interested bodies such as unions. There are key points to be discussed, some of which may involve discussions with senior management:

   Do the statements that are being drawn up reflect the true culture of the organization?

   What changes in the business are possible and will they mean that sustaining the policy will be difficult?

   Can the organization deliver the promises that the policy is making? Do senior and line managers across the organization really believe in the statements of the policy and will they actively reinforce its implementation?

   The learning function must not be associated with a circulated learning policy consisting of a 'wish list' of nice-to-have statements to which the organization and its management does not really support.

5. Once the straw model is accepted, with any appropriate modifications after the discussions, it is presented to senior management, stressing the need for their support of the policy when it is implemented.

6. Taking heed of any comments from the senior management presentation, the policy is completed at a level of detail appropriate to its purpose within the organization.

The policy should include details of:

▌ Individuals' responsibility to prepare themselves for current and future job performance.

▌ The responsibilities of the learning function and line managers.

▌ Eligibility learning programmes and other learning initiatives. For example, are contract and part-time staff to be included?

I Any organizational mandate/recommendation on a number of days each year for each employee to spend in learning workshops and other learning activities.

I Induction processes. When can new people take advantage of all the regular learning activities?

I The possibilities of the organization contributing to an employee's non-vocational development. How can this be discussed?

I The possibilities for external development, such as an employee undertaking a part-time degree. How can these possibilities be investigated?

I The processes through which employees find out about learning initiatives and how they enrol.

The answers to these questions, when they are grouped into the learning policy document, must align with the statements made in other organization documents and internal policies, particularly when they represent legislation. This includes alignment to contracts of employment, equal opportunities, health and safety and data management policy documents.

Maintaining a learning policy

The continuing success of a learning policy relies on responsibilities being followed through by all parties. Learning activities need to be implemented, with a full understanding and application of the overall policy. A learning function monitors the possibility of learning and development initiatives becoming unacceptable to the 'customer community' of line managers and their staff. This may follow the introduction of practices not aligning with the policy: for example, a trainer is ill and another, less experienced trainer is substituted because there is a high urgency for the planned learning workshop. Things could go wrong if the policy stated that only experienced trainers would be used, and this was ignored. A further example of a policy being ignored is a line manager insisting a member of staff attends a workshop, although that member of staff has not completed the prerequisite study. The staff member might be able to take only limited value from the workshop, and the event could be disjointed for the other participants.

The learning policy should be monitored regularly:

I in meetings with line management and with staff by testing knowledge, understanding and acceptance of the policy;

I through benchmarking the organization's policy with those of other organizations whenever possible;

▌ through continuously and consistently analysing all the learning initiatives planned and implemented.

A policy may need to be supplemented when there is significant change in the business environment, or when a significant initiative such as NVQs (national, government led vocational qualifications in the UK) is introduced. Whenever a modification to the published policy is necessary, circulate the changes or a replacement document to all holders of the policy. Broadcast the changes or the whole new document through the organization's IT systems.

CHAPTER SUMMARY

▌ The corporate learning architect manages the learning function at a position on a continuum that is appropriate for the organization. This continuum stretches from a totally reactive 'establishing' mode through to a highly proactive 'guiding' role.

▌ In the establishing mode the corporate learning architect operates in a manner which reflects the fact that the learning function has time, resources and ability to put in place an operation with a rigorously planned strategy and implementation – an operation that will only be slightly modified over time.

▌ There remain many organizations where the frameworks for the successful implementation of learning programmes are built by a learning function reporting into and/or being part of the HR function. These organizations are ones where change is continuous and the traditional approaches to learning management are sufficiently flexible.

▌ Organizational strategies and overall learning needs are planned and monitored through the focus of HR.

▌ There is a regular flow of strategy, plan, implementation and review that results in a framework for learning. This framework encompasses a learning strategy, a learning implementation plan and a learning policy. All these are prepared, used, monitored and updated by the learning function working in close cooperation with all levels of organizational management.

3

A journey to learning excellence

Your career of years of working in learning functions has reached a pinnacle. This year, in your current role as training and development director, you have gained permission to examine the possibilities of initiating a corporate university. Whatever else results from your investigations you know that you will no longer be reporting through human resources (HR). Your new role, possibly to be labelled chief learning officer, will be as a direct report to the board.

You know the organization is about to formulate strategies for the coming years, and your appointment is a public statement of how learning is seen as one cornerstone of the future. This is the time to put the correct 'sticks in the ground': an appropriate learning architecture together with the correct personnel. This is a one-off opportunity to put everything in the right place to start your journey to learning excellence.

This is a time to both examine current internal practice and to benchmark the best of practice outside the organization – in both learning functions and other types of function where there are moves from 'service provider' to 'value-adding partner'. The success you envisage will only come to fruition once you find the best ways to identify and proactively handle both the commercial challenges and the learning challenges of your role. This is a real opportunity for learning to play a major part in the success of the organization. The manner that learning is delivered to stakeholders has to be correct for an organization that prides itself on successfully managing change. Any commercial model needs to be acceptable to the board, including a continuous modelling of 'added value'.

For this organization, unique in its style, where are you to aim? What could be the best approaches? What options are available, what is working elsewhere? What will be the metrics of success? Are there any quick wins? What style of management will be appropriate, what team competences are needed?

The purpose of this chapter is to discuss the role of a corporate learning architect moving the learning function's operations beyond traditional training and development approaches, and describe the activities involved in researching, planning, implementing and communicating that journey.

THE TRANSFORMING CORPORATE LEARNING ARCHITECT

Introduction

A state of 'learning excellence' will be different for different organizations. It will include different strategies with different learning programmes, managed by different styles of people. Equally, there will be many different journeys towards the attainment of learning excellence, with different levels of supporting organizational investment. Critically, the nature of learning excellence and the journey to its fulfilment have to be appropriate for, and almost certainly unique to, any particular organization.

The role of the corporate learning architect and the learning function team is to understand the organization and its future, and to ensure that learning provides the best possible service to the organization. The work of the corporate learning architect centres on the successful management of two interleaving voyages – this work we have designated as 'the journey to learning excellence'. This work will transform the learning function and, more importantly, the service it provides to the organization.

The first consideration concerns the *what*: what learning programmes are to be implemented, where and when, to fully satisfy the needs of the organization? The second, conjoined, consideration is the management of the journey across the corporate learning architect continuum introduced in Chapter 2. This is about identifying the *how*, the correct style of operation of the learning function for the organization's needs. The continuum starts from a reactive 'establishing' style and moves through to a proactive 'guiding' style – see page 46. Our corporate learning architect retains the vision of the optimum positioning on the continuum for equilibrium between the needs of the organization and the capabilities of the learning function, and of the appropriate rate of movement across the continuum as the learning function changes in response to the needs of a changing organization.

As the organization makes progress towards its goals we need to continually identify and discharge the most appropriate role for learning and the most appropriate 'shape' for the learning function. Continually we are identifying the current learning needs of the organization and monitoring current levels of success in discharging these needs. Any gaps in our performance need to be filled – to maintain our current, primary stream of work. In parallel, we are implementing our 'journey to learning excellence', identifying the future direction and changes of the organization and the resulting learning strategies and action plans – our secondary stream of work.

Typical key roles and responsibilities for a corporate learning architect managing the learning function in an 'establishing' status were introduced on page 48 of Chapter 2. This chapter describes the role growing to be about managing the learning function along the continuum to 'positioning' and 'guiding' status. Here there will be additional aspects to a corporate learning architect role as it both deepens and broadens. The role expands in taking on new responsibilities and characteristics, including:

▍ Working as a member of the higher level of management of the organization, playing a fully participative role in its strategic management, ensuring that learning provides acknowledged, vital benefits to the organization in pursuit of its goals.

▍ Managing the issues in maintaining meaningful and consistent strategies, policies and plans for learning solutions in constantly flexing organizations where staff are becoming more active, demanding people.

▍ Having regular access to the CEO on all matters that concern the role of learning within the organization, and using this intimacy to ensure that learning has the correct voice across the organization.

▍ Through the learning architecture (see Chapter 5), our framework for learning, having influence across the organization with all learning initiatives, not only those associated with HR. This involves responsibilities, established through the matrix structure of the organization, for learning being undertaken in line areas where the actual delivery of learning is not 'owned' by the learning function. Vocational training's delivery is managed by the line while responsibility for such training fitting with the organization's learning strategies is owned by the corporate learning architect and the learning function.

I Being fully involved in any organizational development, ensuring its alignment to the solution of business problems, research and restructuring.

I Ensuring that the knowledge and wisdom in any learning intervention for the organization and for its individuals is retained and made available within the organization.

I Building mechanisms to allow a continuous dialogue with senior organizational management of topics including discussion of topics such as:

- the necessity for a corporate learning architect to discharge a role at the highest levels of the organization;
- the potential beneficial role of learning for the success and continuance of the organization;
- the role of senior management in realizing organizational performance and competitive advantage from an appropriately developed 'human resource';
- the added value to the organization of the learning function and of the processes for the provision of learning.

CASE STUDY

An internationally operating information systems consultancy employs many thousands of people and specializes in a number of 'vertical' marketplaces – finance, government, transport and so on. There is an extensive learning programme structured around a detailed competence framework for all staff. A learning function has a mostly strategic and managing role. A profit centre model is implemented. External suppliers deliver all the learning initiatives, and these are charged back to the operating units on a 'cost plus' model to finance the learning function. Administration, evaluation and quality are all highly controlled. A training plan is published each November and covers a wide range of technical and interpersonal skill workshops for the following year. There is a high priority on developing skills of leadership all across managers at all levels.

Each vertical marketplace trading division has its own learning practice manager responsible for staff development and for liaising with the learning function over required learning initiatives. Individuals within the learning function have direct responsibility for working with these practice managers.

In the space of just a few months a highly significant issue for the organization has arisen. The organization has to respond to a 'fracture' in its marketplace brought about by initiatives introduced by its major competitors. This impacts each of the vertical-market operational units. A high-profile learning programme has been identified as part of the organization's response to the market change. Initially the client-facing teams have to be reskilled; a wider educational programme will follow for many in the organization.

The usual well-designed procedures of learning strategy and planning are not appropriate for this situation. They are designed for situations of continuous change and growth, not for a fundamental change in the organization's business needs. There is a significant learning need, but initially little internal expertise.

There is clear ownership and a well-established rapid response process. A senior learning consultant from within the learning function is working with the learning practice manager from an operational team formed to manage the organization's response to the business issue. Together they are building the plans for the appropriate learning programmes across the organization for managers, salespeople, sales consultants and pre- and post-sale project managers. With such a highly important project, the corporate learning architect is much involved. The learning consultant has prepared an invitation to tender for the learning initiatives and managed the process of choosing an external training and coaching supplier. The learning consultant will manage implementation, monitoring and review of the resulting learning programmes, continually working with the practice manager from the operational unit to monitor the usefulness of the learning initiatives and to make any necessary modifications.

Less than four weeks after the vertical marketplace trading division approached the learning function for assistance, the first classroom based workshops for client-facing teams are fully ready.

A scope of responsibilities

Chapter 2 described a familiar organizational structure with a learning function placed within an HR function. With this model the learning function typically only has responsibilities for learning associated with 'people' programmes that originate within the HR function. Terms such as 'human resource development' are indicative of learning initiatives primarily concerned with the traditional 'softer' skills of management and personal development. This approach allows for an efficient concentration on one specific area of learning. However, there is always a danger that, throughout the organization in areas less strongly associated with HR, there may be a considerable number of learning programmes that are poorly planned, poorly implemented, money-wasting initiatives. Organizations can suffer when there is a plethora of learning initiatives across the organization with which the learning function has little or no contact. Typically, these initiatives include activities as diverse as large-scale skills development programmes implemented by sales and marketing functions, and health and safety training programmes delivered to the production line staff by external consultants.

Important decisions need to be made about a scope of responsibilities as the corporate learning architect starts planning the 'journey to learning excellence' for the organization and for the learning function. Are the learning function's responsibilities to extend to involvement with training beyond 'soft skills' directed by HR? If so, in what ways and in which areas of the organization?

It is possible for the corporate learning architect and the team to take total ownership of all learning initiatives in every function of the organization. Experience has shown that such ownership may prove to be challenging for the staff of a learning function lacking knowledge of how parts of an organization discharge their working responsibilities. There is also the question of 'bandwidth' – how many staff are there in the learning function and how large is the organization? A more potentially successful relationship can take the form of a brief for the learning function for consultation and guidance. Here the operational functions take personal responsibility for implementation of learning initiatives. Consultation and guidance is provided by the learning function to ensure that all learning reflects the organization's overall learning strategies and policies – strategies and policies that remain in the ownership of the learning function. The consultation will include working with the functional departments in:

I ensuring that the planned learning has identified goals that are instrumental in establishing the usefulness of the learning initiatives;
I assisting in choosing the most appropriate facilitators of the learning initiatives, whether they be internal or external to the organization;
I establishing facilitator licensing approaches (see Chapter 8);
I framing wise use of organizational resources and budgets.

This 'consultation and guidance' strategy has been shown to minimize potential dangers of poorly focused functional, job-related learning.

CASE STUDY

An international computer company had long been renowned for the prowess of its sales training. The sales training function reported to the sales director and was staffed by a group of the most successful salespeople. A winning two-year appointment within the training team was inevitably followed by a promotion into sales management. A large budget was available, and this ensured that many of the programmes were delivered by high-quality external sales training consultants. There was little common ground between the human resources training team and the sales training function. Salespeople were able to take advantage of HR training programmes although in reality they rarely did so. Separate training records were maintained, and evaluation methodologies were not compatible.

Times changed in the computer industry. The company's market profile changed to a services-based organization and the sales of computer hardware declined. Margins were eroded and less money was available. It became obvious that the sales training function, although still regarded as highly successful in discharging its role to train and motivate the salesforce, could no longer continue in its traditional form.

Merging the two training areas was always going to be challenging. The sales training function, for all the logic of the financial arguments, wielded power, and the sales force had traditionally had a limited appreciation of the HR function. A compromise solution was reached, with the sales training function having a high degree of autonomy although it was absorbed into a newly shaped corporate learning function. The head of sales training reported directly to the corporate learning architect, who was by now reporting directly to the managing board of the organization. Financial savings were made, with sales training staff rather than external consultants delivering the majority of workshops. A new teamworking ethos was established across the corporate learning function, by staff from all parts of the function coming together in work groups to establish new learning management processes – including a learning architecture (see Chapter 5) and evaluation processes.

Positioning of the corporate learning architect

In Chapter 1 we discussed the importance of the corporate learning architect reporting directly to the senior level of management, typically the board – if not actually being a member of that senior management. When the chief information officer (CIO), responsible for knowledge information systems, computing and networking, often has such an elevated level, why not the learning architect? (In fact, it is not impossible to envisage those roles, CIO and the corporate learning architect, as one and the same person.) To operate in the style described in this chapter, with a very proactive mode of implementing learning, the corporate learning architect needs to operate at the highest levels of the organization – closely sharing the vision of the organization's direction, particularly in a rapidly changing environment. He or she must both share and, in appropriate circumstances, impact on that vision.

(We have even shared an ideal with some of our fellow learning architects for a CEO and a learning architect becoming one and the same person, a person who recognizes the absolute importance of learning, leads the whole organization and nurtures a learning-based organization. In reality, it may prove some years before the first person moves directly from a corporate learning architect role to being CEO, retaining both sets of responsibilities. We do know of people in the most senior of roles that have spent formative time as head of HR. All is possible!)

Initially, the suggested elevation of the corporate learning architect may not be acceptable to certain members of senior management. There may well be 'political' blocking by other functional management who see a personal and/or operational threat within the apparent rise of the head of learning. An escalation in stature and status of the corporate learning architect may have to be earned over time. It certainly should be a key factor in the plan for the journey to learning excellence, advocated at every opportunity – particularly when there are clear examples of success to justify the positioning.

When the corporate learning architect is not sufficiently highly positioned, an 'internal salesperson', advocating the learning function in high places and spreading news of the function's success, is vital. This sponsor definitely needs to be a member of senior management, well connected and well respected across the organization and its stakeholders.

Relationships for the learning function

When the corporate learning architect is 'establishing' a learning function, a traditional structure with the function reporting through HR to the organization will be the most likely model in use (see Chapter 2). Table 1.2 on page 37–38 shows this clear relationship. This model is not appropriate for an organization seeking to implement a 'positioning' or 'guiding' style of learning function. The learning function needs to be more in direct relationship with the operational units of the organization, and a model as in Figure 3.1 is appropriate. This is further discussed in Chapter 5.

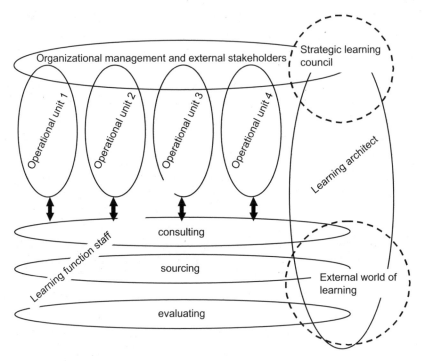

Figure 3.1 New relationships

The establishment of a strategic learning council can be a vital step in the progress towards building a responsive relationship between the organization and the learning function. Permanent membership of the council will be restricted to the CEO, the COO/operations director, the CFO/finance director, the HR director and the corporate learning architect. The council has the responsibility to monitor the progress of the organization's capability to use wisely learning and the associated resources. The strategic learning council should meet monthly, and discussions will include operational priorities for the organization and the most appropriate areas for the learning function to be concentrating, together with the success of the learning function and its learning strategies in providing appropriate learning across the organization.

The meetings provide excellent opportunities to have renowned learning and business 'gurus' address the council and further emphasize the potential importance of learning in organizational importance.

Budgeting for learning

The majority of organizational learning functions, managed by a corporate learning architect, will have a dedicated budget for the learning function, its staff and the implementation of learning initiatives. The size of this budget is quite often a 'top slice', a given percentage of the overall organizational expense budget. Alternatively, the size and 'shape' of the budget and associated resources may be derived through a thorough planning process of the form outlined in Chapter 2 of this book – learning initiatives are defined for the coming period, probably a year, and budget is assigned against the defined initiatives.

In Chapter 5 we discuss a number of current models for providing the budget for learning.

CASE STUDY

A UK-based financial organization is proud of its approach to learning. Its learning function has been celebrated in books and magazines as an excellent example of strategy, planning and implementation. The head of learning, our corporate learning architect, often graces the platform at conferences describing how the large number of people within the learning function work with staff across the organization in developing skills – against a background of a highly active market, significant competition and non-trivial, continual changes in legislation of which staff must be aware. Blending learning is seen to be successful in handling a wide variety of staff skill levels and a widely distributed workforce.

A proportion of the 'middle office' administrative operations are to be outsourced to an overseas country. This will probably lead to redundancies, and a considerable amount of ill feeling amongst staff is predicted. There needs to be training of the managers from the overseas country who will, in future, manage the work of the departments involved in outsourcing. These overseas managers need to be trained in the UK in order that they will have first-hand knowledge of the complexity of the operations and the supporting systems.

One of the most senior members of the learning architect's team, the account manager into the middle-office administration area of the company, is made responsible for this potentially tricky training initiative for the overseas people. Training is organized in a hotel, rather than in the on-site training school, and guest presenters are brought to that location. The overseas managers are only brought into the live middle-office area after the usual staff have left for the day.

The required knowledge level of business complexity, a high level of cultural awareness, the skills to handle the internal politics and the appropriate behavioural style in handling a tricky situation are all challenging for the account manager. The corporate learning architect has very firmly taken on a coaching role with the account manager in bringing this project to a successful conclusion. The learning architect is certainly using these parallel success stories in her work with the organization's strategic learning council.

Staffing the learning function

A traditional model for a learning function team, reporting to a corporate learning architect entitled 'training and development director', is typified in Figure 3.2. This will be a familiar model when the corporate learning architect and the learning function are in the 'establishing' status of the learning architect continuum. The delivery team consists of a number of trainers grouped in specialisms, perhaps by the topics in which they have particular expertise or by the areas and geographies of the organization they serve. In today's team there may well be a group specializing in distance learning, including e-learning. The development team's skills are in the areas of learning and training needs analysis and of learning material development. In the development team there may well be individuals with specialist skills and knowledge in topics such as assessment and evaluation.

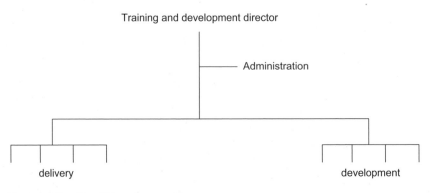

Figure 3.2   Traditional reporting

As the corporate learning architect manages the transformation of the learning function from left to right across the learning architect continuum, and manages the journey to learning excellence, the accompanying skills of the learning function's team are likely to be modified, moving to fit with the model of Figure 3.1. This structure and the associated competences are more appropriate to handle the roles and responsibilities of a fast-changing organizational environment. This will be achieved through a development programme or through a change of staff.

Figure 3.1 shows how a rapid, proactive approach to delivering learning initiatives is served with members of the learning function team positioned close to the business. They operate very much as consultants, and it is likely that their background will be business-grounded rather than 'soft skills' grounded. This is a significantly different working environment from that of the 'establishing' mode of learning function operation. Now things happen quickly, and there may be less opportunity for personal development for the team members – certainly less chance for 'learning by mistakes' than in the steady world of the establishing status. This working environment demands a different set of competences from the team members; it also demands a high level of coaching and encouragement from the more senior team members – right up to the corporate learning architect.

Staff within the learning function may act as 'practice managers', responsible for the relationship with one or more specific functions in the organization, straddling the interface with the learning function. Their practice could therefore be 'marketing' or 'production'. In addition, as experts in their own field of expertise in learning, they may manage, for example, distance learning or mentoring practices within the learning function. In the fulfilment of learning initiatives, the practice manager organizes intervention teams in the topic areas, acting as the interface to the internal client within the other functions of the organizations. This approach will be particularly useful if there is to be charging out of the services of the learning function, since it provides a particular individual with responsibility for particular interventions.

Practices within the learning function may well be organized as centres of excellence available across the whole organization. As 'topic leaders', practice managers are responsible for maintaining knowledge, skill and wisdom for their specific speciality. They facilitate a group of subject experts from a range of functional groupings, and maintain contact with external organizations including academic organizations. In addition, they organize communities of interest with people who are in need of the core expertise and who are prepared to attend seminars and the like. Guiding and coaching for the topic areas are made available across the organization. An example is a learning function practice manager being the 'corporate guru' for teambuilding. In addition to ensuring there are appropriate, proactive learning initiatives for teambuilding, the practice manager will be the owner of the process, tools and techniques of teambuilding. Teambuilding will be consistently implemented across the whole organization under the practice manager's guidance – ensuring the ease of teambuilding and the likelihood of success with team-based projects.

Other responsibilities within the learning function may include client account managers who have, amongst other duties, permanent responsibility to interface with other functions of the organization in discussing that function's needs and proactively promoting the services of the learning function. Learning interventions will involve the learning function teamworking in total cooperation with other organizational functions, managed by the account manager. For example, for an intervention involving the sales function, the team formed will consist of members of the sales function and members of the learning function. Representation from the learning function may be practice-driven or account management-driven, depending on the nature and goals of the intervention. Team leadership throughout the duration of the intervention is with the sales function to ensure its ownership of the whole intervention. This also underscores the understanding of a philosophy of 'handover' and 'ownership' once the intervention and the accompanying paths to organizational learning are embedded. For the duration of the intervention the learning function representatives on the team would supply project management expertise, as well as the expertise in the most effective use of learning interventions and the retention of the learning within the sales function.

When the corporate learning architect and the learning function operate in a proactive mode, our concept of staffing includes a reluctance to establish layers of management structure within the learning function. This reflects an 'inside-out' attitude to working, rather than a fixation on hierarchies. The recommended format is more of a 'peered organization', with a group of equal-level professionals teamed, when necessary, by project. In reality, any decision as to structure will have much to do with the size of the learning function and the maturity of the function's staff. The decision may have to take account of a certain number of specific situations. For example, care needs to be taken in a totally flat structure with performance management, appraisals and career development – particularly as such procedures must be seen to be effective within the learning function, one of the obvious role models across the whole organization.

The extended team, virtual resources

In order to provide solutions rapidly to a wider variety of learning needs there will be the need for a wide range of implementation capabilities. All styles of learning architect and, when appropriate, the practice managers and account managers discussed above need to build extended teams of expertise in business and learning. These teams will include personnel from external organizations as well as internal people; all have rich, scarce knowledge needing to be shared with others.

Using resources outside the direct team (see Chapter 8) always leads to challenges. The learning architect together with all the other staff of the learning function has a brand to protect. Material needs to be developed and delivered in a consistent, learning-focused manner. There will always be the need for an element of policing when other resources are brought into play.

One corporate learning architect, hundreds of 'learning architects'

Transforming the learning function and its contribution to the organization will involve focus and exceptional leadership, particularly when the work has identified that the 'journey to excellence in learning' is one with a number of challenging hurdles. Individual corporate learning architects will work in different ways to handle particular hurdles and to provide the most appropriate benefits to their organizations; journeys will never be dull!

In the straightforward model we propose, to provide an appropriate level of control and leadership, there is one corporate learning architect within an organization: the one senior person owning the vision, well supported by everybody within the learning function. In addition, in that same organization there must be hundreds of learning architects who understand and 'buy in' to the vision. These are others, passionate about learning, who are dedicated to employing the power of learning for themselves, their teams and everybody with whom they work. They share the values and the focus of the learning architect without having the overall organizational responsibilities. A prime vision for the corporate learning architect is to have everybody in the organization fully competent and fully committed to being a learning architect. The vision for each learning architect is the use of learning as a full contribution to organizational performance in conjunction with the attainment of personal goals and needs.

In support of the development of all of the learning architects, the corporate learning architect and the learning function team carry a full responsibility for communication all across the organization about learning, its successful involvement in assisting organizational performance and its further potential. (See 'Branding and communication for a learning function' in Chapter 5.)

Providing learning initiatives: tools and processes

Learning professionals have become used over the years to a well-structured approach to the delivery of learning initiatives from a stable organization managed by a training and development director – stability that provides time to build and implement robust learning solutions. This is described in Chapter 2 as the establishing status of a learning function. Well-planned, firmly implemented lines of control and fully planned learning initiatives are the order of the day.

In response to a highly complex, oft changing organization, our corporate learning architect will need to manage the learning function on a journey to a more responsive, more proactive role. This involves a move across the learning architect continuum to a 'positioning' status, and eventually to the 'guiding' status. Time may well not be available to implement well-structured mechanisms, and a different model for strategizing building, implementing and evaluating is available. This is built around a highly professional learning function team, working consultatively across the organization and its stakeholders (see Figure 3.1). It centres on mechanisms to provide degrees of control in highly flexible situations. These implementation models and the overall control mechanism, our learning architecture, are described in Chapter 5.

THE JOURNEY TO LEARNING EXCELLENCE

Introduction

Through careful attention to the approaches outlined in the paragraphs above, we have our corporate learning architect in place, with an initial level of acceptance of how the challenges of the role are to be delivered – a first 'licence' from the most senior organizational management. Now our attention is turned to implementing the organizational journey to excellence, a journey that will result in a learning function with the correct 'style' of operation for the organization, and a journey that will result in the implementation of the correct learning programmes for that same organization. This needs to be a journey managed by our corporate learning architect.

In Chapter 2 we described the tools and techniques for a corporate learning architect to establish an efficient learning function. This chapter discusses the planning and the implementation of a journey to result in a learning function which, in addition to being efficient, is highly effective in the development of organizational performance.

Our considerations will be:

I Making the decisions about where the journey is aimed. What is the vision for learning that we are to follow? For this organization, as it moves forward, what will be the appropriate style of operation of the learning function, and what will be the learning programmes that can contribute to superior organizational performance? How exactly should the corporate learning architect be operating within the organization?

I Planning the journey to excellence and gaining approval for the key stakeholders who must support the journey. Initially considering from where we start, what needs to be done to reach our goals and what is a realistic timeframe? It must consider short-term goals to plug any gaps in the current learning programmes, and longer-term goals as we build a strategy for learning. What can we learn about effective learning that is being implemented elsewhere? What processes, tools and techniques are we to employ? What are the considerations for the many people involved?

I Continuously reviewing progress as we undertake the journey, checking that the journey remains the appropriate one and evaluating progress against the plan. Communicating success as we go.

Figure 3.3 plots the approach to our journey, using tools and techniques from project management, client relationship management and customer service. As with all journeys, things will change along the way and there will be need to review and refocus as we journey – internal and external organizational changes will have an impact, and our journey will need to be modified. Figure 3.3 shows the sophistication of what we are undertaking, the 'double loop' nature of our task. As learning has a real impact on the organization, the organization will change and thus our journey will need to change in response.

There is always a danger that organizational change will take place faster than we can provide stable learning initiatives. Trying to have useful learning initiatives catch up with their potential for the organization has been likened to 'nailing jello to the wall'. Flexibility in the architecture of

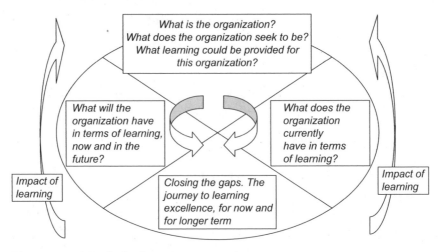

Figure 3.3   Needs for learning

learning and its implementation will be of paramount importance; flexibility, too, in the competencies of those implementing the learning.

Whatever is the result of the deliberations associated with these pragmatic questions, the visioning, strategizing, planning and implementation of new learning approaches will require strong management and leadership. This is the management and leadership role given the title of the corporate learning architect throughout this book.

Based on the research that is described in the following paragraphs, decisions will be made concerning the style of the learning function, its staff, its capabilities and its approach to its performance goals – all agreed with the management of the organization.

RESEARCHING THE JOURNEY TO LEARNING EXCELLENCE

This section concerns the understanding of the organization of the way that we can plan to ensure the foundations of learning are strong and that we build the correct journey to future learning excellence. It provides tools and techniques to analyse organizations and to make the correct decisions about these foundations of learning. It goes much further than a traditional analysis of learning needs, discussed in Chapter 2, where analysis begins with organizational strategies handed down to a learning function through a (possibly filtered) HR function view. Analysis in the approach followed here starts from a core assessment of the organization with which we are dealing together with its people, particularly its senior management.

Our research involves:

I interviewing senior stakeholders of the organization, internal and external, to gather views on the future of the organization and the potential 'involvement' in organizational performance of learning;

I identifying the style and culture of the organization, and predicting the most appropriate ways that learning could play a role in the organizational journey to superior performance;

I building a benchmarked view of the possible: what is happening elsewhere and what might be appropriate for our organization?

The results of all this research are key to identifying the styles of learning programme and learning function most appropriate for working with the organization.

As with all projects of this nature, our consultative research will follow a cyclical pattern. As answers are forthcoming, further questions are identified, thoughts and findings need to be reconfirmed and possibly modified. Essential to our work is an acceptance of rigour in planning and implementing all these research activities, with sufficient time allowed to confirm results.

Choosing who will undertake the research is an important consideration. An experienced external facilitator of the process may be appropriate in the early stages, to plan and initiate the research project as well as to establish its importance within the organization. Our own recommendation will always be that members of the learning function themselves should undertake the research – with appropriate training when necessary. The ability to discuss key issues for the organization, including the potential of learning through an effective learning function, particularly with senior people, is a desired quality of staff across the learning function (see Chapter 7). As soon as is feasible, take ownership into the learning function – grow its people and signal those people's capabilities within the organization. When appropriate use the external experience in a mentoring role for the learning function staff. It may be new work for those staff if their background is a traditional training and development function.

Working with internal and external stakeholders

Whatever the tactical considerations, our strategy will be to advocate an approach with learning given a higher, more proactive importance for the organization. As part of this strategy, the potential for learning needs to be consistently and knowledgeably discussed with senior stakeholders of the organization, both external and internal. Our goals are to understand views on a range of topics including:

  ▌ the perception of the current status and contribution of learning;
  ▌ the level of understanding about what learning could provide as an integral part of the organization's performance;
  ▌ an indication of the level of investment and risk that might be acceptable in absorbing new approaches to learning.

Conversations with senior stakeholders are all-important throughout our research, and later during our negotiations towards an agreement about what will be implemented. Within the organization senior stakeholders are key in terms of their support for appropriate learning initiatives. In addition, their organizational role may have a significant impact on a learning function's role and budget; at times, its very existence. It is not impossible that such senior stakeholders may have little real idea of the importance of learning and its possibilities for an organization. In addition, their current belief into the effectiveness of the learning function may well be a perception built on unstructured comments and rumour from unconnected sources across the organization. Thus, our role in these conversations will be partially questioning, partially educating, partially defending and justifying.

There are a wide range of possible external stakeholders, differing between different types of organization. These include:

  ▌ Government bodies that prescribe a wide range of learning topics such as those associated with corporate governance, risk, health and safety for a variety of staff, and legislative awareness for individuals selling financial products to the public.
  ▌ Bodies that can provide guidance, experience, and possibly funding in such areas of learning as literacy, young people's development and specific trades.
  ▌ An organization's clients involved in initiatives such as quality, where there may well be an insistence on levels of competence across their supplier's staff – resulting in imposed learning initiatives on the organization.
  ▌ An organization's suppliers where there are agreements about supply chains that will allow the supplier's impact to be deeply embraced within the organization. There may well be the need for such initiatives as education for the supplier staff and joint workshops to capture maximum benefit from the association.

Conversations with these important people need to be fully prepared and carefully orchestrated. Our experience is that there is only small real return from 'tick list' surveys. To interview senior individuals requires innovative approaches, allowing the interviewer to lead the discussion in a positive manner. Such innovative approaches include 'four by' matrices, an example of which is shown as Figure 3.4. These matrices, used as the centrepiece of an interview, encourage active involvement of the interviewee, allowing interviewees a framework to place their own 'crosses' on the matrix as to where they think things are currently and where things might move. This naturally leads into questioning and discussion about why the interviewee has these opinions.

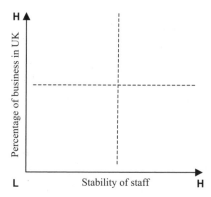

Figure 3.4   Analysing by 'four bys'

Figure 3.4 would prompt a range of discussions whose results are important to the plan for organizational learning. Do we intend to change the mixture of business across the countries in which we operate? How, with what objective? What impact will that have on the stability of staff? Will we be employing more or fewer people? What will be the profile of any new people? What will be the window for any necessary training? Will we be doing more outsourcing of work? Will people be hired on short-term contracts or as permanent employees?

'Alternative view' questions are also useful in interviewing people, particularly in engaging senior people. 'Why is this company not positioned in a similar manner to the ABC corporation when we advertise to potential clients?' 'How do you think that person would handle such a situation?' 'Which of our major competitors would we most like to be like, and what would help and hinder us in such a strategy?' 'Within the organization, which department in which country do you consider the best managed, and what would it take to catch up with them?' 'If there is one person with whom you could work, who would it be and why?'

Before 'going to print' always 'play back' to senior people any recording, paper-based or otherwise, that you have of conversations, and particularly the conclusions you have come to from those conversations. These busy people are much-needed allies and will need to be correctly quoted.

Characterizing an organization: introduction

Organizations are shaped and reshaped by a host of factors which are themselves changing. The external evidence of the 'way an organization is' includes its structure, its alliances, where and how it is active and its reputation for working with stakeholders. Internally, organizations exhibit a 'way of being' in many, often conflicting, ways – the organizational equivalent of an individual's personality. Just like personalities, internal 'ways of being' are difficult to measure and understand; we see only behaviours. The corporate learning architect's challenge in understanding the organization is to make sense of the observed organizational behaviours.

Our aim is to build a 'model' of the organization, its culture, its values and the manner in which it operates, and subsequently to design a journey to learning excellence that is specific to this organization. Included in the organizational characteristics to be considered are:

I the physical and controlling structures in use across the organization; is power distributed and communication organized with centralized or distributed models, or with some combination thereof?

I the culture and values of the organization, the 'way things are done to achieve success';

I the organization's relationship to its people together with the attitude to, and the use of, learning for its people;

I the rate of change within the organization, its marketplace and within particular functions.

Characterizing an organization: structure and power

The first set of variables that we consider in categorizing organizations are size, structure and impact on the business world in which they exist, a 'business world' which could be commercial, central or local governmental, or a not-for-profit world. The nature of an organization provides a fundamental shaping for the appropriate learning initiatives for that organization. A top-down, centralized organization will need learning implemented with a different approach to a decentralized, team-oriented organization. An organization where legislation or financial ownership means that there is a considerable amount of acknowledgement of stakeholder wishes will be best served by learning initiatives far different from those appropriate to a private organization with high internal focus.

Structures and power within an organization are identified through a series of questions including:

I What is this organization in existence to achieve? What are the vision, mission, values and strategic direction? What are its success criteria and who measures its progress against what rules?

I Who are the stakeholders in this organization? How do the stakeholders measure the organization and its progress?

I What shape is the organization? Is it hierarchical, distributed or team-based?

I Where is the decision-making power in the organization: centrally located, distributed, totally decentralized?

I Is power and authority granted down through the organization by line or by project?

I What is the power and role of the HR function, now and in the future? Is it perceived as a personnel role, an organizational development role or a combination of the two?

Characterizing an organization: organizational style

The style of an organization, 'the way it is around here' through the nature of its people, will have full impact on the way learning is viewed in importance and taken to the heart of the organization's life. A driving, time-conscious organizational culture will almost certainly be less open to learning than a slower, caring culture unless learning can be proved to be a 'sharp tool' in cutting the organization's success.

In investigating organizational style and its relationship to a role for learning, we ask what built the individual style and culture of our organization. What were the drivers that resulted in this style and culture? Things can change quickly in today's dynamic world. What are the drivers that may quickly change style and culture again?

The factors that contribute to the style and culture of the organization include:

I The organization's development and history. Mature organizations will carry the scars and experience of changes in external environments, expanding and contracting workflow. Newer organizations will experience the pangs of growth, particularly when others with different skills and motivations join the founding members. Other new organizations, perhaps the result of mergers, acquisitions and downsizing, will have inherited all manner of individual cultural drivers.

▌ The people who make up the organization. People with many years of experience may have a deep-felt belief in the organization, having seen it grow and develop. On the other hand, perhaps they feel cynical and disassociated with new directions being taken, particularly when they no longer feel consulted and involved. People newer to the organization may be determined to improve the organization or they may deliberately recoil from its history, never feel part and never become motivated.

▌ External factors, typically the marketplace and the environment in which the organization works. Smaller entrepreneurial organizations in fast-moving environments will obviously be different from organizations in more structured situations. This is true even when those more traditional organizations are changing themselves to mimic some of the success of more nimble, smaller organizations.

▌ Stakeholder expectations. The manner in which an organization performs is highly dependent on external stakeholders in particular. Shareholders, financial institutions and governmental legislation impact on commercial organizations. Governmental and public service organizations are having to live with 'market testing' and continuous appraisal.

These key factors result in the essence of an organization, its culture, its style and the values that its people hold dear. All these have an influence on what learning is required and how learning is best implemented and marketed.

We can identify organizational style through the matrix shown as Table 3.1, providing a mechanism to allocate an organization into one of three 'styles'.

Characterizing an organization: people considerations and the acceptance of learning

What is the level of acceptance for learning and investments in learning in this organization? Are there organizational drivers to use learning as a strategic tool on the journey to success?

We are analysing an organization in pursuit of appropriate methods of implementing the most appropriate learning initiatives for organizational success. Key to this process is the understanding of the organization's relationship with its people. Is this a paternalistic organization with much thought applied to its people, their welfare and their development?

Table 3.1 Styles of organization

Style A	Style B	Style C
Stable organization, low external turbulence.	Changing environment; external environment has extensive impact.	Complex business environment. Highly flexing organization; possible radical changes associated with process re-engineering.
Change is continuous and at a constant rate.	Rate of change is considerable and varying.	Mergers and acquisitions are frequent; a complex business environment.
Process-oriented.	Project-oriented. Processes are modified frequently.	Project-oriented. Processes are modified frequently.
Domination from a single point of authority. Within single country, or multinational dominated from one country.	Growing decentralization. Possibly growing to a multinational controlled from one country.	Globalization. Centralization versus decentralization issues. Introduction of matrix management features.
Mainly stable relationship with stakeholders.	Growing expectations of stakeholders.	Stakeholders are involved with the development and success of the organization. A culture of working in partnership.
Structured, hierarchical.	Less structure, reducing layers. Reorganizations, need for management of change throughout the organization.	Possibly a virtual structure; many non-core functions are outsourced. Matrix and team structures.
Cost budgeting and control.	Cost reduction focus.	Intense analysis of resource usage.

Is it, on the other hand, an organization that tends to hire experienced people, use their talents and recognizes that people may well move on? Tangible rewards may well be high, other considerations not so important.

What are the key factors for the organization in its interaction with learners? Learners may include staff and contractors together with people who work for customers of the organization, people who work for the suppliers to the organization and people who work for other stakeholders of the organization.

For its own staff, is this an organization that encourages learning to help people increase their contribution to the organization's success? Are there genuine attempts to have people develop their own competences? Is the practice backing up the theory? Are there training courses and are people encouraged to attend them? Is there a 'manager as leader and coach' mentality? Is the managerial route the only way to the top? Are there development paths for people who want to reach a senior technical level and would rather shun a traditional senior staff-management development route?

What is provided for other stakeholders? Does the organization make information available to its suppliers and customers in the form that makes it simple for them to understand its products, services and values and therefore to do business with it? Or is it working in a highly confidential situation?

We also consider the organization's attitude to learning in general. Does the organization and its senior management appear to believe in learning and development as key factors for organizational success, or is learning often seen as an expensive, unfortunate necessity? In the latter case we may need to recognize that any new ideas that we are to recommend will need to be justified extensively, and that the 'journey to excellence' may be slower and more challenged than we would wish.

Characterizing an organization: future changes

In the paragraphs above we have set out to analyse the shape of the organization and make initial conclusions about the nature of learning that is best for it. Now we must ask about the impact of future change on the organization. The organization's character will obviously have impact on the need for learning and on the appropriate mechanisms to supply that learning. We should be considering and debating with a wide range of stakeholders:

▎ Are there any significant changes planned in any of the explored areas of the organization, its structures, values and culture?
▎ Is the organization going to change in size or shape in the near future?

▌ If the organization is to change, will the change be consistent or ever-increasing, and with what timescales?

▌ What can be done to increase the level of acceptance of learning at an organizational and an individual level?

▌ Are we to take an overall 'change reactive' mode or should the learning function be proactive in causing change to happen in serving the organization? What will be our agreed role in the future; where will we be operating on the continuum from 'reactive supplier of training workshops' to 'strategic tool' of the organization?

CONSIDERING THE LEARNING POTENTIAL

The results of the work described in the paragraphs above will be a clear picture of the style of the organization now and in the future. We now investigate:

▌ What learning approaches – strategies, plans, staff competences, learning function model – are possible for an organization of this style?

▌ What are best practices elsewhere in organizational learning?

Three styles of relationship between organizations and the provision of learning have been identified to match the three cultures of organizations identified above. These are not, in full reality, three separate, disjointed styles of relationship. They form a continuum of styles.

For a Style A organization the relationship between the organization and the provision of learning is predominantly reactive. This fits most comfortably with organizations of low overall change and/or constant rates of change. Organizational relationships with stakeholders, together with processes such as production, distribution and marketing are well established. Learning needs are generated through the operational, line and staff units of the organization, and the learning function's prime role is the reactive implementation of the appropriate learning initiatives. This style of the learning architect is the traditional 'training and development' style still found in many centralized, hierarchical organizations with low rates of change. This obviously matches the 'establishing' status on the continuum for the learning function that forms the background to Chapter 2. The prevalent style of learning provision throughout the 1960s, 1970s and early 1980s, it continues to be seen in many a large and successful organization in this next century. Overall, the organization is evolving continuously and consistently, while the learning function and its responsibilities evolve at the same rate as the organization to ensure organizational learning needs are being fulfilled.

For an organization showing a Style B identity, the relationship with learning follows the increased rates of change within the organization. This style of relationship initially appeared in the early 1990s as organizations started to react to changing conditions and underwent massive internal reorganizations. The learning function adopts new methodologies to play its part in these reorganizations, and often to prove its worth. The Style B relationship between an organization and the provision of learning is the aspiration for the learning function in many organizations. Processes and stakeholder relationships of the organization's operation are more complex and more flexing than with the typical Style A organization. The organization adopts a 'project' mentality rather than a 'process' mentality; there is a parallel need for a more responsive style of provision of learning. As the necessary skills and the knowledge for the business grow in intensity there will be a change in the style of the learning architect, the learning function and of the implemented learning initiatives. The working processes of learning architects become more consultative and more proactive as they become closer to the deeper learning needs of the organization. Many of the basic processes used within the framework of supporting learning have not significantly changed from Style A, though they are now sharpened and focused to allow for a more responsive handling of change. This is the movement to the positioning status on the continuum for the learning function.

The move to this more proactive and consultative process may be not just the response of the learning function to a changing organization, a pull from the learning needs of the organization. It may, in parallel, be associated with the natural development and maturity of the learning function team and their desire to be more proactive with the organization, a push from within the learning function. Many authors have advocated a proactive approach to learning provision for the learning function, even if only to protect the function's own existence.

For organizations that can be categorized as Style C, the relationship between the organization and the provision of learning is highly sophisticated. It may well involve revolutionary learning function structures and high levels of empowerment. It is the level at which the learning architect and the learning function can truly 'add value' to the organization. This is the movement to the guiding status on the continuum for the learning function. Fundamental changes in the operations of the organization require proactive, fundamental operation by the learning function, the learning architect and individual learning function team members. The learning architect will be continuously working to transform the operation of the learning function. The aim is to continuously bring the function's operation into alignment with the overall operation of the organization, strategically and tactically – and to proactively use learning to move the organization forward. The learning function takes on a full partnership style of operation in its provision of learning initiatives for the organization. It is with Style C that a learning architect has the largest challenges as well as the most potential for impact as a change agent within the organization.

Typical characteristics demonstrated by the learning function and its relationship to the organization are identified in Table 3.2.

We now make a decisive step in planning our journey to learning excellence by identifying which of these styles of relationship is appropriate for the organization today. This decision will be part of the 'primary work' discussed in the first paragraphs of this chapter, moving forward learning for the organization to fill any gaps in the current provision. Of potentially greater importance is the identification of the style of relationship to which the organization and the learning function should aspire. This is the first step in the 'secondary work' identified above, towards providing the learning for the organization longer term.

Best practice: benchmarking organizations and learning

As we make decisions about our organization's specific journey to learning excellence, we examine the possibilities that exist elsewhere in the world of learning – particularly if our goal is a more service-led, value-added learning function. There are a host of published material and many gurus of learning. Across organizations there are many highly creative learning initiatives being implemented, and there are many ideas that may be shaped for your own organization.

Access to the internet has made the accessibility of benchmarked data far simpler than in days of old. Information about learning initiatives in a wide variety of organizations is available through specialist websites, often those of commercial benchmarking companies, through academic papers and through the more general websites of national learning and development organizations including CIPD in the UK and ASTD in the United States.

With the proviso that material is not commercially sensitive, our experience has been that learning professionals across organizations often share views and experience of best practice. There is normally sufficient benefit to each side to make infrequent meetings interesting and profitable for each party. Plan to minimize commercial embarrassment. Exchange

Table 3.2   Styles and learning

Matching learning with a Style A culture	Matching learning with a Style B culture	Matching learning with a Style C culture
	(Builds on the framework of matching Style A)	(Builds on the frameworks of matching Styles A and B)
Probably called 'training and development'	May well be called 'human resources development'	Growth of an organizational development (OD)-focused learning function
Clear path from organizational strategies to planning of learning	Clear alignment to strategies and staffing processes	Clear alignment with prime organizational strategies
Learning initiatives are reactive	Sometimes a proactive function, taking service to the organization	Problem diagnosis, tailored interventions
Learning highly structured and planned: the classic training needs analysis etc	Involved in organizational design as an enabler	Focus on change and change models
A large function, reporting to HR	Medium-sized function, a key part of HR	Smaller direct team, probably 'virtual working', learning architects developed throughout the organization. Learning architect at board level
Much internal delivery. High use of distance learning, including e-learning as a solution to the volume of low-level learning	Extensive use of external learning facilitators, sophisticated use of distance learning including e-learning and learning centres	Growing use of innovative methods of learning associated with motivation, culture change, personal life/work balance

Table 3.2 Styles and learning (Contd.)

Matching learning with a Style A culture	Matching learning with a Style B culture	Matching learning with a Style C culture
High concentration on traditional training assessment and evaluation, constant need to 'prove worth'	High concentration on assessment and evaluation, and proving worth, but time is a factor	Continue to use traditional assessment. Evaluation is highly short-term, results-focused – if time and change allow
Focus on training plans flowing down from business strategies. Learning initiatives are reactive.	Learning plans and activities linked directly into operational plans	Learning highly short-term focused, reacting to needs. Learning function expected to be proactive in developing the success of the organization
Training highly structured and planned: the classic TNA etc	Learning highly structured and planned: the classic LNA etc	Learning is highly focused, less structured, more job-focused
Predominantly a delivery/ implementation function	Predominantly a learning consultation and implementation function	Predominantly a business consultation and sourcing function. Recognized as business partners

information about the way in which you plan, prepare and evaluate learning rather than the actual content of any particular initiative. Discuss the manner in which learning strategies are developed rather than the actual content.

Networks of people from learning functions exist in most geographic areas, some organized formally by training organizations and professional bodies, others informally. Groups meet regularly and exchange a lot of highly useful information. In addition there are web-based groups. All tend to be reasonably informal. Should such an appropriate network not exist, it could be worthwhile to consider starting one. The contact through such groups can be of immense value to the organization's learning initiatives as well as to your own development. There have even been examples in which a number of organizations have worked together with an external training consultant on a programme that each team needed. Recognizing the need for commercial sensitivities, the pooling of expertise and the minimization of cost proves mutually beneficial.

If necessary, use external consultants to benchmark for you when the cost is appropriate. They should have a wide bank of experience and data as well as the contacts to undertake further searches on your behalf.

For all the availability of material, using benchmarking to provide really useful material is not always that straightforward. Typical of the sort of information that organizations store and possibly are willing to share are statistics on training days per employee, per year and training investment per employee, per year. And this shows the potential issue with this type of benchmarking initiative – numbers are an interesting guide but lack real substance as to the benefits of learning. The issue with much information is its depth and its reality; information is often qualitative rather than quantitative, and of limited use in understanding the key metrics for how other learning functions and individual learning professionals really work. Benchmarking is a powerful business approach, though it needs to be recognized that it is not a trivial initiative. It may well take time to start, and the results can take time to turn into really useful information that you could use to improve your organization.

Benchmark beyond the arena of learning within your own organization, particularly with functions that are acknowledged for their excellence in internal and external value-added client service; information services, procurement or even HR might fall into these categories. Typical of the points that could be discussed are:

▍ the manner in which the function employs benchmarking and how the results of benchmarking are analysed and communicated;
▍ the manner in which benchmark information assists in the way in which strategies, goals and plans are built;
▍ experiences in building relationships across the organization and in being recognized as providing a value-adding capability with the organization.

THE PLAN FOR LEARNING FOR THE ORGANIZATION

Introduction

The results of the work described in the paragraphs above will be a clear picture of:

I the style of the organization now and in the future;
I the expectations and overall goals for learning within this organization;
I all the possibilities for learning for the organization.

We know where we could go on our journey to learning excellence; now we plan where and how we are actually going! We are now in a position to investigate:

I What is our starting point on our journey to learning excellence? What is happening in the provision of learning, here and now within the organization? What is the current situation within the learning function and its work with the organization and with its learners?
I What is our goal? Where do we want to be in terms of delivering learning for this organization?
I What do we have to do to get to our goal? What are our plans, both short and longer-term, for the appropriate learning approaches for the organization?
I What is the appropriate overall strategy and 'brand' for the learning function together with mechanisms to communicate them?
I How will we monitor progress?

Once the plan is complete we will agree with stakeholders, document and 'go'. Once the plans are in place and agreed we can implement our journey.

Where are we starting from?

Our process centres on the questioning discussed in the earlier parts of this chapter: questions to senior management of the organization, to learners and potential learners, and the managers of those learners. The answers will enable us to:

I identify the current positioning on the corporate learning architect continuum;

I plan for a realistic future aspirational positioning on the continuum;

I develop insight as to how quickly the passage along that continuum can be achieved;

I identify gaps within the provision of the appropriate learning programmes for the organization, which will need to be filled through the implementation of the work scoped in our plans.

Questions we wish to debate include:

I Has the method of operation of the learning function that has developed over the years recently, if ever, been considered in terms of its fit with the style and culture of the organization and/or the organization's potential future?

I Is there in place a coherent, agreed, defendable strategy on handling evaluation and investment return for learning initiatives across the organization?

I Would the learning function and the learning initiatives it delivers be sufficiently capable of rapidly absorbing fundamental change in the activities of the organization?

I Has senior management recently been engaged in discussion about developments in learning, together with the potential power of knowledge and learning in contributing to success for the organization?

I Is the learning function regularly having to provide, often at short notice and with stretched resources, highly effective learning initiatives to learners who are themselves already overtly busy and sometimes openly cynical about 'training'?

I Has the learning function ever won a nationally recognized award or something similar that recognizes a learning initiative significantly moving forward the business situation and significantly benefiting the staff?

I Have the activities and metrics of the learning function ever been effectively benchmarked against other similar functions, particularly those viewed as 'best in class'?

I Has the staff of the learning function sufficient competence in working with senior line management, in providing coaching improvements in behaviour, in understanding the business needs of the organization and in building appropriate learning solutions?

I Are senior people in the learning function aware of and capable of debating the potential significance to the organization of the latest developments in the arena of learning? These include such developments as blended learning, outsourcing of a training department, the corporate university, the power and role of coaching and mentoring, as well as many, many more.

I Was the role of learning in the organization agreed with senior management or has it grown almost under its own initiative?

I Is the learning function suitably positioned in the organization to have the authority to discharge its responsibilities?

I Has the learning function sufficient resource to discharge its current responsibilities?

I Is there a current view of the learning function as a proactive servant of the organization?

I Is there a current SWOT analysis of the function's role with the organization, and has it been confirmed as the perception of senior organizational management?

I Are there strategic and operational plans in place and agreed?

I Are the roles of the team within the learning function identified and operational, with team development plans in place?

I Is there stakeholder relationship mapping in place to identify the key stakeholders and their potential influence on success of the learning function and its contribution to the organization's future?

I Are there long-term strategy, key performance indicators and critical success factors for the learning function, with staffing and competences mapped to support the vision?

I Is there a shorter-term view, including commitments made to the organization and the labour/competence plan necessary to discharge those commitments?

I Is there a realistic, agreed monitored budgetary plan?

I What are the operational considerations across the organization, including spread of language and functions?

I Are the strategies and plans being exercised correctly, producing the planned results?

I Are the most appropriate learning tools and techniques in place?

I Are stakeholder expectations and processes being managed in the correct fashion?

For any of these questions that result in a negative or incomplete answer, there will work to be done in building the journey to learning excellence.

Planning the journey: closing the gap and providing the appropriate learning

Through careful implementation of the processes described in the material above we have arrived at a point where:

▌ We understand the nature of the organization for which we are to provide learning initiatives, now and in the future. We understand how it works and how key influences dictate its operation and its future.

▌ We have examined the potential use of learning in this organization for establishing how learning can play its part in the success of the organization, in the short and long term, as the organization is subject to change, both internal and external.

▌ We have documented the current learning processes within the organization, how they are supplied and their level of success.

We are now ready to use the results of these investigations to decide the path forward for learning, the 'journey to learning excellence' for this organization. This path will build learning initiatives for the organization and, when appropriate, its external stakeholders.

Building and communicating the plan

The results of the investigations described above will allow the first definition of the manner in which a learning architect should work with an organization, now and in the planned future. The initiatives to be pursued, both strategic and tactical, are recorded in Table 3.3. Only those initiatives that are known to be of high value to the organization should be included on this list. The initiatives listed include both those for the development of learning for the organization, and those for the development of the work and the staff of the learning function.

The learning initiatives listed as A, B, C... in Table 3.3 will each be projects. They will each have:

▌ project objectives: 'By end of March implement a new sales workshop to move the north-western sales force up to competence level 7 of Consultative Selling', 'By end of September have established a fully operational learning centre, according to operating standard xyz, in the Paris factory';

▌ identified sponsors and project managers;

▌ identified risks to success, assumptions made, critical success factors, evaluation metrics;

▌ impact on the organization, benefits to its people and its overall success;

▌ budgets and return on investment calculations;

▮ probable methods of delivery: for a learning initiative one or a combination of methodologies such as training workshops, coaching, e-learning and work shadowing.

Table 3.3 Learning projects

Learning initiative	In place, fit for purpose Score from a possible maximum of 10	Needed now, work to be done	Short-term need	Longer-term need	Comments
A	3	Y	Y	Y	
B	8	Y	Y	Y	
C	–	Y	Y	N	
D	6	Y	Y	Y	
E	7	Y	Y	?	
F	–	–	–	Y	
G	–	–	Y	Y	
H	4	7	N	N	

In the example Table 3.3:

▮ Initiative A is an important project that is needed now and in the future, but is not currently providing the required results.
▮ Initiative C is a short-term fix, not currently in place, though unlikely to be required in the longer term.
▮ Initiative E is a current project that is working reasonably successfully; we are not sure about the longer term need for this initiative.

Confirming with stakeholders

Part of confirming our initial assessment of the future direction of learning and the learning function is to discuss our findings and recommendations with stakeholders of the organization. It is worthwhile plotting a 'stakeholder analysis' for the people involved in learning and its use for the benefit of the organization. The aim is to understand the relative importance of each stakeholder in making decisions about learning, and the resources allocated in relation to their relative influence on the success of learning. Thus, the stakeholder analysis is a graph of an individual stakeholder's importance in influencing any decisions about learning against the potential impact of the success of a learning project. Depending where stakeholders fall within the graph they will need to be influenced (high importance, high impact) or informed (low importance, low impact). This plot should include internal stakeholders at all levels, including people who regularly take advantage of learning initiatives and those who never seem to do so. It may include whole groups of people in a particular department or team. It also includes external stakeholders who are involved in the use of learning initiatives.

Strategy into action

Having undertaken our research and confirmed our plans with stakeholders with a range of interests, we now present our findings to senior management of the organization in seeking their sponsorship for our work. The aim is to have agreement about the role and the style of the learning function, together with an agreement to our plans for short and long-term implementation of learning initiatives. Now we use the tools available to us in building the details of our learning programmes. Chapter 2 of this book deals with a number of the traditional aspects of implementing learning, probably mostly associated with the Style A organization described earlier in this chapter. As an organization's style matures towards Styles B and C, there will be increasing call for a selection of the tools discussed in Chapter 5 of this book.

Within our overall, agreed strategy there will be plans for learning initiatives to plug any immediate gaps, and plans for longer-term work. All of these will be detailed on our work matrix, Table 3.3.

In addition to overall strategies, individual plans for particular learning initiatives and tools to monitor and review progress, there will be need for a communication plan. It is important that we are able to communicate progress and success. Both the matrix of Table 3.3 and the 'rainbow diagram' of Figure 3.5 are highly effective mechanisms for visually plotting and publishing progress on a path to learning excellence. The rainbow diagram can act as a stimulus to discussion within the learning function team and with other stakeholders in using learning wisely. The format of the rainbow diagram will be different for each learning function, but it provides a highly useful tool to demonstrate and discuss the stages required for a successful journey to learning excellence. For each diagram effective use of colours will assist in stakeholder understanding: green for things on target, yellow for items that are being closely monitored and red for anything 'off plan'.

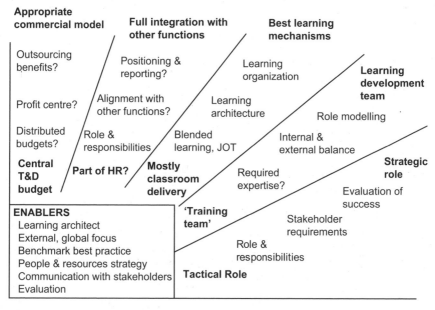

Figure 3.5 Journey to excellence

CHAPTER SUMMARY

▌ The bringing of appropriate learning to an organization is a sophisticated challenge.

▌ Many of the traditional processes of analysing, monitoring and recording are not appropriate for today's rapidly changing, highly responsive learning tranctions. New approaches are appropriate.

▌ True understanding of any organization includes an investigation of its culture and style and its distribution of authority and power. Once these have been identified, the appropriate style of learning and learning management for the organization can be predicted.

I There are external sources of information with which benchmarking can be significantly useful in understanding different approaches to learning that may be shapeable for our own use.

I There are a wide selection of tools to analyse and record the current learning initiatives and their usefulness, together with methodologies for building and publicizing the future strategy.

4

Managing learning without a team

So this is what it feels like to be involved in a management buy-out! You knew it was going to be a different, slicker, faster, focused world in the training department once the new organization had taken shape. What had not been initially obvious was the fact that you were going to be the only surviving member of the training and development function! In addition, that there seems to be an understanding that the level of service that has always being provided in the realms of learning will continue.

There's a recognition that many people in the organization are going to experience a far higher rate of personal change than before. Implementing a top-down, really effective change management initiative might be a fine way of scoring a quick win in the new organization; it might even provide a space for some planning for longer-term learning initiatives.

Time to start talking to the external learning suppliers who have done occasional work over the last few years. Time to investigate budget possibilities. Time to consider some innovative ideas for learning provision.

The purpose of this chapter is to discuss a number of different approaches to the provision of learning when a conventional learning function does not exist and there is only a tiny handful of people, perhaps only one, involved in the management of learning.

THE TACTICAL LEARNING ARCHITECT, THE 'ONE-PERSON LEARNING FUNCTION'

Introduction

As this book was researched and developed and we talked with a wide range of learning professionals, we became more and more aware of a situation prevalent in many organizations. There are many people with responsibility for learning across significantly large organizations who have to deal with (often enormous) challenges without any sort of direct team working with or for them. These people, who we have called learning architect type 2, tactical learning architects, have many of the responsibilities of the corporate learning architect that we described in the previous chapters but no 'learning team'. The tactical learning architect, in similar fashion to the corporate learning architect, is positioned within the corporate functions of the organization. His or her challenge is to discharge his/her responsibilities without the assistance of a direct team, other than perhaps an administration person, who is often shared with others in corporate functions.

In general, people handling this role are experienced learning professionals, having developed, for at least part of their career, through a range of trainer, training manager and facilitator roles. Their role most often reports through to the head of a human resources (HR) function.

We have seen this situation arise in a number of circumstances. Three typical examples that we have observed are:

I When an organization has scaled down its learning function in one or more cost reduction exercises, leaving the minimum of resources in what is seen as a service department to the core business. One, often senior, member of the learning function has been retained.

I When an organization has scaled down its central HR function, possibly in a cost reduction exercise, possibly by splitting much of the HR function across the functional units, learning has been 'forgotten' in the new structure. Almost as an afterthought somebody, appropriately multi-skilled, has been requested to undertake the responsibility for learning across the organization.

I When an organization has been split into a number of functional, operational units where there is a decision to have no corporate functions, and each of the operational units is not large enough for a fully fledged learning function. When the original organization was split up individual members of the function were placed, one by one, into the organization's new functional units to manage learning within that unit, leaving a single person as a token corporate learning function representative.

Budgeting for learning

The reduction in staff described in the previous paragraph, resulting in a one-person learning function, is quite often accompanied by a movement of budget away from the function. The funding for learning sometimes moves into a general HR fund, sometimes into operational unit budgets and occasionally into the ether. The manner in which the tactical learning architect can discharge learning responsibilities is obviously dependent on the size of any available budget and its ownership.

Working alone it is unlikely that the tactical learning architect will have the time to undertake an in-depth learning analysis within the organization. A budgeting plan based on a wide-scale learning needs analysis will simply not be possible. Two models can be considered:

▌ The learning architect is given a fixed amount of budget and is authorized to make prioritized decisions about how that budget is to be used. Although time once more will limit the activity, these priority decisions should be made after significant conversations with senior staff in operational units.

▌ The budgets for training are allocated to the functional units and they 'spend' those budgets with the learning architect, who will bring expertise to bear on the functional learning needs and the best use of budgets.

The second of these approaches particularly may lend itself to difficulties for our tactical learning architect. There may be no effective corporate limitation on how the functional units utilize budgets, including training budgets. The functional units may be tempted to spend their budgets away from the organization and make their own decisions about learning – decisions that may be detrimental to a growth of good learning principles across the organization. The learning architect wishing to establish a strong position within the organization will be highly reliant on strong interpersonal influencing skills and key examples of success. A strong mandate from senior management is a key factor, as is a learning architecture (see Chapter 5) supporting an organizational learning approach that is easy for the functional units to understand and use.

Models for financing of learning functions are described in Chapter 5.

Operating model

The learning architect type 2, the tactical learning architect, is highly likely to be operating primarily in a reactive mode. Operational units from the organization will be generating requests for learning directly to the learning architect.

Whenever possible, the tactical learning architect should be working to agree one direct contact within each operational unit of the organization, and concentrating on all requests flowing through that person.

CASE STUDY

One division of a major engineering organization is devoted to servicing a rail network. The operational director has 20 direct reports, geographically based, each with between 8 and 14 engineers. The size of the task to manage learning for the division was far beyond the normal scope of the learning function, recently reduced in size to one person. Margins were small and the organization under great pressure. For all this, safety training was a key issue. Every engineer had to maintain knowledge to be certificated to work. Self-certification had to include proof of attendance at appropriate current courses.

There were a host of courses at different proficiency levels for different types of engineer. A matrix of engineers against chosen courses at different levels had a potential of more than 10,000 cells. Overall cost of training was also a concern. Courses were provided by external agencies and a highly *laissez faire* attitude to people booking on whatever course they wanted had grown up.

An attempt at a web-based learning needs analysis to populate such a matrix proved a disaster. Only a small number of people had easy access to computers and the replies generated more questions than answers. Similarly, piloting e-learning to provide much of the knowledge parts of the required competence had not been a success even when well-furbished learning centres had been available. There was simply no history of this being seen as 'the way to do training'.

The designated tactical learning architect implemented the following plan:

1. An agreed budget per engineer per annum was agreed with the operational director. This was allocated across the 20 branches depending on numbers of engineers and a simple formula based

on the importance of the work done and the general experience level of the engineers in the branch.

2. Each of the 20 branch managers was made responsible for identifying the training requirements for each engineer, selecting courses within the calendar quarter, within the overall cost for the branch.

3. The learning architect then outsourced the booking of the necessary courses with the external training companies, and established a web-based tracking system – fed by the external training companies as engineers completed their courses.

The learning architect's approach was broadly successful, although several issues took time to eliminate. These included:

I Engineers failing to arrive at designated courses or cancelling very late. This was mostly overcome when managers' bonuses were partially linked to wise use of the allocated training budgets.

I A higher turnover of staff than had been initially considered. Extra training budget had to be allocated as initial training for engineers occupied more days than training for experienced staff.

There will be little time for a tactical learning architect to be able to develop the learning strategies, policies and plans associated with the stable, traditional world of training and development (see Chapter 2). The need will be to build the more 'rapid response' type of learning architecture framework described in Chapter 5 of this book.

Personal proximity to the organization and its needs, combined with budgetary constraints, almost certainly mean that the tactical learning architect will personally deliver learning interventions.

In forging a longer-term approach, consideration should be given to building a 'virtual learning team' of line managers from the units of the organization who will accept some of the challenge of providing the appropriate learning programmes. As well as assisting the tactical learning architect with identifying and prioritizing learning needs, unit managers should be prepared to themselves implement learning initiatives. The tactical learning architect needs to provide training initiatives for these unit managers on topics such as 'performance growth', 'manager as leader and coach' and 'train the trainer'. (See the discussion of trainer licensing in Chapter 8.)

Identifying external organizations to deliver learning programmes is also key to discharging the tactical learning architect role. Learning requirements will be identified frequently, and will need to be responded to rapidly. Using resources outside of the direct team (see Chapter 8) always leads to challenges and the need for a monitoring role. Such a monitoring role is particularly tricky for the tactical learning architect with so many personal responsibilities; agreement has to be reached with external providers to faithfully undertake monitoring and reporting themselves.

A more proactive role?

There may be the opportunity for the tactical learning architect to take on a more proactive role for the organization. He or she will work with many parts of the organization and may well see the need for learning programmes to fill capability gaps for people in many functional units. Particularly if the HR function, in common with the learning function, has been stripped to bare essentials, nobody may be taking care of such situations. Typical of the learning initiatives that might be suggested by the tactical learning architect are a management development programme and a 'handling change' programme. The implementation of such programmes would involve our learning architect in applying a wealth of skills and techniques:

I working with operational function managers to scale the project and its potential impact for the organization;
I calculating budgets and potential return on investment;
I deciding on the most appropriate ways of delivering the learning, assessing it and evaluating its actual impact;
I forming an overall argument for learning and an associated budget, presenting, influencing senior management.

THE FUNCTIONAL LEARNING ARCHITECT: MANAGING LEARNING WITHOUT A LEARNING FUNCTION

These are a group of people who have a role in which they are tasked with the provision of learning programmes for one portion of a very large organization, or perhaps for the whole of a smaller organization. We have labelled these people learning architect Type 3, the functional learning architect. They are positioned within organizational units and not, as with the tactical learning architect discussed above, within a central corporate function.

This situation often arises because of an extension of what was described in previous paragraphs. We described how the tactical learning architect is often coping with a situation where a reduction in size of a learning function has resulted in that function having almost no remaining resources. In the case of the tactical learning architect, we now are discussing a situation where the organization has completely removed the central learning function. Each functional unit has been made individually responsible for its own people's development in line with that function's path to success.

A highly significant difference here from the case of the tactical learning architect discussed above is that the functional learning architect typically has no personal learning and development background – and no internal access to such expertise if the learning function has gone. Senior management has given responsibility and authority for learning across a portion of the organization together, possibly, with a learning budget to somebody with little or no learning background.

Operational challenges and opportunities

There are a number of issues that may surface with this approach:

▎ The functional learning architect often continues to have responsibilities as part of any other role held before his or her appointment as the functional learning architect. This may lead to a priority challenge where learning takes a secondary priority, particularly if other organizational pressures grow.

▎ The role for learning in this situation is a reactive one. Only when there is a real need for a learning programme will something be implemented. Department managers within the organization, frustrated with the lack of any formal learning strategies, are likely to organize their own learning programmes using whatever means they can. There is every chance these initiatives, poorly scoped and implemented, will be less than effective, and lead to an environment across the organization where learning initiatives are poorly supported.

There is one possible optimistic strain here. If the organization has been broken up into self-supporting units, there may be a number of functional learning architects, one per operational unit. All will have the same challenges, and should be working together to use budgets well and to establish some of the aspects of best practice in implementing learning.

CASE STUDY

The once-large automobile company had been significantly reduced in size in only a few years. The central training function had long ago disappeared. One particular production unit had survived, though without any guarantee of a future unless new markets and new customers could be found and the whole operation made quicker and with far less manufacturing faults. Call-backs due to faulty work were identified as a massive cost to the organization, one that could bring it down whatever creative and innovative plans were implemented.

The newly appointed CEO of this division recognized the need for a learning-focused approach, and personally took on the role. He had no training staff, and appointed one of his managers as his learning architect, albeit without the title.

There was an immediate need for implementing change, an improved attitude to quality, and creativity in marketing. Money was available, though recruiting talented individuals to what was seen in many external circles as a lost cause was far from easy. The CEO and his newly appointed learning architect identified learning as a keystone of the division's strategy, although the competences that were identified for improvement were all known to be highly difficult to change in classrooms, being largely about attitude as much as skill and knowledge.

There was little time to undertake a traditional learning needs analysis, and the new learning architect really did not have the appropriate background to organize such an initiative. Most of the useful material on competency frameworks, individuals' training records and appraisals had disappeared. What was done, through a number of workshops facilitated by an external consultant and involving senior management, was the production of an outcomes-based framework of how the people in the division were to work in guaranteeing survival. Key performance indicators, objectives and critical success factors were put in place for individual groups of people on a master plan for survival. Learning gaps were identified at a high level, mostly in the areas of change management, coaching and influencing for managers. A small 'learning team' of line managers and supervisors, reporting for the duration of the project to the learning architect, was put in place to monitor this programme, as well as to be the 'learning eyes and ears' of the new company into the outside world. It was their role to identify new initiatives in other places and to communicate such ideas within the company.

Although training was mostly aimed at management, it was also key to success to engage the remainder of the workforce. What was needed were opportunities to communicate plan and progress to the staff, to have them truly engaged with progress, and at the same time to allow management to evaluate progress in the attitudinal change they were personally coaching in their teams. The engagement with the workforce was brought about by what was once called 'quality circles', where the topic of output quality was a constant theme linked to survival, with many illustrations from other organizations.

Straightforward, pragmatic approaches to learning focused around an obvious set of goals were instrumental in this business survival scenario. Nobody was a learning professional except for the external learning consultant whose role was to facilitate coaching abilities and an understanding of motivation into the division's management group. True to say, some implementation was ragged and not everything was totally successful. However, particularly as a result of the CEO's continual involvement and encouragement, the learning programmes were heralded as a highly motivational and practical contribution to the eventual success of the production unit.

After some time initial enthusiasm for learning began to visibly dwindle as the unit became more busy and people's minds, including the CEO's, became focused on newer initiatives. Recognizing this, the management group made the decision to bring on board a learning professional, and established a training manager position. This role was filled by an experienced learning professional who built and implemented a highly successful, sustained development programme, including an appraisal/personal objectives initiative. The development programme was supported by a learning architecture (see Chapter 5) appropriate to the structure and learning needs of the production unit.

Operating model

The functional learning architect requires a budget that can be spent in obtaining external professional assistance. Unlike the tactical learning architect, the functional learning architect does not have the competence to personally strategize, plan and deliver learning initiatives. A reputable learning consultancy may be contracted to build at least a framework for the implementation of learning programmes – a framework including the need for learning objectives, an appropriate delivery methodology and a level of evaluation of learning benefit.

When time and budget allow, a virtual team of line managers, competent in identifying learning needs and delivering appropriate learning programmes, can be built through programmes such as 'manager as leader and coach' and 'train the trainer'. These programmes will be implemented by the external learning consultancy. Employing external consultancies will result in challenges (see Chapter 8), and an agreed programme of quality control is important. This is highly problematic for the functional learning architect who, with a range of personal responsibilities of which learning implementation may only be one, may have little or no knowledge of learning programmes. Agreement needs to be reached with external providers to faithfully undertake monitoring and reporting themselves.

Implementing learning

In common with other styles of learning architect, the functional learning architect is likely to face requests for training in a number of fields. Line managers will be seeking knowledge and skill development for their teams, and there will be requests for 'legislation' training, typified by such things as health and safety training. These requests will originate from line managers aware of their legal duties, as well as from any HR function. In today's legalistic world, even the smallest of organizations has to take 'personnel' advice, possibly supplied by external consultants retained for such duties.

The approaches that the functional learning architect may take to provide learning for his or her 'internal customers' include the following:

I   Agreeing a budget process for learning in the arena to be served. This is likely to be a self-funding model since the learning architect is unlikely to have a learning budget. Approaches to budgets for learning are discussed in Chapter 5.

I   Seeking an external learning professional, or a training company, to assist with all the stages of learning initiatives.

I   Establishing an operational mode in which line managers take much of the responsibility for the development of their people. To promote the success of such an approach will require a programme of learning events, centred on coaching and train-the-trainer events for line management, provided by an external provider of learning initiatives.

I   Establishing a simple framework of learning event management, assessment and evaluation to be shared with line managers. Time constraints will limit this to an approach typified by:

- Testing the priority of this learning. Is it really necessary and can it be clearly cost justified?
- Treating any learning programme as a project; being clear about objectives and deliverables.
- Building the learning event, always focusing on the objectives and examining each potential learning session as a contribution to the objectives; taking input from delegates as to the perceived success of an event in pursuit of personal and organizational objectives.
- Ensuring the delivered event is highly practical and focused on skills to complete a delegate's role, rather than a theoretical background.

A more sophisticated approach could be to form a type of strategic learning council (see Chapter 2) of the senior management in the arena that is being served, an approach often taken by a corporate learning architect. Use this council to debate learning priorities and to gain people's commitment to sharing the load in implementing learning.

It is unlikely that a tactical learning architect will have time to establish a significant learning framework unless extensive assistance is taken from external sources. In this circumstance a simple version of a learning architecture (Chapter 5) may be appropriate.

THE INDIVIDUAL LEARNING ARCHITECT: MANAGING LEARNING FOR INDIVIDUALS

Our learning architect type 4, the individual learning architect, encompasses the approaches to learning and the associated personal skill sets for a variety of people responsible for the development of individuals. We have encountered five major learning situations that fall within the learning architect type 4 role. These are:

▮ Across many organizations, the coach, providing continual, proactive support and development of individuals or small teams (see Chapters 6, 7 and 8). This may well include the line manager who is operating as 'manager as leader and coach' for the team. Possibly without any formal assistance from an organizational learning function, this is an individual who wishes to develop the performance capability of the team and its individual members.

▮ The mentor, providing similar facilities of support for individuals as the coach, though in a far more reactive mode. We see the mentor operating as the experienced hand guiding a less experienced person in the ways of life within the organization. Interestingly, although an important role, it is one for which people are not too often trained. We find in many organizations coaches have learning programmes to develop their coaching abilities while mentors are expected to perform using simply their own wit and experience. This is definitely an example of an individual learning architect whose performance would benefit from a learning initiative.

▌ The part-time trainer. This is a growing role in many organizations, and has grown to a large extent out of the development of shared services and help desks. When assistance is required by people using a help desk, it is frequently the case that the support person will provide more than a 'fix the current situation' approach. It is frequently more efficient to train the requester to ensure that the 'fix' is a permanent one.

▌ The branch trainer, providing learning programmes for all the staff in one location of a distributed organization. These are not members of the corporate learning organization. Typically they are supervisory-level staff with an operational role in addition to their learning responsibilities. They deliver programmes sent from a corporate learning function, but have no other contact with that function. Parcel delivery companies are typical of the organizations that use this variety of individual learning architect.

Whereas people requested to take on a role of coaches normally are provided with training in the appropriate skills to undertake such roles, the part-time trainer and the branch trainer, in our experience, rarely have such opportunities. If they are at all formally trained, it will have been through attendance at traditional train-the-trainer workshops, which often prove to be of only limited use to part-time trainers. The majority of train-the-trainer workshops are designed to prepare classroom trainers for their role. There are an increasing number of these part-time trainers who obviously need the opportunity to develop their skills – the requirement is a mixture of developing workplace skills, how to coach, and how to train one-on-one.

▌ The individual learning architect whose focus is on developing him or herself. Often these are people who wish to enhance their career, perhaps who are planning to take an entrepreneurial step towards self-employment. They may be using the organizational learning opportunities to develop their competence for both their current role and their planned future. They may possibly be doing completely 'private' study – a self-funded MBA, learning Chinese at night school. This is a highly interesting arena for those responsible for organizational learning. There is often an enormous pool of potential abilities and energies that are directed outside the organization. Should ways be found, through job enrichment and the like, perhaps a higher proportion of the entrepreneurial spirit could be focused internally for organizational benefit.

CASE STUDY

A senior business analyst in a financial institution has the responsibility to assist senior managers whose role is to write market analysis reports for major clients. This assistance takes many forms, from assisting with simple IT issues (how to switch on the machine in the most frustrating of cases), to advising how to best use the templates for the reports. The reports and the client service are highly confidential, the senior managers very busy. There is no possibility of any formalized training involving the learning function of the institution – its role is all about worldwide, large roll-out, blended learning initiatives.

The volume of report writing is growing, and in consequence so is the number of calls for help to the senior business analyst. There needs to be a transfer of learning, a transfer of expertise to the senior managers to make them much more self-supporting.

Having no personal formal training in any aspects of the provision of learning, the senior business analyst, on the path to becoming an individual learning architect, employs an external learning consultant. This external consultant, during two highly intensive sessions, coaches the analyst through the stages of developing a learning programme – clear objectives, metrics of success, making sessions interactive and so on.

The individual learning architect now makes the simplest of learning contracts with each of the people who seek her assistance. Every time she works with one of her 'learners', normally at that learner's desk, prior to handling the direct inquiry, a 10-minute learning session is undertaken. The learner acquires at least one new item of competence on the way to independence. Obviously, whenever possible, the individual learning architect ensures that today's learning is coupled to today's request for assistance.

The external consultant sat in on two of the less confidential sessions with the individual learning architect and one of her subjects, to provide further encouragement, feedback and motivation. The individual learning architect is measuring the success of her approach by monitoring the number of calls she receives, particularly the volume of repeat calls from any one senior manager. If all goes well, the 'learning contract' will be extended to 20-minute sessions.

Relationships for the individual learning architect

We have seen in previous chapters how corporate learning architects and tactical learning architects, having responsibility for learning and performance development across organizations, build a range of strategic frameworks for learning. It is important to their success that they are cognisant of the people across the organization acting as individual learning architects, and any learning initiatives that these individual learning architects are providing. For the corporate learning architect a pool of individual architects can be a boon or a problem. It is a boon if the individual architects can be brought within the learning function strategies and given appropriate competence to undertake their role; the 'learning architects' mentioned on page 75 in Chapter 3. It is a potential problem should the reputation and effectiveness of learning in the organization be damaged by a raft of poorly implemented learning activities from an individual learning architect.

Building the organizational coaching culture described in Chapters 8 and 9 is a key responsibility for the learning function, harnessing the potential of individual learning architects. A role of coordinating the development of all styles of individual learning architect could be the responsibility of one of the practice managers discussed in Chapter 3 on page 85. This role would include ensuring that people who undertake occasional training workshops are themselves trained on a suitable train-the-trainer programme, and that coaches and mentors are themselves developed and supported.

CASE STUDY

The teaching staff of an institute of higher education (HE) consists of a bewildering range of talent, backgrounds and personal development needs. Recruited from other HE institutes, colleges of further education and from the profession that the institute supports, their learning needs defy any conventional form of training needs analysis. All are highly conscious of a need to keep their professional skills – delivering courses to students, mentoring, evaluating, presenting and so on – and their subject knowledge up to date. The issue is that every continuing professional development (CPD) path is different. In fact, each individual regards him or herself as an individual learning architect with a heavy emphasis on one person's competence – his or her own.

There is no training function, only an HR department with an interest in development of the staff – a necessity, as the institution needs to fly its flag in seeking funding with external, often governmental, sources. There is a strong concentration on an appraisal system, after which staff are encouraged to organize their own learning paths. HR does organize a small range of workshops, centrally funded and provided by external providers and by (as often as possible in minimizing spend) 'subject experts' who are staff members. Workshops include 'teaching in higher education', 'diversity', 'reflective learning' and 'mentoring/tutoring'.

Departmental managers are made responsible for their staff attending the basic workshops listed above. Managers also have a learning budget for their department, with a recommended amount per member of staff, though with some leeway as to how it is actually split.

There is, overall, a significant emphasis on personal development. Each person, in a very flat, web-culture organization, has a very personal set of talents and interests. There is an understanding that individuals will seek funding for their learning, often in parallel with their own research projects, from the departmental funds and from external sources.

CHAPTER SUMMARY

I There are a number of situations in which learning has to be implemented without the assistance of a centralized learning function. These situations may well arise following a cost reduction exercise resulting in the total or almost total removal of the central learning function.

I A tactical learning architect operates in a centralized learning function role but has no staff; he or she is a learning professional and operates in a mode of working focusing on the highest priority learning initiatives.

I A functional learning architect is responsible for learning within one unit of an organization. This is often one of many jobs for an individual who is often without any formalized background in learning and development. This architect is likely to be reliant on external expertise in providing learning programmes.

I There are many individual learning architects, often working as coaches, who provide learning and development to individuals or small teams. It is important that the potential of the learning architects is harnessed by the corporate learning architect in building effective learning performance.

5

The business of learning

It seems as though the struggle is beginning to be worthwhile! The plans for the corporate university are all agreed and things are generally starting to fall into place. A strong learning culture is being acknowledged with significant learning initiatives in most areas of the organization. The learning function team is building an impressive image in parts of the organization. Units across the organization are voicing their admiration for the work of the learning function.

Yet there truly are exceptions to every rule. There is always so much to do – being popular and proving worth immediately means there are more requests, and some people seem to think that they are not having their share. Your own team are proactively identifying opportunities for learning to assist organizational performance and those ideas generate work. Success has a price. And of course there is always the need to justify both the budget and the time that knowledge workers are taking up with learning programmes.

What is required are some effective processes, professionally implemented and maintained, that will allow control of the operation while you grow its impact even more. Where are the pragmatic, quicker approaches that can replace or be added to the traditional approaches to learning when those traditional approaches are proving insufficiently successful or proactive? What models can we implement to be more proactive while maintaining control?

The purpose of this chapter is to describe:

I methods of operational budgeting for the learning function;
I the way that the learning function can communicate its brand, its success and its value all across the organization;
I a range of methods of evaluation for the whole learning operation;
I the development of a learning architecture that will allow a rapid response to organizational change and a vast range of learning needs;
I new ways of working across the organization to proactively provide a 'rapid response' framework for learning.

COMMERCIAL MODELS

Introduction

Wise management of the budget for learning will be fundamental to success, irrespective of the nature of the learning function and of the role of the learning architect. Wise management that includes choice of the correct budgeting model and its implementation, followed by rigorous monitoring of the use of resources and of a return on investment. The most usual budgeting models are summarized in Table 5.1.

Cost model

As is customary with budgets for 'service' functions, the most commonly used budgeting framework for a learning function is a cost model, or as it is sometimes called, a centralized budget. An amount of money and other resource is directly allocated to the function, and the management of the function is charged with the responsibility for its wise use. Additional costs, typically the travel and accommodation costs for learners, are usually budgeted within the operational functions. This approach provides a simple form of budgeting and an accurate picture of monies dedicated to learning activities.

The cost model has a major operational advantage in that once the annual negotiation for budgets is complete, the learning function can concentrate on learning programmes. Not that the possibility of budgets being altered during a financial budgeting period can be ignored! Budgetary control in most organizations these days means that the learning function budget

Table 5.1 Financial models

Type	Details	Comments for learning function
Cost Model	Budget controlled by learning function. Allocated percentage of overall organizational expense budget, or plan budget through building learning strategy and full learning needs analysis across organization.	Simplest operational model. Can be easy for organization to readjust budget, for people to see learning as expensive function. Could lead to complacency and/or 'operational' focus within learning function, which only 'faces' the organization once a year.
Profit Model	Learning function has to be self-sustaining by charging out services into organization, and possibly beyond. Learning budgets in operational units.	Operational units may spend budget with third-party suppliers; difficult to control learning strategy of organization. Danger that learning budget is spent elsewhere than learning, or not spent. Difficult model to manage.
Outsourcing Model	Third party provides some or all learning functions. Organization is charged for services by third party on overall price or transaction basis, against contractual service level agreements.	Needs management from the organization; a level of learning function must be maintained. Can be highly inflexible as situations change. With proper management, potential to be cheapest approach.

may well be reviewed at least once every six months, not annually as was the once-accepted norm. The cost model provides for high levels of control over how and where budgets are spent, and the learning function is able to report upwards on the wise use of funds. Initially gaining sufficient funds, particularly in a top-slice approach, relies on powerful networking and influencing skills with senior management. They will recognize that funds made available to the learning function and its learning programmes may mean less operational spend for them. The learning architect's submission must be strong and coherent.

Perhaps the learning function's largest problem with a cost model occurs at times of organizational cost cutting. Should the senior management be looking for areas to prune costs, the fixed allowance allocated to the learning function can always appear as an easy target for reduction. A major operational disadvantage is that operational units, seeing learning as a free, bottomless service may well abuse their position, pulling people from learning initiatives while always believing that another one will be available. Another major detraction is the ability of the management of other functions to manipulate the use of those amounts that are budgeted under learning travel and accommodation. Also to be considered is those managers' ability to minimize learning attendance by their staff by 'saving' this same budget. To negate this some organizations have moved to central budgeting for all aspects of learning, including travel and accommodation.

There are a number of ways to decide the extent of an allocated budget in a 'cost' model. Chapter 2 described a formalized approach to linking learning needs to the planning and implementation of learning programmes, an approach suitable for organizations with a low rate of change allowing sufficient time for effective information to be built. This approach can be extended to pricing for each aspect of learning programmes, and an amalgamation into a bottom-up budget for agreement with senior management.

A simple budgeting method is allocation of a fixed percentage of the turnover of the organization, an approach known as top-slicing. The challenge is the decision on the top slice percentage. It is possible to research typical percentages in organizations in a particular business or governmental sector through organizations such as CIPD in the UK or trade organizations. Typical figures are between 0.5 per cent and 3 per cent of turnover in a commercial organization, or of allocation in governmental organizations. The figures themselves need to be viewed with care, as they can represent a variety of different things. We need to really understand any quoted figures – is the figure the amount of budget allocated to learning delivery, or does it include costs of the learning function and its salaries, transport and accommodation for learners and so on? We may define the most accurate figures through discussion of such topics with networking colleagues (see benchmarking in Chapter 3).

Another view for the top-slicing approach is to allocate a specific amount of money for the development of each person in the organization for the year. There may be a weighting associated with the functions whose staffing include new entrants with an associated high learning load. Once more, benchmarking between organizations can be helpful, provided care is taken with the exact meaning of any figures.

A pragmatic approach is often taken with these approaches. In the first year of operation one of the methods described above is used in a rigorous allocation of a learning function budget. Should the learning function subsequently be seen to manage its budget effectively, further years are budgeted by the addition of an agreed rate of inflation. Bottom-up budgeting – the full process – is then undertaken every three or four years.

Profit centre model

There is a vogue, in these days of functional responsibility and cost control, for learning and development functions and other non-core functions to embark on the implementation of profit models. Learning budgets are not maintained in the learning function. Rather, those budgets are placed into operational units who internally purchase learning initiatives from the learning function. The learning function then charges market rates in such a manner it generates a profit, or at least breaks even. The financial transactions are book ones within the organization, and the system allows the learning function to be self-sustaining, with an opportunity to discuss its return on investment to the organization.

A small allocation of organizational funding can be made to the learning function to handle the very basics such as salaries and facilities. This is particularly important with a new initiative for functional budgeting. Once the model is fully operational then this small central budget can be halted and a full self-sufficiency model implemented for the learning function.

When learning is to be provided for external stakeholders such as supplier and client staffs, the profit source model has obvious advantages in that a market rate is available for negotiation, and systems to bill are already in place. Otherwise, there may have to be resources applied to working with internal financial units when billing of the stakeholders is necessary.

Often the budgeting system is arranged in such a manner that any operational unit does not exclusively have to spend its budget for learning with the internal learning function. Should it choose, the operational unit can purchase learning initiatives directly from an external supplier. In this situation the learning function's control over organizational learning, wise budgeting for learning and the integrity of the learning architecture for the organization (see below) may all be under pressure. This is a significant detraction from the use of a profit centre model.

Intra-organization billing allows other functions to be charged directly with the cost of learning services by the learning function. Although this may involve high management process overheads, it allows the most appropriate cost and benefit calculations to be undertaken. A real 'business' sense can be felt within the learning function. Once again, this approach leaves other functions free to buy services from external providers. The internal function needs to be able to prove its competitive worth and experience, but in common with external providers, the learning function has the discretion of being able to charge for all its services.

Tracking real spend on learning and development can often be difficult, and accounting functions need to take responsibility to collect sufficient information to account for overall costs to the organization. Whenever line managers are able to use learning budgets as they wish, there will be difficulty in tracking expenditure centrally.

Outsourcing

For many years organizations have been leveraging benefits from outsourcing organizational functions to specialist companies. Included in the list of departments that have been outsourced in a variety of organizations are accountancy, information technology and systems, customer service, catering, cleaning and fleet management. Significantly, one area that has recently become a topic for much consideration and discussion is human resources (HR). Despite continued discussions about the ethics of outsourcing information about people, let alone the ramifications of legal control of personal data, the transactional elements of HR functions are increasingly being outsourced. Payroll has become a prime objective of outsourcing.

Learning functions are now high on the list for outsourcing consideration. As yet, there are not as many organizations offering outsourcing of learning functions as in other areas of business. There is not yet an extensive list of partners, though many outsourcing specialists are beginning to use their expertise in other outsourcing areas to enable them to move into the learning and development arena.

Organizations have a need to be more cost-effective, to have immediate access to solutions that are tried and tested, and have their leaner management structures focused on the core business activity. Outsourcing has enabled some organizations to achieve this. Specific challenges for a learning function that have led to the investigation of outsourcing possibilities have included:

I to do more with less resources;
I to embrace e-learning, which has required big investments in terms of time, money and knowledge;
I to deliver just-in-time solutions to pressing business needs, interventions that are up to date, compliant and effective.

The claimed benefits that organizations gain from outsourcing are generally all or some of the following:

I Investment in assets is reduced.
I Funds for capital purchases are available.
I Cost structures can be variable.
I Operating expenses are reduced or controlled.
I Management can focus on core business activities.
I Activities are better managed by specialists in specialist companies.
I Internal resources are freed up to handle other activities.
I Expertise is easier and quicker to access.
I World-class expertise and solutions are available.
I New and tested ideas are acquired.
I Competitiveness is increased.
I Flexibility is increased.
I Risks are reduced.

The particular benefits for learning architects where the learning function has been outsourced is that they have more direct time to:

I Create and implement a learning architecture (see below).
I Raise the profile of the learning function.
I Contribute to the strategic direction of the organization.
I Define long term, strategic learning requirements for the organization.
I Monitor and evaluate the quality and effectiveness of the learning function.

The disadvantages of outsourcing for the learning architect are potentially:

I a loss of control;
I limited inability to change if the organization changes – the initial contracts have to be well engineered with full consideration of appropriate exit strategies and contingencies;

▌ financial penalties for changing an outsourcing partner or ending the agreement; particularly with a first experience of outsourcing mistakes can be made.

As a learning architect who is involved in any move towards outsourcing you may wish to consider the following points:

▌ The learning architect role in the outsourcing process. The learning architect will probably stay in the organization that has outsourced as the 'interface manager'.

▌ Learning, development and training are more aligned to the culture, values, priorities and strategy of an organization than some other areas of the business. With this in mind you need to consider how well the outsourcing partner will fit with your organization's strategy, culture and values. The work on influencing in Chapter 6 will prove useful in these considerations.

▌ Be very clear about the rationale for outsourcing, and make that clear to the outsourcing partner. If the rationale is really about cost savings and the outsourcing partner is led to believe it is about access to expertise, the relationship will run into difficulties.

▌ Partnership arrangements need to stand the test of time, so the outsourcing strategy should look beyond the here and now and beyond the length of the agreement.

▌ Create an end of agreement strategy, an exit strategy, so that the organization is not left with nothing at the end of the relationship, particularly if the possible exit strategy is to (re)in-source.

▌ Consideration should be made about the large investment in terms of money, time and effort during the first year of the agreement. You will need to look at the benefits gained beyond the initial transition.

▌ Plan for effective change. Organizations under-estimate the effect that outsourcing has on all stakeholders. Managing change needs to be a top priority for the outsourcing team, including the outsourcing partner.

▌ The experience of organizations that have outsourced indicates that it may be preferable to have more than one outsourcing partner, particularly with a first outsourcing initiative. Each partner is picked for its expertise, some examples being a learning management system expert and a knowledge management expert. This makes the role of 'interface manager' more tricky but provides more control and experience than with an all-out 'eggs in one basket' approach.

▌ Establish clear accountability, monitoring and evaluation processes. The use of service level agreements is common practice and enables all parties to have a sense of what is expected of them. The levels of service must seem fair to all parties.

I The benefit of outsourcing a function like learning and development needs to be evaluated in terms of adding value, not just in terms of cost savings. Learning activities are a means of improving an organization's performance, in whatever way that is measured.

I Consider a halfway option whereby the provider manages aspects of the function, choosing from a menu that may include training administration, training delivery, evaluation, venue booking, marketing, assessment centres and training needs analysis. The organization retains full control of its assets and the accompanying spend.

I Develop and use a checklist for assessing potential partners, covering the following: past experience, learning management systems, customer support, quality systems, strategy for transition, location, global support, other value added services, metrics, references, and financial status.

Choice of budgeting model for corporate learning architects

For the corporate learning architect there are a number of considerations involved with choosing the appropriate budgeting model:

I The ease of control and straightforward nature of a direct cost model lends itself to consideration as the commercial model for a learning function when it is in an establishing status (see page 48 in Chapter 2). In this status the learning function has time to work through detailed analysis of learning needs across the organization, resulting in a firm costing of the learning function and its learning programmes. In addition, there is a host of published materials from the CIPD in the UK, ASTD in the United States, and on websites to provide assistance in modelling the full costs of learning after learning needs analyses are completed.

I With the learning function moving to a more consultative, business-focused unit charged with implementing learning initiatives in shorter timescales in a more intense manner, the careful planning of a budget, described in the paragraph above, ceases to be possible. The profit-based budget model becomes more attractive, with budget lying with the operational functions and being spent into the learning function. This arrangement will sharpen the focus of the learning function in providing the most appropriate learning initiatives into the organization.

Choice of budgeting model for other learning architects

For the tactical learning architect, carrying many of the responsibilities of the corporate learning architect while operating as a one-person function, there is much to recommend the profit model. Shortage of time does not allow the tactical learning architect to undertake detailed learning needs analysis in generating an acceptable model for budgeting purposes. Tactical learning architect time is better spent developing learning programmes, with budgets under control of the functional units.

Outsourcing has attractions for the tactical learning architect, with the assumption that the architect is retained as the link between the outsourcing provider and the organization. The architect can manage the interface with the supplier, and in addition manage the expectations of the learners, their management and all other stakeholders.

For the functional learning architect, involved within one particular area of an organization, a directly costed model is most appropriate. Whatever learning initiative is agreed with unit management, that agreement will include an allocation of financial and other resources. The functional learning architect, having no experience in the field of learning, will struggle to provide an accurate budget figure. This exercise may require the assistance of an external learning consultant (see page 122 in Chapter 4) in providing an appropriate concept of budget to be allocated.

The individual learning architect, especially when operating in a coaching and mentoring role, will only have the direct cost of his or her own time. A financial modelling exercise is almost certainly not worthwhile.

EVALUATION AND ASSESSMENT

Introduction

Continuous monitoring, evaluating and improving of all aspects of the operation and its deliverables is a key role and responsibility for those charged with the management of learning across the organization. We must be able to monitor the impact of all types of learning initiative and their contribution to the performance of individual learners, their teams and to the organization. In addition we must monitor the use of resources and funding. Overall, we require to know which of our activities are delivering value against organizational priorities.

Across many years within the arena of learning, 'evaluation' is possibly the topic most discussed, sitting as it does at the heart of the debate about the worth of learning functions seeking to add value to organizational performance. Many learning professionals advocate measurement and metrics, with the view that only what is measured is held in value. Others believe that much evaluation is quite artificial, and that resource, time and effort would be better focused into implementing learning initiatives that really bring value. A mature learning function will want to understand its value, and its success and evaluation plays a significant part in this. Certainly well-planned operational learning initiatives will always be focused, with a pay-back philosophy. There is room for an argument that majors on stating that a pay-forward of some programmes is highly difficult to measure, and has to live within the strategy of the organization and the professionalism of the learning function. These programmes include such things as building an organization's knowledge management capabilities, or changing its future culture in response to a changing world – possibly survival programmes.

The take-up of e-learning and other remote learning initiatives is a challenge to those who wish to use a metrics-based approach to evaluation of learning. Counting the number of 'clicks' or measuring times online is little more than an analysis of activity. Even in-place testing, linked to new skills and knowledge, is little more than assessment and is some distance from a true evaluation of new competence.

Our maximum focus should be with 'evaluation.' Evaluation refers to the bigger picture, monitoring the overall (business) impact of learning programmes on the performance (in terms of both competence and attitude) of individuals, teams, functions and the whole organization. For learning professionals this is key as we strive to monitor the added value to the organization of our work. It is also the key area for consideration by an organization, monitoring how the learning function is fulfilling its commitments to achieving its goals.

We also address other terms. 'Assessment' is generally used to refer to on-time monitoring of learning initiatives. The 'happiness sheets' that finalize the majority of learning workshops remains the most familiar form of assessment. Assessment results promote the opportunities for short-term continuous improvement of learning initiatives. 'Validation' is the term often ascribed to testing materials and methods for their suitability for the job to be done with a focus on design, structure and completeness.

A process of evaluation

Evaluation promotes improvement through a cyclical process:

1. The standards, expectations and goals for the learning function and all aspects of its operation are agreed. At a macro level these are expressed through learning strategies and policies. At a micro level they will include many detailed aspects of the function's operation, such as performance development plans for individuals in the learning function and the criteria for success in a learning programme.
2. Activities are initiated and monitored, and the results are analysed, interpreted and reviewed.
3. Any necessary changes are made in an appropriately timely manner.
4. Further evaluation is undertaken.
5. Standards, expectations and goals are reconfirmed.
6. The process continues.

In evaluating learning activities and their potential contribution to organizational performance, evaluation begins during the design of the initiative, continues through its piloting and implementation, with the bulk of evaluation occurring after delivery. In the design stage, the focus is on planning:

▌ What does this learning initiative seek to achieve; what will be success, for the learners, their teams, the organization?
▌ What aspects of results of the learning should be evaluated?
▌ What methods and models of evaluation will provide useful results as we seek to improve the learning initiative and continually provide value to the organization?
▌ Considering the costs of evaluation and ensuring that those costs are included in the overall learning initiative costings.

Once the learning initiative has been completed focus shifts from planning to implementation:

▌ collecting evaluation data;
▌ analysing and interpreting the data; asking the critical question, 'What value has the training delivered to the organization?' which any evaluation process should ultimately aim to answer;
▌ presenting your evaluation findings and agreeing any necessary improvements;
▌ modifying the learning initiative and starting again.

Evaluation of the evaluating methods

The structured approach to analysing the success of a learning initiative described in the sections above raises an interesting point. The process is cyclical, as was explained – and around it there is another cycle to be considered. Wrapped around the cycle of evaluating the learning initiative is the cycle of evaluating the evaluating process itself. Care needs to be taken that we are evaluating the correct aspects of the learning, that we are using the correct evaluation processes, and that we are making the correct decisions about what is required as the outputs of the learning. These are sophisticated points, but if ignored they could result in the evaluation results being challenged, and our professionalism questioned.

The environment of evaluation

Consider training somebody with the skills of making a cup of acceptable tea; consider this everyday task in the way it illuminates the challenging topic of evaluating learning. To evaluate the success of the training will involve a long list of questions including:

■ What does 'acceptable' mean? Who is the judge? What are the criteria? Where are those criteria recorded? When were they last agreed, by whom, against what standard?
■ What useful skills did the trainee have before the training started?
■ What will be used as a test of success? How will this test be used? When will it be used again – are we organizing to check whether the trainee retains the skills?

For this simple task the questions appear endless. And then there is consideration of all the possible variables that will impact the cup of tea while having little or nothing to do with the training. These variables will have a major impact on whether the cup of tea made by a trainee is deemed acceptable – china or plastic cup, hardness of water, quality of tea. What about the trainee's level of motivation? Does he or she like tea, does he or she see any point in the exercise? And the trainer: sufficient expertise and experience? Motivational, involved, trained as a trainer? These and many other types of issue will have significance as we seek to evaluate our success with this training initiative.

Establishing measurable benefits of learning has always been a primary challenge, although there are legendary difficulties in evaluating the true impact of any learning initiative. The performance of the organization, individual functions and individual people are subject to a number of influences in addition to the benefits taken from learning activities. So how can we split the impact of learning from the other factors? An objective of a 25 per cent increase in production after all shop-floor operatives have attended a workshop is a tangible standard, but can we decide how much of any improvement will be attributed to:

 ▌ new skills learnt in the workshop;
 ▌ the motivation due to selection for the workshop;
 ▌ any new reward and recognition that is introduced;
 ▌ any new machinery and working conditions introduced in parallel to the learning initiative;
 ▌ what happens directly after the workshop; how quickly can the new competence be applied, how much encouragement will the newly trained operative receive?

The permanence of each of these factors is different, and will depend on what happens during and after the workshop. Evaluating the workshop's benefits is a highly subjective concept in these circumstances. Similarly, monitoring and evaluating the impact of the whole learning function is challenging. Measuring the spend, especially with a cost model (described earlier in this chapter) is comparatively simple, but evaluating the value from that spend is difficult when all the possible variables are taken into account.

The majority of learning professionals agree the key to working with the challenge is realism. Once learning is part of the overall approach of the organization and everybody from senior management downwards recognizes the potential benefits of learning, do not become paranoiac about measuring its impact. Spend time and effort in providing the 'correct' learning initiatives. Develop and apply the appropriate strategies and meaningful, inspirational learning activities. Discuss progress with line managers, use 'happiness sheets' and talk to individual learners and constantly keep in touch with senior management who will wish to be informed of progress. The vital point is that standards are agreed and are realistic for the overall good of the learner, the trainer/facilitator/coach, the learning function and the organization.

Be aware that there may well be cynicism about the presentation of evaluation results. Senior managers have been known to dismiss this work as groundless; these are often those senior managers who have not been convinced about any aspect of learning and the resources applied! Unfortunately, there are colleagues amongst learning professionals who are also highly sceptical about evaluation, and particularly the amount of time and resource applied to it. The learning architect needs to ensure the team is all working on the same script.

Evaluating the learning function

Standards against which evaluation can be made for the learning function are established through:

▌ agreement of the objectives and plans of the function with senior management;
▌ recognizing an expectation of the learning function's performance detailed in the contents of the function's published strategy, policy and implementation plan;
▌ an emphasis on sustaining improvement month on month, year on year;
▌ benchmarking the function with those in other organizations (see information on benchmarking in Chapter 3);
▌ the budgetary/resource allocation methodology for the organization.

The learning function is evaluated from data gathered through:

▌ Proactively monitoring the perception of the function across the organization as to the function's use and usefulness. This is done by regular questionnaires sent to a variety of people in the organization, and when appropriate beyond it, followed by in-depth interviews. With a learning function integrated within the HR function this needs careful organizing, ensuring that any 'customer service survey' is done in conjunction with the other function. Otherwise the 'customers' may be confused, particularly if a number of similar surveys are sent out. An example survey is shown as Figure 5.1.
▌ Discussions with members of the strategic learning council, described in Chapter 2.
▌ Summarizing learner feedback from all activities.
▌ Summarizing changes in performance of learners as the result of attending all activities.
▌ Monitoring the commitment, competence and personal growth of the function's own staff.
▌ Continually reviewing the use of budget and resources.

LEARNING FUNCTION – SURVEY

Please circle your level of satisfaction using these scores:

Very satisfied	Satisfied	Somewhat satisfied	Dissatisfied	No experience
4	3	2	1	X

NAME .... ORGANIZATION UNIT....................................

My level of satisfaction					The learning function	Importance to me				
4	3	2	1	x	Is clear about the role to support the organization's performance	4	3	2	1	x
4	3	2	1	x	Is aligned to the strategy of the organization	4	3	2	1	x
4	3	2	1	x	Is aligned to the work of this unit	4	3	2	1	x
4	3	2	1	x	Has an appropriate /understood strategy	4	3	2	1	x
4	3	2	1	x	Meets regularly with unit managers	4	3	2	1	x
4	3	2	1	x	Aligns with the 'people strategies of the organization / HR	4	3	2	1	x
4	3	2	1	x	Focuses on learning needs of the organization's stakeholders	4	3	2	1	x
4	3	2	1	x	Actively monitors effectiveness and efficiency	4	3	2	1	x
4	3	2	1	x	Uses feedback to continuously improve	4	3	2	1	x
4	3	2	1	x	Seeks to identify ways of adding organizational value	4	3	2	1	x
4	3	2	1	x	Continuously demonstrates a professional brand	4	3	2	1	x
4	3	2	1	x	Consistently provides high quality learning solutions	4	3	2	1	x
4	3	2	1	x	Provides high-quality consultancy into the organization	4	3	2	1	x
4	3	2	1	x	Proactively partners with people in this business unit	4	3	2	1	x
4	3	2	1	x	Understands and implements new learning approaches	4	3	2	1	x
4	3	2	1	x	Benchmarks best practice with learning functions	4	3	2	1	x
4	3	2	1	x	Continuously improves the competencies of its own staff	4	3	2	1	x
4	3	2	1	x	Manages budgets and with a sense of business urgency	4	3	2	1	x
4	3	2	1	x	Operates reflecting the vision and values of the organization	4	3	2	1	x
4	3	2	1	x		4	3	2	1	x
4	3	2	1	x		4	3	2	1	x

Figure 5.1   Customer satisfaction survey

The information that results from all this data is used by function management to continuously evaluate the role of the function against the agreed standards, for discussions with senior management and for making any necessary modifications to the operation. More insight can be gained with another form of survey, one based around conversations triggered by use of the 'four by' model shown in Figure 5.2. This is particularly powerful when reviewing the function with senior stakeholders.

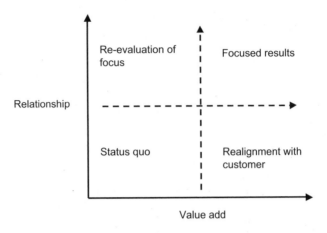

Figure 5.2 Value add and relationship

Conversations based around use of the model in Figure 5.2 may prompt views including:

▌ Low relationship, low value add: the learning function is seen as a low-value service provider. A state of status quo may easily lead to stagnation.
▌ High relationship, low value add: a respected learning function that probably needs an overhaul in its contribution to the organization, particularly its alignment with the organization's strategies. This is a potentially dangerous scenario for the learning architect where 'talk and no substance' is a criticism that could be directed by 'political' enemies.
▌ Low relationship, high value add: the learning function is probably seen as highly capable, but not really partnering with the organization or, particularly, with the person being interviewed.
▌ High relationship, high value add: the ideal situation. You should really understand the reason for the interviewee's perception in order that what is behind it can be maintained and reproduced elsewhere.

Evaluation of learning activities

Each learning initiative is critically evaluated, whether it is a month-long senior management learning workshop or an individual coaching event. Evaluation will lead to change, improvement and business benefit. The most common methods of evaluating a specific learning initiative are:

▌ Completion of evaluation forms by learners involved in the initiative. These forms are traditionally labelled 'happiness sheets', and continue to be viewed with intense cynicism in parts of the learning community.

▌ Examinations and practical tests, possibly both before and after attendance at the initiative.

▌ Discussions concerning the effectiveness of the initiative, particularly after one-on-one sessions of coaching or mentoring.

▌ Reports by line management and supervisors of changes in skills, knowledge, behaviours and overall performance.

▌ The introduction of a control group, people with similar roles and current competence who are not to have the benefit of the group who do attend the learning initiative. This is a sophisticated and time-consuming approach though it has some possibility of providing at least an indication of the return on investment of the learning programme. Care must be taken that the two groups, the learners and the control, are similar and that other factors do not influence the research.

The outcomes of only certain types of learning activities can be directly measured. A typist makes fewer mistakes and/or completes more letters. An accountant prepares the monthly accounts in days, not weeks, using his/her new spreadsheet skills. In many managerial posts, such measurement is not as easy. However, indicators of improved performance may include:

▌ lower staff turnover and absenteeism;

▌ fewer disciplinary matters;

▌ less use of the grievance procedure;

▌ better use of management techniques like joint problem solving and quality circles;

▌ improvements in interdepartmental relationships;

▌ fewer delays in getting information.

Evaluation of learning activities – pilot activities

A new learning initiative will be piloted when it is designed to have a significant business impact and/or when the initiative includes a lot of new learning or a number of new learning techniques. This piloting approach will increase the probabilities of a successful event when the first regular initiative is launched. The most common form of piloting is to have the initiative facilitated as if it was one of the regular events and to include extra levels of evaluation. Delegates on such a pilot initiative should include learners with a similar background and potential learning needs to the learners who will eventually attend the regular initiative. In addition the delegates may include members of the business function that has sponsored the initiative, and facilitators who will subsequently deliver the initiative. Time should be made available for the pilot activity to run one day longer than the planned regular activity. This will provide sufficient opportunity during the pilot for detailed discussion, and even, should it be necessary, for sections of the initiative to be tested more than once.

Evaluation during a pilot will be even more detailed than for a scheduled initiative:

▌ The facilitator and the sponsor should agree SMART (specific, measurable, achievable, realistic, time-bound) aims and objectives for each session as well as for the whole initiative.
▌ Assessment forms will be completed by the learners at the end of each learning session or each module of the initiative as well as at the end of the whole event.
▌ The progress of the pilot should be reviewed regularly, either at the end of each day or first thing each morning.

Another familiar approach to piloting is the use of a preview panel. These are a group of people, normally a mixture of people from the sponsoring function and from the learning function. Each will use a pre-prepared scoring sheet in examining the materials that have been built for the initiative. These will include descriptions of the objectives for the whole activity and for its components, learner materials, facilitator materials, descriptions of facilities and so on. Each panel member scores his/her sheets and then the panel meet to discuss their scorings, in particular those scorings that have a wide variation – the aspects of the planned learning initiative that may provide problems.

Monitoring one-to-one learning activities

With a formalized coaching and mentoring programme the coach/mentor and the learner schedule the last few minutes of every session to review progress and the coaching/mentoring techniques that are being employed. An open relationship built in support of the coaching/mentoring is a perfect environment in which to make this assessment of the usefulness of the session. The coach/mentor questions the learner's view of the success of the session and of potential improvements in the coaching/mentoring process. Agreement is reached about changes and how they will be introduced.

On regular occasions, a session should be devoted to a more robust evaluation of the progress and success of any coaching and/or mentoring intervention. The facilitator and the learner should agree that:

▌ their agreed objectives for the coaching/mentoring programme are still appropriate;
▌ the sessions are working towards those objectives;
▌ appropriate techniques of coaching/mentoring are being used.

Reviewing the impact of learning activities

The manager responsible for the staff who have attended learning activities should be asking:

▌ Are learners able to do their jobs, or some aspect of them, more effectively as a result of the learning initiative?
▌ If there is no discernible difference in work performance, is this because:
  - the real problem is job design and organization structure, not skills, knowledge or abilities?
  - the learning needs were poorly defined/delivered?
  - the employee lacks the ability or motivation to change behaviour?

The manager should debrief his/her member of staff on return from the learning initiative. Where possible, they should agree goals for putting the learning into operation, for ongoing coaching and checkpoints for assessing progress. The changes in performance should be encouraged through coaching, and monitored through the appraisal process. One model for this is to discuss with the learner, after the learning event:

▌ L What was learnt from the workshop?
▌ R What learning was particularly relevant to this delegate from what was learnt from the workshop?
▌ I What does the learner now intend to do to use the new competence, and what will he or she do to maintain and increase the competence?
▌ M How can the manager monitor progress and assist in the implementation and development of the new competence?

These post-learning debriefing sessions will be most effective when the manager and the learner have had a briefing session before the learner attends the initiative. This will establish the motivation of the learner and set the agreed expectations of the learnings from the event. Tests of proficiency before and after the learning initiative all lend more depth to the approach.

A similar approach needs to be taken by the manager over the period following the learning event. The manager continues, as part of a 'manager as leader and coach' relationship, to discuss how the learning event has impacted the capabilities of the learner. There may even be the opportunity, through some subtle questioning, to begin to form an impression of the real return and value of the learning initiative.

We firmly believe that this involvement of the learner's manager/coach/mentor before, directly after and then in the period following the learning event is one of the most important components, if not the most important, of this challenging topic of evaluation. A learning architect building a true learning culture across an organization needs to fully consider this aspect of 'buying in' management. It may require an extensive programme of management development in terms of both knowledge about a manager's role in developing his or her people, and the interpersonal skills to implement the appropriate evaluation. It will be money and time well invested.

An added dimension to this approach to evaluating learning is to add a 360° approach. This not only has the direct manager/coach working with the learner to evaluate performance improvement; it uses the input of others. Whether by personal contact and conversation or by completed form, possibly using a computer-based approach, several people can be asked to assist in evaluating a learner's improvement in capability. Pre- and post-evaluation, before and after the learning initiative, can always provide greater significance to the results of a 360° process of evaluation. Learning architects and their staff need to be aware, however, that there are some people who doubt the validity of 360° commentaries. They will argue that personalities and personal issues between people may well override any truth in evaluation.

Learner action plans

In gaining commitment to implementing new competence following learning activities, learners need to be encouraged to complete an 'action plan' at the end of the session. This provides a vehicle for discussion with the learner's line manager or supervisor, and encourages target dates to be set for action to be completed. Typically, the action plan will include:

▌ The most important actions to improve his/her performance the learner will undertake personally as a result of the learning initiative.

▌ The expected job-related results of these actions with, if possible, outcomes expressed in terms of time, quality, quantity or cost.

▌ Any action the learner can suggest for the organization/function to consider in assisting him/her to implement the listed actions.

Evaluation models

The majority of models that link together all the aspects of evaluating learners – from their attendance on a learning initiative through to their 'bottom line' benefit to the organization – are based on the Kirkpatrick model. This model comprises four stages:

1. Reactions, during and directly following the event, using facilitator questions and formal end of initiative evaluations by the learners.
2. Learning: as the final stage of the initiative or back in the workplace, a short time after the initiative, learners are tested by quizzes, job activity or in-depth interviews. This is designed to test understanding of the learning initiative.
3. Behaviour: the testing of the learner's enhanced performance in the workplace resulting from the learning initiative through specifically designed tests or, most often, direct observation by line managers and supervisors.
4. Results: the measurement of a contribution to the bottom line from an individual or a group of individuals participating in a learning initiative. For a production staff member this evaluation is normally undertaken by monitoring times, error percentages and the like before and after the learning initiative. For a knowledge worker it could involve 360° feedback from customers, suppliers, line managers and/or team members.

This model provides a set of standards rather than a process, and is often used with two other stages. A stage 0 concerns the setting of objectives and criteria for success. A fifth stage, return on investment, is also discussed, though it is known to be highly difficult to fully justify any results because of the situations described in the 'Environment of evaluation' paragraphs above.

There are many models for evaluation, mostly derived from the Kirkpatrick model. An interesting website with mention of a wide range of these models is www.campaign-for-learning.org.uk/pdf/LAW2004/history%20_evaluation.pdf

There are also models to capture a cost-benefit analysis approach to the evaluation of learning. One equation used is:

$$\frac{\text{Financial benefit of business change}}{\text{Cost of learning initiative}} \times 100 = \% \text{ return on investment}$$

This equation requires data from before and after the learning initiative, typically from sales performance, number of errors, staff turnover rates, number of health and safety incidents.

Assessment of learners

There will be situations when a learning activity includes the evaluation of learners and their competence development. This evaluation may be in one of several forms:

I The facilitator writes a report to the management of the learner(s) after the activity. This will detail the learner's performance during the activity against an agreed set of standards.
I The learner undertakes a skill test or written examination at the end of the initiative. This may be balanced against a similar evaluation done at the start of the initiative.
I Learners may be evaluated against their personal or team performance in a business game included as part of the learning initiative.

It is key to the success of these initiatives that the learners:

I are aware that they will be evaluated;
I understand how the evaluation will be conducted and what reports will be submitted;
I understand what criteria will be used for pass or fail, and what could be the results of failing to attain a particular standard.

If the learners are not aware of these facts and subsequently find out about the evaluations and its consequences, the learning function and the facilitator may be severely criticized, and future trust could be impossible to achieve.

Although not every situation will allow this to happen, the results of evaluation of the learners should be discussed with the learners as soon as possible after the learning initiative. In fact, if at all possible, this feedback should be provided as the final stage of the initiative. This will ensure that facilitator and learner have a clear memory of the event and can most fairly discuss the learner's performance. The provision of effective feedback is dependent on the inclusion of evidence. If the facilitator is to provide feedback to learners, the facilitator should proactively note evidence of each learner's performance all through the initiative.

Assessment centres are also a useful mechanism to investigate individuals' abilities and capability to successfully use skills and knowledge. They are particularly used in a mode of judging future potential. Detractors often discuss the artificiality of such events, with delegates on their best behaviour, and warn that assessment centres are only a fraction of the overall process of identifying and developing talent.

Assessment of individual facilitators

Facilitators working in learning functions of medium and large organizations will be subject to performance management and appraisals. These should include overall performance evaluations and personal development plans. This may be structured around a competency framework for the job. In addition, a facilitator can build evidence on personal performance against which he/she can evaluate himself/herself and monitor progress. The sources include:

I the results of 'happiness sheets' from learners;
I feedback from learners who are receiving monitoring and coaching;
I feedback on performance from his/her manager;
I personal benchmarks against acknowledged excellent facilitators.

The facilitator is key to the success of the learning. Without his/her excellence of performance all the remaining work can be wasted. Facilitators should be reminded constantly of the importance of self-evaluation and personal improvement. They are encouraged to benchmark themselves against colleagues and facilitators in other organizations. Facilitators should attend learning activities within the organization as well as external activities, partially to learn and partially to observe other facilitators – giving, when appropriate, suitable feedback.

BRANDING AND COMMUNICATION FOR A LEARNING FUNCTION

The learning architect role is full and demanding. Building, implementing and managing a successful learning function is a key role within an organization. It is only appropriate that our success is known throughout the organization. The learning architect's abilities should become recognized and acclaimed, and should be part of learners and their managers recognizing the 'brand'. It is appropriate that everybody concerned, internally and externally, knows what to expect when dealing with the function. The brand should be inspirational and provide a consistent message of professional people, meaningful processes and policies and fit-for-purpose facilities. Whenever an individual interfaces with the learning function, that interface should be managed in a predictable, consistent, agreeable manner.

The learning function and all its activities should be aligned to the 'learning intensity' and sense of urgency that will have them highly regarded throughout the organization. The real point of learning is at the workplace, and here learners, potential learners and their manager/coach should be:

▌ clear about their role in the development of their people in terms of interaction with the learning function and its initiatives, particularly in areas of coaching and post-initiative evaluation;
▌ clear about the role, importance and value of the learning function;
▌ clear about their relationship and the processes of contact with the learning function;
▌ always prepared to provide references to the contribution of the learning function, regarding it as a practical, pragmatic assistance to their own attempts to be successful.

A learning function brand is one to which the learning function staff have contributed in design, build, implementation and reinforcement – with the guiding hand of the learning architect.

The relationship that the learning function has with the organization could be illustrated with a diagram similar to Figure 5.3, and progress by the 'rainbow' chart of Figure 3.5. All contacts between the learning function and the stakeholders are those 'moments of truth' that are the opportunities to demonstrate the function's professionalism, and more importantly, its worth to organizational success. Each and every learning event, every inquiry handled, every complaint response and every other interaction must support the brand. This is not an easy goal to attain when we are striving to be proactive, flexible and quick to respond. However, our continual high standing within the organization will be more easily achieved by consistent branding of our actions – although it can never compensate for inappropriate learning programmes!

When branding is a common theme in the organization, ensure the learning function brand is not at odds with the organization's. Its brand should be supportive of the overall organizational brand while being individually distinctive, showing clearly the nature of the function.

Figure 5.3   The relationship

The website will be a major statement for its branding. The website needs to be:

▌ stakeholder-focused, particularly for users and potential users of learning programmes;
▌ regularly updated and not allowed to look stale;
▌ informative, easy to access and use, effective – just like the learning programmes;
▌ an opportunity to broadcast the success of the learning function in supporting organizational performance;
▌ entertaining, with quizzes, games, articles with a learning bias – and as interactive as possible;
▌ an opportunity to tell people about the learning programmes that are being implemented and their success – particularly in parts of the organization where there is perhaps less expectancy of any learning function involvement;
▌ layered: quick visitors can find out what they seek with ease while those with time and a specific purpose find depth with intellectual content and challenge.

The website will include the entry point, the portal, for accessing the learning available throughout the organization – the access to the learning architecture (see below).

Update the whole community of the success of learning initiatives, individuals and the learning function using the 'interesting' website together with any other forms of mass communication, including organization broadsheets and staff magazines. Launch new programmes of learning in a way that ensures the community recognizes the proactivity of the learning function and its alignment to organizational success and talent development.

The signs of success

The establishment of a strong, consistent brand, and a proven ability of the learning function to effectively communicate with all the learning stakeholders of the organization, are amongst the signs of success that we seek. Others, some tangible, some less so, include:

I Recognized, applauded and rewarded across the organization for adding value to organizational performance.

I Overall value being greater than cost; for many initiatives, where true evaluation is a reality, capable of proving an actual positive return on investment.

I 'Intimate' with senior stakeholders, contributing to the organizational strategies.

I Renown externally as an organization providing effective learning, 'world-class training' or similar things; invited to speak at conferences, invited to be the subject of case studies in research and benchmarking initiatives, winning 'training prizes'.

I Internal conversations are not about the cost of training, rather more about the proven value of learning.

I Staff throughout the organization are curious about themselves and their potential, actively undertaking continuous development and visibly learning to learn.

I People want to work with and for the organization, quoting the learning possibilities and talent development as a major reason.

I There are genuine performance improvements through people having access to knowledge and the ability to turn that knowledge into applicable wisdom.

I People across the organization wish to work within the learning function fold. People within the learning function are approached with job offers by line management, since the function staff are seen to have the ability to contribute so significantly to organizational performance.

I The 'journey to learning excellence' is clearly understood and applauded through all the organizational stakeholders; the learning architect and the staff of the learning function are clearly aware of the current position and the next activities of the journey.

▮ Members of the learning function team are seen as role models. They are actively pursuing personal development and are part of the continuous improvement across the function.

TRANSFORMED LEARNING STRATEGIES AND IMPLEMENTATION

Introduction

A learning function 'strategy for learning' needs primarily to be realistic. It can be aspirational, although if those people who own it and those people who work with it have no faith in it, it is worthless. A strategy needs particularly to allow its users to recognize priorities from all the things that could be pursued, and to concentrate on those things that will be achieved. In today's busy climate this prioritizing is vitally important in the challenge to develop talent for the organization, and learning processes that will benefit its operation with its stakeholders.

In situations where there are high levels of change and organizational churn, plans can be made and rapidly have to be changed. An overall strategy can be far from easy to define in these circumstances. Perseverance brings rewards; at the very least an outlined strategy has the ability to have resources facing the same direction and accepting what is to be achieved.

When the situation is appropriate we advocate an intense, proactive style of operation for the learning architect and his/her team. The strategy, its documentation and its communication should reflect that style: brief and to the point while containing sufficient detail for the direction of the learning function's operations to be agreed and understood with management across the organization. A traditional training and development strategy, described in Chapter 2 for an 'establishing' learning function, may be several pages in length, the result of a detailed working process. For learning functions in either the 'repositioning' or the 'guiding' status (see page 46 in Chapter 2), the recommendation is for a simpler document, easily constructed and focused on gaining acceptance from management at the top of the organization.

The strategy will include:

▮ A brief description of the function's 'journey to learning excellence' in parallel with the organization's journey to success and the overall talent strategy for the organization – probably owned by HR. It will include sentences such as 'Develop a culture and mindset based around the five key values and around cross-organizational communication to fuel organizational transformation strategies' and 'Develop senior leadership capabilities against the HR competency framework' and 'Promote a learning organization'. Each of these strategies will be amplified, with a brief recording of critical activities, critical success factors, any identified high-level risks and assumptions.

▌ An outline of engagement methodologies with operational functions as described in the next section of this chapter.

▌ An outline of any high-priority tactical initiatives that need to be addressed through learning initiatives or the management of resources: 'Conduct rapid learning needs analysis on the staff on the newly (re)insourced customer service division', 'Acquire a (replacement) learning management system capable of supporting all the staff of the newly merged organization', 'Identify a high-quality external workshop facilitator with international, virtual team experience and a sales and marketing background'.

▌ Staffing, budget and other resource considerations.

▌ Frameworks for prioritization of potential projects and of the most appropriate manner in which to provide learning programmes.

▌ Approaches for monitoring, any high-level metrics to be employed together with any critical success factors. These topics are discussed in the earlier pages of this chapter and in other chapters of this book.

The strategy is unlikely to have detailed descriptions of general types and examples of learning initiative that will be implemented.

As Dennis Waitley (1984) is much quoted as saying, 'Winners can tell you where they are going, what they plan to do along the way and who will be sharing the adventure with them.'

LEARNING FUNCTION ENGAGEMENT

The learning strategy documentation will include outline details of how the learning function engages with the organization for a variety of learning initiatives. The professionalism of this 'contracting' with the operational units is vital; it must be seen as a two-way process with hard measurable outcomes. It will be seen as part of the learning function's value-add to the organization's performance, and will encourage the 'customers' to call again. The engagement proposition needs to be powerful, clear and easily taken up by the customer. In addition to the obvious conversations about learning needs, costs and the 'best' learning methods, the learning function representation must clearly debate such 'business' items as evaluation, risk and ownership.

Responding to 'today's' operational learning needs

The learning function's 'today' focus is on responding to learning requirements from the operational units and other stakeholders in identifying, prioritizing and implementing learning for the shorter timeframe. Change in legislation, new business opportunities, competitive activity, changes in budget, new people acquired in a merger, new operating procedures and many other situations will produce these shorter timeframe needs. Such responses are focused through the relationship that is mapped in Figure 3.1.

The engagement strategy should be underpinned by regular meetings between the 'practice managers' and representatives of the operational functions, who may be labelled 'function learning managers' when they are in place. Frequencies of such meetings are dependent on the numbers of people in the learning function and in the operational functions, the manner in which the practice manager/account manager model is organized, and – most important of all – the relative importance of the operational functions in terms of their learning needs, particularly towards achieving organizational success as defined by the strategy of the organization and the CEO. When appropriate, agreement about the priorities between learning needs from the different operational functions will be a decision made between the learning architect and other senior management, normally at meetings of the strategic learning council described in Chapter 3.

The generated learning needs are handled in a rapid reaction process:

I Learning needs are identified within the operational functions and notified to the practice manager in the learning function, possibly through the learning account manager within the operational function. It would be usual for the practice manager, constantly in touch with the operational unit, to have prior warning of such a request for learning. Indeed, the practice manager may even have personally instigated conversations about the potential benefits of the learning with the unit's management.

I The practice manager works with representatives of the operational unit in preparing a short report that scopes the project and details:

  - the benefits and objectives of any learning aligned to an operational programme;

- budgetary considerations and the most effective learning mechanisms to be applied;
- any operational 'quick wins' in a learning programme that will help in its implementation.

❙ Having agreed the accuracy of the report with the operational function, the practice manager discusses the priority of this project with the learning architect. It may also need consideration with the strategic learning council.

❙ Agreement is reached on whether this project will be handled with the assistance of the learning function. If it is, a level of priority is given to it and a project manager appointed – possibly a suitably qualified practice manager from within the learning function, possibly a nominated person from within the operational function.

❙ The learning project, as part of the operational project, will now be unfolded. The learning aspects will be implemented using the most appropriate sources (as discussed in Chapter 8), as managed by the project leader. Figure 5.4 shows the interaction of activities for this process and Figure 5.5 shows a typical project flow including the evaluation of the results of learning.

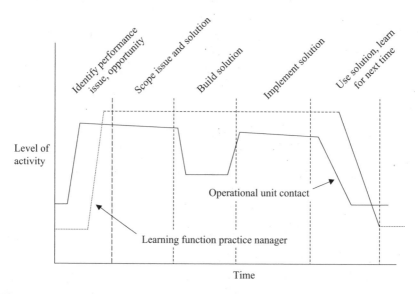

Figure 5.4   Working with the organization

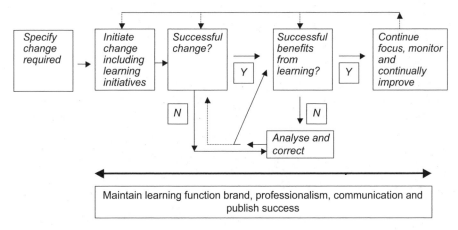

Figure 5.5   Operational change and learning

Should it be decided that the learning function will not be involved with the project, it will be passed back to the operational function. The function may decide to pursue the learning aspects of the project, since it has the appropriate budget, using external resource. There will be a strong recommendation, if this is the case, that the function takes advantage of the briefing provided on the learning function intranet site for such eventualities (see below).

Short-term learning initiatives

There will be a wide variety of learning requirements identified by the operational functions:

▌ Skill development programmes at the workplace, job-focused with high-intensity learning, concerning knowledge workers applying wisdom and available knowledge to their role. A learning professional, probably from within the learning function, will most probably facilitate any planned learning event, possibly with content provided by a co-facilitator, an experienced topic expert from the operational unit. Working together the facilitator and the topic expert, having agreed the objectives of the event, ensure the objectives are met for the learners.

▌ Focused programmes of learning aimed at an identified group of managers and supervisory staff for 'immediate' improvement of their leadership, coaching and facilitating capabilities in assisting the performance of their knowledge workers.

I Programmes of project management and change management for teams at the workplace, aligning theory and a project management toolbox of techniques with the actual jobs the staff undertake.

Such skill-focused programmes can be supported by knowledge-focused programmes available through e-learning materials, at learner desks or within dedicated learning centres, and through classroom-based 'knowledge workshop' events.

Longer-term learning programmes: a strategic approach

The second arena of engagement of the learning function and its operation concerns longer-term learning initiatives available all across the organization, and in some circumstances to the organization's suppliers, clients and customers.

These learning initiatives may have originated proactively within the learning function, and are programmes that will have deep impact on the organization for several years. They will include such concepts as the development of a learning organization and of a mentoring and coaching culture. These may be launched as large organization-wide initiatives, or they may be treated as new, as yet less well-developed ideas, piloted with a single unit of the organization.

The development of these proactive, learning-function-generated ideas should follow this sort of path:

I Having discussed the ideas with the strategic learning council, described in Chapter 3, or directly with senior management within the organization or within an operational function, the learning architect seeks a sponsor to support further investigation.

I The sponsor provides contacts within the organization and/or its stakeholders for research by the learning function team. The sponsor grants the learning function or its representatives a 'hunting licence' to discuss the ideas with all appropriate people.

I A costed, business success-focused presentation is then made to allow decisions to be made about the possibilities of the potential learning initiative.

I A staff member in the learning function, or even a 'function learning manager' from an operational function, may manage such a longer-term project as a personal developmental project.

Chapter 3 describes methodologies for identifying what learning programmes will be appropriate for a particular organization. Although a complex process, it provides a deep insight into an organization's learning needs. It asks more fundamental questions than the learning needs analysis with which many are familiar. In essence, the process has the following steps:

▍ Examining what learning strategies, methodologies and programmes are appropriate by researching a series of parameters about the type, culture, size of organization, processes and successes, together with indications of what is to change in future for the organization.

▍ Examining the gap between this ideal and the actual, together with examining the gap for the organization's staff – the difference between ideal and actual for skills, knowledge and attitude.

▍ Proposing an action plan for agreement with senior management and methods of communicating with the workforce, paying attention to variables including funding and the availability of dedicated and co-opted resources and facilities available to the learning architect.

Proactive learning initiatives generated within the learning function may take the form of large programmes across the whole organization, a mixture of classroom, on-the-job learning, coaching and whatever else. Such programmes will entail deep research in analysing the investments involved. On the other hand, the initiatives may involve recommendations and guidelines for learning-rich activities that have little involvement with the function, such activities as work shadowing and project work (see Chapter 8). The role of learning function and the learning architect may only be to encourage these activities and provide a framework, detailed on the learning function architecture, of key checkpoints to follow. Checkpoints include criteria for a successful learning event, the agreement of learning objectives, planning activities, and methods to monitor and evaluate progress. Line managers would use these lists to orchestrate appropriate activities for their staff.

The learning architect as a 'player'

The idea of 'players' was introduced in Chapter 1, as people who perform in the work of the learning function. Perhaps one of the most powerful engagements from the learning function into the organization is personal work with the senior management group by the learning architect. This includes involvement in the strategizing and planning for the organization, and should also include more proactive initiatives.

In terms of showing added value and the power of amalgamating learning, knowledge and wisdom in a most powerful manifestation, few things could be better than the learning architect facilitating scenario playing with the senior staff – the organization's thought leaders and decision makers. The engagement could take one of several forms involving simulations of the future of the organization, access to knowledge and the application of 'wisdom' through decision making and conflict resolution techniques. The learning architect demonstrates the real value of directed learning, and significantly enhances the brand image of the function. The trick for the facilitator, of course, is to be both the orchestrator and a contributor who is perceived the equal of the other senior people.

The role of facilitator is significant. When the senior management believe they have somebody they can rely on, both in terms of ability and confidentiality, they will be far more comfortable to take on the planning challenges associated with today's world of ambiguity, complexity and uncertainty. This is a considerable contribution from the learning architect.

A TRANSFORMED LEARNING ARCHITECTURE

Introduction

The learning architecture is the framework for all the operations of the learning function and its interactions with all its stakeholders – from its 'customers' who will take advantage of learning initiatives through to the most senior management of the organization and any bodies external to the organization. It is often the physical presence that sums up the brand of the learning function.

For the stakeholders in learning across and beyond the organization, the architecture is about access. It makes available all the information and processes that allow these stakeholders to take advantage of learning to complete their own work. It is the source of everything to do with learning, including an explanation of the significant work of the learning function. It encompasses everything from a fully descriptive catalogue of training workshops through to a source of information about the 'whys', 'whats' and 'hows' of learning in and beyond the organization. The architecture also provides access to records, those managed by the learning function and those maintained elsewhere – typically in the HR function.

For the staff of the learning function, the learning architecture is the framework that supports all their work. It provides guidance, tools and techniques in allowing them to respond to their customers in the most appropriate manner. It outlines the manner in which relationships are managed, how the correct learning processes are selected and implemented, how records are maintained, and how information is stored for future improvement of their work.

For the learning architect, the architecture provides an overall control and management framework. It provides one of the largest opportunities to have people across the organization understand and buy in to the role of learning, and an appropriate learning function for their personal performance and success.

Today's learning architecture

The simple training and development framework that is described in Chapter 2 continues to supply a learning architecture for many learning functions. This architecture supports the detailed planning, publication and implementation of learning initiatives. It is appropriate in a stable environment when there is time to adequately plan learning initiatives over a longer time horizon, and where the learning function is regarded as a service function. Customers need to know what learning initiatives are being made available and how to take advantage of them.

A number of factors are working in parallel in organizations to result in the traditional learning framework being replaced with a different form of learning architecture. These factors include:

I Rates of both internal and external change coupled with increased workloads in organizations mean that everybody and everything needs to be highly flexible and responsive. Planning horizons with which we were once familiar no longer are appropriate.

I Learning functions are seeking to build a learning culture that is regarded as an integral part of the organization's successful performance, one that develops the talent available to the organization. This requires a 'pull' from a knowledgeable organization and its staff. Important to this is the easy availability of information about learning, reinforcement of skill sets and much more that makes access to learning and its application to performance simple for the customer.

I There is a wealth of material and technology, including off the shelf learning management systems and intranet-based knowledge, that we can make available to the organization to make people feel that our learning culture is appropriate to them in their roles.

I The traditional training and development frameworks were often quite academic in nature, often paper-based, and were clearly 'owned' by the learning function. In the modern organization the function needs to be regarded as part of the solution, and therefore be seen as open and available.

Ideally, today's approach to a learning architecture will provide the necessary access to a flexible knowledge-based learning environment while retaining as much as possible of the planning rigour and successful branding of the more traditional approaches.

Hosting the learning architecture

The learning architecture will result in large databases of information and a considerable amount of traffic as people access the information. Traffic will also be encouraged by building the type of access portal that was discussed under 'Branding' earlier in this chapter: fun, games, quizzes and timely information about the world of learning are all designed to have people involved with the portal and with learning. When an electronic learning architecture is being designed, it is imperative to discuss these issues with the information systems function and with other experts. Several major catastrophes have occurred when learning functions have not fully integrated with other functions when implementing learning management systems and online learning systems: system crashes, appalling response times and high levels of user dissatisfaction have occurred. There has been a trend to host large learning architectures on systems external to the main organization.

Although it is not unusual for an organization to be extensively wired in its headquarters location, be wary of networks that do not function in a satisfactory fashion in remote locations, and of situations where hosts of fieldworkers do not have full availability of central systems. This may have resonance with learning architects who have experienced immense frustration with e-learning initiatives that have failed because of technology. Do be aware of these situations, and that it may be necessary to rely on more old-fashioned communication mechanisms in some cases. Discuss with other operational functions how they keep in touch with their staffs; you may be able to piggy back on existing processes to move information about learning. It has also been recognized that take-up of learning tends to decrease, the farther away people are from a corporate headquarters. This trend may well be amplified by learners who are frustrated by failed attempts to access an electronic-based learning architecture.

Do not be overwhelmed with technology; there are many experienced people to contact. Always maintain the vision of what the learning architecture means to the 'customers'.

The conceptual model

The conceptual model for the learning architecture is shown as Figure 5.6. This formation allows the learning function to establish the relationships with all interested parties, and to consistently monitor the appropriate nature of the constituent portions of the architecture.

The engagement layer of this model is the portal that is described in the paragraphs above concerning branding and communication. It enables stakeholders across the organization to have full access to information about learning, and acts as a window into other databases. It should act as a sophisticated form of help desk built on the principles of 'pull' from the customers of the learning function, having them sufficiently involved that they come to the architecture for information and assistance.

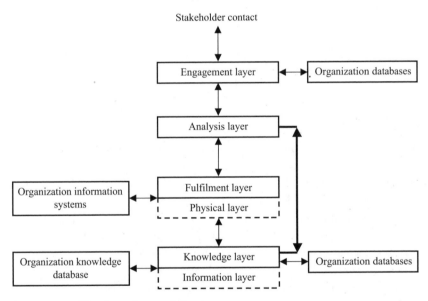

Figure 5.6   The learning architecture

Be ready to interface with other functions in the organization. Encourage the HR function to maintain useful records, job descriptions, performance management data, competences of job families and the like. Encourage operational functions to maintain the records of their people's development programmes and the evaluation of how those programmes have developed their performance contribution to the organization. The learners are the operational function's resource and responsibility. The learning architect is the consultative source of assistance to the learning community rather than a librarian or a statistician.

The analysis layer conceptually shows that decisions are made about such items as the best method of fulfilling a learning need, the best method of evaluation, whether a particular learning need will be handled directly by the learning function or passed back to the operational unit. Decisions can be made using considerations recognizing:

▮ the size, location, delegates for the learning initiative;

▮ the available learning technologies (classroom, distance learning, coaching and so on), including both their availability in the locations required and the richness of the technology in answering learning needs;

▮ costs using the potential learning technologies;

▮ access to best practice about this sort of learning initiative, from the databases connected to the information layer of the architecture;

▮ available facilitators, internal or external, with the appropriate abilities in the locations required.

Originally these decisions will be based very much on the individual expertise of members of the learning function team, filtering learning needs through the points above. As best practice builds, a database can be built to assist the decisions and stored on the information layer of the architecture. The project manager appointed for each learning project will have, among his or her responsibilities, a need to contribute 'lessons learnt' to this best practice database.

The fulfilment layer conceptually represents the methodologies that can be applied to implementing the learning initiatives. Many will be supplied through electronic technology, and therefore the fulfilment layer is shown symbolically attached to the physical layer. Even when the learning initiative is implemented with a traditional classroom workshop, it is highly likely that it will be supported by knowledge made available through electronic technology.

Information is generally brought into the architecture from the web, possibly from supplier and customer databases and from internal databases. When information has been processed and becomes available for future use and best practice it is stored in the conceptual knowledge layer. The knowledge layer is also conceptually a recognition of the storage of a series of checklists to assist with the implementation of learning, particularly with initiatives where the learning function is not directly involved. These would include primers on coaching processes, choosing an external supplier, setting up a learning initiative with appropriate standards and evaluation. Should time, budget and resource be available, these primers could be built to support the brand of the learning function by being interactive, colourful and fun to use.

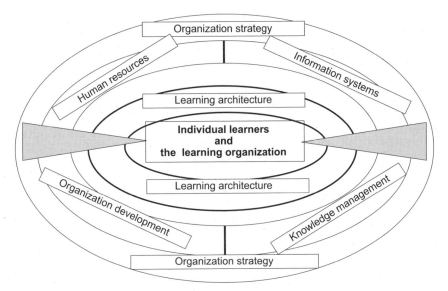

Figure 5.7   Concept of the learning architecture

CHAPTER SUMMARY

▌ There are a number of commercial models available for the management of a learning function. The learning architect needs to work with senior organization management to implement the most appropriate model.

▌ The learning architect and the learning function team need to implement a series of evaluation methodologies to monitor learning initiatives. The results of these will allow the function to focus continuous improvement on its activities and ensure that learning can prove its worth to the organization.

▌ Branding and effective communication are key to the perception of the function across and beyond the organization.

▌ The learning function works with a strategy and a learning architecture that allows close management of the learning activities.

Part II

The rise of the learning architect

6

Skills of a learning architect

The purpose of this chapter is to:

▌ outline the skills required by all types of learning architect;
▌ identify with which players a learning architect will most frequently have to use the skills;
▌ provide examples of how learning architects have used their skills in the workplace;
▌ highlight areas for skill development.

This chapter explores the skills required by learning architects when they are managing the players. The different types of learning architect we have identified (corporate, tactical, functional and individual) will use all of the skills, but may only use those skills with some of the players.

The skills we have outlined are developed from observing and working with successful learning architects who use these skills to create a learning architecture. While the list is not definitive it does reflect the current skill set required by learning architects who are working in organizations requiring effective solutions provided through learning.

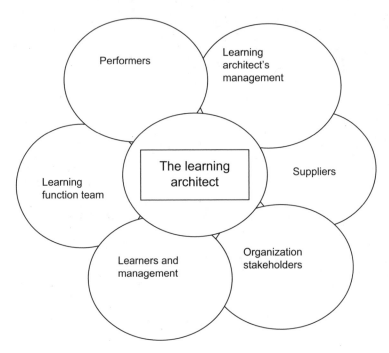

Figure 6.1 The players

SKILLS OF A LEARNING ARCHITECT

▌ Influencing.
▌ Project managing.
▌ Coaching.
▌ Mentoring.
▌ Facilitating.
▌ Marketing.
▌ Negotiating.

By creating a matrix which combines the skills and players we can identify which skills a learning architect is most likely to use with each player. Not all skills will be used by each type of learning architect with every player, but it is a requirement that each type of learning architect has each skill.

Table 6.1 Players and relationships

	Influencing	Project Managing	Coaching	Mentoring	Facilitating	Marketing	Negotiating
Learning architect's manager	LA1	LA1	LA1			LA1	LA1
	LA2	LA2	LA2			LA2	LA2
	LA3	LA3	LA3			LA3	LA3
	LA4		LA4			LA4	LA4
Suppliers	LA2	LA2			LA2		LA1
	LA3	LA3			LA3		LA2
							LA3
Organization's stakeholders	LA1	LA2	LA2	LA1	LA1	LA1	LA1
	LA2	LA3	LA4	LA2	LA2	LA2	LA2
				LA4	LA4		
Learners and their managers	LA2	LA2	LA1	LA1	LA2	LA1	LA1
	LA3	LA3	LA2	LA2	LA3	LA2	LA2
	LA4	LA4	LA3	LA3	LA4		LA3
			LA4	LA4			LA4
Learning architect's team	LA1		LA1	LA1	LA1	LA1	LA1
Performers	LA2	LA2	LA2	LA1	LA1	LA1	LA1
	LA3	LA3	LA3	LA2	LA2	LA2	LA2
				LA3	LA3	LA3	LA3
				LA4	LA4		

INFLUENCING

To have an effect on a person or their behaviour in causing or persuading someone to act in a particular way without the use of direct force or command.

(Longman's Contemporary English Dictionary)

In the context of managing players, influencing will mean that a learning architect senses:

▌ agreement not acquiescence;
▌ commitment not compliance;
▌ wanting to, not forced to;
▌ that the concept or idea is bought not sold.

Influencing without force or command is paramount for a learning architect. We are in the people business, and our success with building an architecture for our organization comes from the belief that people have of us. Our ability to influence for the long term comes not from what we force people to do, but from how we respond and react to others and how we conduct ourselves.

Every human being is influenced by many things, but mostly by other people. We can influence via requests, the nature of our conversation and how well we 'walk our talk'. Organizations are made up of a range of individuals and groups who are attempting to satisfy their own needs as well as those of the organization. The interplay of power exercised by various stakeholders, both internal and external, is what enables an organization to achieve its objectives with some unity.

At the core of influencing is power. If we take our definition of influencing, we mean power in the context of causing or persuading someone to act in a particular way without the use of direct force or command. Not all individuals or groups use power in such a way. Those who use power to force or control others usually do so out of fear of what might happen if they do not control. Short-term control may be gained at the expense of long-term trust and positive relationships.

The source of power varies from one organization to another, and can shift within an organization. Learning architects need to be aware that sources of power can be within (managers, functions and learners) and outside the organization (shareholders, government departments, interest groups).

Many of the qualities of a learning architect, outlined in another chapter, are required for a learning architect of any type to have influence. Successful influencing comes from combining qualities such as being motivated, informed, able to create a network, building trust and rapport, being recognized as a contributor, understanding the organization and knowing who to influence.

Understanding how individuals and groups, within each group of players, are likely to influence the work that a learning architect does in an organization will enable the successful learning architect to know who, how and when he or she needs to influence:

▎ Learning architect type 1 (corporate) will need to know who to influence when seeking a change to how the learning and development budget is allocated.
▎ Learning architect type 2 (tactical) will need to know the most appropriate people to use influencing skills with when proposing a new management development programme.

▌ Learning architect type 3 (functional) is probably going to need to know who to influence in order to gain assistance with the implementation of health and safety training.

▌ Learning architect type 4 (individual) will use influencing skills with managers who are reluctant to involve a third party in the training of their team.

Example 6.1: Learning architect type 2 (tactical) influencing external stakeholders in connection with the implementation of national vocational qualifications (NVQs)

This example features a tactical learning architect, operating without a team, with many years' experience gained from working in other parts of the organization before moving into learning and development. Like other organizations within the sector, the learning architect's organization was experiencing a skills shortage with its existing staff, and an inability to recruit people with the skills required for the future.

The strategy to improve this situation was based around introducing NVQs to the organization. One of the first objectives for the learning architect was to identify the external and internal stakeholders. Once these had been identified, the learning architect would be able to understand where they had the power to influence. In turn the learning architect would have a clearer sense of where to use her own influence to best effect:

▌ Internal stakeholders:

- learners;
- learners' supervisors;
- learners' managers;
- senior management board;
- workplace trainers;
- learning architect.

▌ External stakeholders:

- learning skills council;
- sector skills council;
- local college;
- local schools;
- customers;

- suppliers;
- chamber of commerce;
- unions;
- trade association.

The learning architect believed that influence usually occurs only because individuals share expectations with other individuals or groups, and thus become a stakeholder group.

Most individuals belong to more than one stakeholder group. People will identify with the aims, ambitions, values and needs of a stakeholder group. These groups may occur because of geographical location, level in a hierarchy, different departments, gender or specializations. External stakeholders can seek to influence an organization through connections with internal stakeholders. There was no official union recognition within the organization, but some individuals were members of unions. Local colleges may have influence because of past students who now work for the organization and through staff with children who attended the college.

In order to analyse and assess stakeholder influence, the learning architect used a couple of models. The models had been used to good effect for a workplace assignment for an open learning programme.

The objective was the introduction of NVQs to the organization. Using the beliefs she held about the needs and attitudes of the various stakeholders, the learning architect identified the likely responses of the stakeholder groups to the objective. Using the broad terms of approval (A), opposition (O) and indifference (I), she came up with the pattern shown in Figure 6.2.

As some of the groups (such as learners, unions and customers) had two possible responses, the learning architect broke down the membership of the individual stakeholder group further to identify subgroups. She used a matrix to plot the interrelationship between all the stakeholder groups, then constructed a force field analysis to identify and consider the driving and restraining forces. Economic security, fear of change, increased work load, recognition and targets met are some of the forces that came into play.

Having collated this information she had a clearer sense of where and who she needed to spend time with, and which would be least and most influential in the successful introduction of NVQs into the organization. This was a long and careful process in which the learning architect used initiatives to help overcome limiting beliefs and encourage those beliefs that were enabling a group or individual to embrace the objective.

Some of the initiatives taken by the learning architect were: small discussion groups, evidence of past success, regular communication, visits to and from other organizations that had introduced NVQs, attending

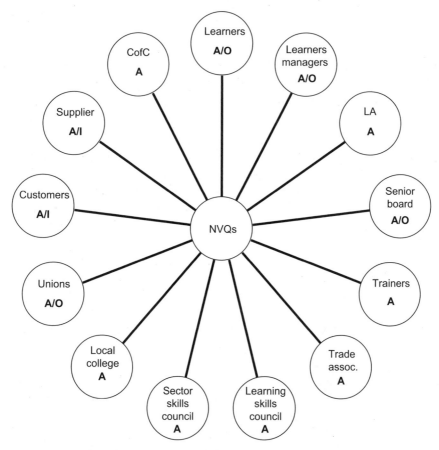

Figure 6.2   Influencing

meetings of external stakeholders, being part of the working party developing new standards, and visits to and from local colleges and schools.

The learning architect believed that it was more beneficial to influence through changing people's behaviour or beliefs because they want to, rather than employing coercion or sanctions; gaining long-term commitment for success rather than a short-term fix.

PROJECT MANAGING

Amongst the most powerful of the tools and techniques available to the learning architect are those grouped under the heading of project management. With many parallel programmes a project management approach ensures a consistency of approach, appreciated by all stakeholders, together with a maximum chance of success.

For learning programmes and all other activities associated with the learning function, a four-phase project management approach is the most obvious. As with many things in life, doing the early phases well is all-important. There is less chance of failure as we get deeper into the detail of the later phases.

When analysing a project there will always be hard measures of success about bringing a project in on time, to expected cost and with the correct deliverables. For the learning architect the softer side of evaluation is also key. Did the project team work well together? What did the people involved in the project learn? What aspects of the work did they enjoy?

I Learning architect type 1 (corporate) may be involved in project managing the outsourcing of a function, or other strategic changes in the organization such as the purchase of a new company. Typically he or she will hand the project management over to one of the learning function team.

I Learning architect type 2 (tactical) could be project managing the implementation of a graduate trainee development programme.

I Learning architect type 3 (functional) might project manage the training of first aiders for a company.

I Learning architect type 4 (individual) could be involved in project managing the coaching programme for a department.

Example 6.2: Learning architect type 3 project managing his manager, suppliers, stakeholders, learners and their managers and performers

In this company a strategy to diversify into providing packaging for the food industry meant that all the production staff were going to have to receive training in basic food hygiene. The day shift line manager, with responsibility for training, was tasked with managing the project. Following the four-phase project management approach he was able to keep track of the important initiative along with all his other responsibilities.

Phase one, the preparation phase, is about identifying clear objectives for a project: describing in detail what the food hygiene training will achieve, framing the exact definition of how production will be affected by the implementation of the standards, the changes needed to changing rooms and wash areas, uniforms and so on, clearly listing the objectives for the training. Phase one is also the time that the business owners of the benefit of the project are clearly involved in discussing with senior people exactly what they are expecting from the learning initiative, what role they will play before, during and after the event, what the motivation is of the people who will attend, and so on.

The (line manager) learning architect facilitated meetings with all managers and supervisors, at which roles and responsibilities and expectations were discussed. What objections to the change in procedures would be raised by the shop floor? Where would the money for the training and additional facilities come from? What would be the result of increased production time?

As phase one was conducted the learning architect built a project brief, which is a collection, a statement of everything to do with the project. By the end of the phase it contained all the details of the planned project, and allowed confirmation and sign off with any stakeholders involved: managers of people who would be attending the training, senior directors who were sponsoring the change to providing food packaging, accountants and so on.

The learning architect used a number of project management tools, which proved essential for phase one of the project, and which he was also able to use in later phases:

| **SWOT analysis** to investigate the situation faced at the start of the project and where the project was going.
| **Spider diagrams** as a lateral creative way of identifying questions to ask stakeholders and to identify risks. He involved small groups from all work areas in order to gather as much information as possible. From these diagrams many issues were raised: what happens at break times when people need to change out of work wear to get to the canteen? How quickly can the changing rooms be fitted out? What happens when a member of staff has a cold or an upset stomach? Who will train new starters? Who will translate the mandatory hygiene signs?
| **Force field analysis** as a mechanism of identifying those factors that will accelerate our plans, and those factors that will work against us, and therefore need handling. The learning architect was able to use the spider diagram information to feed into the force field analysis. Factors that were for the project were such things as training already established through manual handling and health and safety training, training provider able to provide service quickly, facilities existed on site for training. Factors against were shift working, need to translate material, written tests would have to be changed to oral or translated, and holidays.

By the end of phase one the project brief was complete and the manager had sign-off from all the stakeholders as to the exact nature of the project.

In phase two the detailed resourcing plans are put together for the project. He put together a bar chart of all the factors that made up a project, the owners of the tasks together with their start and end dates and their interdependence. The learning architect knew that other people in the organization had used software for such detailed planning. He asked for help with installing and using the software, to ensure consistency and that all plans would be available for future review and inclusion in other initiatives. Software tools also allowed for modelling: that is, aspects such as the impact of changing the resources can be investigated. The learning architect heeded the warning given to him by a colleague: 'Be clear about the tasks and their ownership before you load them into a piece of planning/modelling software. Have a clear picture before you turn on the computer. These can be wonderful examples of garbage in/garbage out!'

To assist with identifying all the tasks involved in a project, the learning architect constructed a work breakdown structure (WBS) of the components of the project, to identify all the tasks before loading them into the planning software.

By the end of phase two he had a detailed plan for the project signed off by all the appropriate stakeholders. In addition he had written a communication plan detailing how progress on the project would be communicated to all involved, listing dates of meetings, expectations of contributors and so on.

The learning architect was aware that in the planning of larger projects, the project would be split into stages as it develops. Each stage would be identified by a start and end point, generally called milestones. This was not a very large project, and the milestones were at the end of stages such as training facilities booked, translations complete, invitations distributed, holiday schedule checked, and certificates issued.

Phase three is when the work on the project is undertaken. The milestones were acknowledged at meetings and reviews. The manager believed it was key to have the sponsors and chief stakeholders involved at these milestone reviews so that those who would be receiving the benefit of the project were fully involved. The senior manager team, all line managers and supervisors were able to look back at work done on the project since previous milestones, checking progress and putting into place any actions to put the project back on schedule. The breakdown of machinery meant that production slipped, and one training course had to be postponed in order for the staff to be available to catch up the lost time.

The review meetings were also about looking forward to ensure that everything was in place for the work to be done between this and the next milestone.

Phase four occurred after the handover of the project. The trained production teams were handed over to the managers and supervisors who would manage them in implementing the new procedures and practices in the workplace.

Phase four is a time of evaluation, lessons learnt. The learning architect asked himself and others: overall did the objectives get achieved across the project and at individual milestones? Were there better ways of doing things? Were the right approaches used in the right ways? What would he do differently with a similar task in the future?

COACHING

Coaching can be viewed as a distinct style of management, and can also be a set of skills that are used by learning architects as they operate within other styles of managing. Coaching as a discrete skill can be used when you facilitate, mentor, counsel, negotiate and project manage. A useful indicator of whether a conversation can be called a coaching conversation comes from Julie Starr's _The Coaching Manual_ (2003):

> If someone acknowledges the following to be true after a conversation they would probably accept that it was coaching:
>
> I The focus of the conversation was primarily themselves and their circumstances.
> I Their thinking, actions and learning benefited from the conversation.
> I They were unlikely to have had those benefits in thinking or learning within that time frame if the conversation had not happened.

Key components of coaching

I **Building rapport and a relationship based on trust.** 'Rapport is that state in human relations where there is an agreed, sometimes silent, recognition and acceptance of common issues' (Seán Weafer, 2004). The person in the coaching role will establish some common point of interest; will engage with the other person through demonstrating interest by smiling, listening and asking questions. Use words, tone and expressions that match the other person's language and remain outside the person's personal space.

- **Asking questions.** Use questions that are predominately open: what, where, when, who, which, how. Ask questions that stretch or shift the person to enable him or her to learn and develop. People can then gain an understanding of personal strategies and find answers or solution for themselves:

  - 'If you did know the answer, what would it be?'
  - 'What do you have to believe about the situation to be able to move forward?'
  - 'When have you been able to do that in the past?'
  - 'When you have achieved that what will you know?'

- **Listening.** When you ask a coaching-type question you need to listen. Give the person you are coaching time and space to work through the internal process of thinking without interruption. Being able to listen without comment, suggestion or interruption requires the learning architect in the coach role to let go.

- **Let go.** Many people who start to coach find the transition from being experts, in their own role, to being coaches a difficult one. Expectations of other people are that you will be the one who provides the answers. This will have come from the belief that you are the expert in your function; or as a manager you are expected to provide answers. A learning architect who is a successful coach makes the shift to the coach role through allowing and encouraging others to find the answers and develop into experts for themselves.

  In your role as a coach you require the ability to let go of your own beliefs and needs while being present for the other person. Make the shift from directing to allowing, and from telling to asking.

- **Providing supportive feedback and a way forward.** Praise, ask questions, provide constructive comments and encouragement are the key components for effective feedback.

The person who is the focus of the coaching conversation may have some actions or changes he or she wants to make. The coach will provide motivation for him or her to make the changes. The use of goal-setting models such as: SMART (specific, measurable, agreed, realistic, timed) and well-formed outcomes may be used:

- Learning architect type 1 (corporate) will use coaching to develop members of his team.

I Learning architect type 2 (tactical) will use the skills of coaching when her manager has asked for some feedback on a presentation he is to give to the senior management board.

I Learning architect type 3 (functional) coaches an external provider when explaining the procedures and policies of the organization.

I Learning architect type 4 (individual) uses coaching skills with the learners he is developing to broaden understanding and enhance skills.

Example 6.3: Learning architect type 1 coaches his learning and development team to enable them to move from trainers to learning partners

Many corporate learning architects are fighting for the survival of the learning function. Organizations are demanding that learning solutions are provided quickly, that their employees are able to take advantage of any learning opportunity, and that the return on any learning investment can be demonstrated in the terms of benefits to the organization.

The strategy for many corporate learning architects is to move their teams from traditional 'deliverers of training' towards 'learning partners' who are proactive in the organization. Other functions are making the same transitions. Personnel/HR managers and advisors are more frequently referred to as HR partners, taking a more proactive business-focused role in organizations.

One such corporate learning architect understood that he was going to have to use his coaching skills, along with some other initiatives, to shift his team from trainers to learning business partners. The team identified that they had been fulfilling the role of passive providers for such activities as:

I training needs analysis for individuals and departments;
I booking, developing and running training courses;
I providing legislation and health and safety based training;
I implementing appraisal systems for departments;
I responding to changes in the workplace that required a training initiative such as new equipment, or changes in procedures.

The team identified that they would have to change their role to more of a change agent and do the following:

▌ diagnosing and working on organizational and inter-functional issues through being more proactive and getting involved in operational issues;

▌ individual and group coaching, facilitation and counselling;

▌ acting as a third party, a catalyst, sounding board and coordinator;

▌ facilitating workshops;

▌ providing ideas, concepts and theories for other functions;

▌ liaising with internal and external stakeholders;

▌ assisting HR with policy making and implementation;

▌ connecting themselves to business issues;

▌ suggesting and providing learning solutions, not just training courses.

In one sense the trainers were having to become more like learning architects, and probably most closely associated with type four, the individual.

The corporate learning architect decided to use Robert Dilts's Logical Levels as a framework for coaching his team. He understood that in order to make the transition from traditional trainer to proactive learning partner, the individuals in the team would have to do more than learn some new skills. He believed some members of the team would find the change difficult, and through coaching he hoped to help them discover what the blocks might be.

Of the many theories that attempt to gain a better understanding of what motivates people, what enables or limits us from making changes, the learning architect believed that Logical Levels would help him provide a context for his coaching:

> In our brain structure, language, and perceptual systems there are natural hierarchies or levels of experience. The effect of each level is to organise and control the information on the level below it. Changing something on an upper level would necessarily change things on the lower levels; changing something on a lower level could but would not necessarily affect the upper levels.
>
> (Dilts, 1991)

The corporate learning architect used the Logical Levels in two ways. The first was by asking questions which explored each level in turn, and the second was through listening to answers to more general coaching questions. The answers gave an indication of where and what would enable or limit the individual team members in moving into their new role.

Statements made in the course of the coaching conversation indicated different logical levels.

Identity

I am the person people come to for help.
I am a specialist trainer.
I am the expert in health and safety.

Belief

It is important to create a good reputation with the sales department.
The line managers are not going to like the change.
It will take us longer to get things done.

Skills and capability

I can make a difference.
I know I am able to adapt to change.

Behaviour

I listen well.
I talk with all the line managers now.
I do that sort of thing when I am running a workshop.

Environment

In my new role I will work from home.
I will spend more time in the car.

From the coaching conversations the learning architect discovered the following issues:

- resistance to being proactive rather than reactive;
- concerns about the response from other departments and functions who may believe the learning partners are interfering;
- lack of business skills and knowledge;
- concerns about breaking up the team as the working environment becomes more flexible and virtual;
- preference for delivering rather than facilitating, suggesting and consulting.

The learning architect was able to assist his team to develop individual development plans to overcome some of the concerns and fears. These plans were tailored for the individuals and covered the following initiatives:

▌ workshops in which to practise facilitation;

▌ short secondments with other functions combined with project-based feedback;

▌ mentor/buddy link with trainers in other organizations who are operating as learning partners;

▌ a training day on consultancy skills delivered by an outside provider;

▌ attendance, as observers and then contributors, at department and line managers' meetings;

▌ communication plan, developed by the team, to inform and educate the organization about the change to the learning function.

The learning architect supported the team members through ongoing, regular, individual and group coaching using an external coach as well as himself. He was delighted that the fears and concerns originally expressed by the team gave way to positive intention gained through experiencing new initiatives and self-discovery through supportive coaching.

MENTORING

A mentor represents a wise and responsible tutor. He or she is an experienced person, who advises, guides, teaches, inspires, challenges, corrects and serves as a role model. The term 'mentoring', used in the context of personal development, had been used by organizations and individuals well before coaching arrived in the form that many of us know it today.

Many pages have been written and much discussion has taken place trying to define and make the distinction between coaching and mentoring. Mentoring involves coaching, counselling, consulting and teaching, and when effective is a powerful catalyst and support for individual and organizational development and change.

So what role does a learning architect take when he or she is mentoring as opposed to coaching or counselling? The learning architects who shared their mentoring experiences with us made the distinctions between mentoring and coaching that are listed in Table 6.2.

▌ Learning architect type 1 (corporate) may act as a mentor for a newly appointed member of a learning skills council.

▌ Learning architect type 2 (tactical) could mentor a student studying for an MSc in Human Resource Development.

▌ Learning architect type 3 (functional) can be a mentor for a recently promoted line manager.

▮ Learning architect type 4 (individual) fulfils the role of mentor for a less experienced workplace trainer.

Table 6.2   Mentor and coach

Mentor	Coach
Has knowledge and experience of the role and the organization.	Coach has knowledge and experience of coaching, not necessarily the role or organization.
Provides advice, makes suggestions, arranges introductions and creates openings. More proactive with the person's job role and function.	Asks questions that enable the person to discover, experiment, make his or her own connections. Stands away from getting involved in the everyday job role.
Mentoring relationship is more open to the rest of the organization. People often choose their mentor. Confidentiality of content of meetings is agreed and maintained.	Coaching relationship is not so transparent to the rest of the organization. Greater level of confidentiality.
Mentoring relationship is often longer than in coaching. It can span many years, and survives changes in roles and organizations for both parties. More about relationship than specific outcomes.	Coaching relationship usually shorter. Often related to successful outcome of coaching arrangement.
Usually mentors someone less experienced, may be younger, more junior in the organization.	Status and experience of the role is less relevant for the coach. Can coach across, above and below formal hierarchy and structures.
Acts as a mentor for people from other organizations (within and outside own sector), the community, educational establishments.	More likely that a learning architect will be a coach for someone within his or her own organization. External coaches are usually from an external coaching resource.

Example 6.4: Learning architect type 3 is a mentor for a graduate management trainee

The organization's graduate management trainee scheme had been running for many years. The number of intakes have been reduced over the past couple of years because of a downturn in business and redundancies that followed. The functional learning architect, type 3, was a general manager of one of the production units and was a product of the trainee scheme. Although the learning architect was up to her neck with work, she remembered the value she had gained from having a mentor. When the operations director asked for volunteers for mentors she agreed to be part of the scheme.

The mentor relationship started for trainees after their initial induction training. They were then assigned to a department for three months, before moving on to other functions within the company. The trainees had the opportunity to choose their mentors from reading profiles and meeting the mentors in person.

The learning architect worked with the trainee to establish a framework for the mentoring relationship. This provided some terms of reference for both parties while allowing flexibility. The following topics were identified:

- outcomes for both from the relationship;
- what they expected from and of each other;
- frequency, length and location of meetings;
- events and functions that the learning architect could attend with the trainee;
- confidentiality boundaries;
- style of mentoring: directing, coaching, counselling, teaching;
- connections that the learning architect could help make for the trainee;
- assistance with open learning programme.

The mentoring relationship lasted for the two-year training period. The learning architect found it difficult to keep to the meeting schedule, with the pressure of a shortage of staff and tight deadlines. Her belief in the value of the mentoring programme, for both parties' development, enabled her to keep the relationship going by using phone calls and e-mail when a face-to-face meeting had to be changed.

Her trainee successfully completed the training programme and took up a permanent position in the organization. Both parties kept in touch with each other, and it was a delight for the learning architect to witness her mentee's progression through the organization.

The learning architect gained the following benefits from participating as a mentor:

I She broadened her own knowledge of the organization through keeping in touch with what was happening for someone else as she moved through different roles and functions.

I She gained respect and kudos from other management, both senior and junior.

I She was able to build the learning structure by providing a means of personal development and more self-directed learning for others.

I The opportunity to use her skills of coaching and counselling.

I A chance to reflect on her own position, knowledge and skills, therefore creating an opportunity for self-development.

I She broadened her knowledge and experience of other organizations as she attended meetings and events with the trainee. These opportunities would have been lost had there not been a compelling reason to attend.

I She was able to reflect and challenge personal beliefs and assumptions as both parties became exposed to new situations and individuals.

FACILITATING

Facilitation is more commonly associated with group or teamworking. The existence of groups and teams, in the structure of 'the players' that a learning architect has to manage, would indicate that facilitation is a useful skill to use. We have identified that the learning architects of today are working in organizations which are:

I leaner, more globalized;

I changing from a command and control, directive style of management to one where individuals are encouraged to take more responsibility for their development;

I using more team and cross-functional teamworking, and adopting a more matrix style of managing a function.

All these trends lend themselves to the use of facilitation and a shift towards a facilitation style of management.

The use of facilitation as a method and as a skill will help increase your standing as a role model for other managers in the organization. It will help you to create a sustained environment of learning in which individuals learn to work in teams, solving issues for themselves and creating a more informed organization.

Kurt Lewin recognized that successful groups were those who focused on team processes as well as team procedures. The assisting of team process is a key part of the facilitator's role, and to do this the facilitator must remain independent and as impartial as possible. The facilitator's role aims to create an atmosphere in which a group can clarify its goals, review its options and formulate its approach to common challenges. The role requires the learning architect to:

I remain neutral;
I encourage participation;
I help create and achieve outcomes for the group;
I assist the group's process, not content;
I protect individuals;
I liaise and assist the group or team pre- and post-meeting;
I clarify goals;
I help resolve conflict;
I help review progress and performance.

The learning architect uses facilitation to effect change through enabling groups, teams and individuals to discover their own resources and outcomes. The aim is to create an environment in which groups of people can create sustainable working models for themselves, to help make the shift from chair-led meetings to ones in which the whole group participates:

I Learning architect type 1 (corporate) would facilitate a meeting of senior partners in their law firm.
I Learning architect type 2 (tactical) would use facilitation skills when assisting with the running of a workshop on a new project.
I Learning architect type 3 (functional) uses facilitation skills when attending a weekly line managers' meeting.
I Learning architect type 4 (individual) would facilitate a meeting between different departments in a call centre.

Example 6.5: Learning architect type 4 facilitates a meeting with a group of learners and their managers about customer service issues

A learning architect type 4 provided workplace training and coaching to customer service advisers (CSAs) working on a help desk in a call centre.

The learning architect was aware that the service levels had been falling over the previous two months. Senior managers were concerned that the falling levels would compromise the agreements they had with their client. This could result in financial loss through penalty charges, and ultimately the client could terminate the contract.

Through the one-to-one work the learning architect did with the CSAs she was aware that morale was low, in part because of IT problems which had occurred after a rewrite of the system. The number of customer calls had increased, and the CSAs' tolerance level for callers had fallen as the problems were not fixed. Productivity was being affected through more people taking time off sick. This was adding to the pressure already felt by the remaining team members. The message being repeated, by all the CSAs with whom the learning architect worked, was that the management did not understand.

Her solution was to provide some facilitated forums to which CSAs, managers and team leaders were invited. Her impartiality, independence and well-practised skills of asking questions and listening gave her a unique position in being able to offer this initiative. Her credibility within the call centre was high and she was respected by all groups.

The output of the facilitated meetings varied depending on the mix of people present and their experience of attending other meetings in the organization, where a manager usually led and controlled the meeting. The learning architect was able to provide an environment in which everyone felt able to contribute, no one took over the meeting and everyone felt comfortable to contribute as much and as little as they wanted. The outcomes from the facilitated forum were:

I increased understanding of the issues facing all staff of the call centre;
I an opportunity to spend time communicating with each other;
I joint problem solving for current issues;
I measures to improve communication for the future;
I reduced absence rate.

MARKETING

The business process of managing the flow of goods, services or processes from the producer to the end user or customer, involving assessment of sales of the product, services or processes and responsibility for its promotion distribution and development.
(_Chambers Dictionary_ definition of marketing)

Whatever type of learning architect you most comfortably align with, it is likely that you will have to market yourself, your function or your services to your customers. Successful learning architects have used the skills and processes associated with marketing to promote themselves and their initiatives within and outside their organizations. Finding customers for the service you can offer and then delivering it in an acceptable format and price may seem alien to the world of learning. Many learning functions might have survived for longer if more attention had been paid to using the principles of marketing to secure their future.

Carrying out an audit of your marketing activities will help to identify whether you need to raise your profile or change the product or service. This audit is applicable whatever type of learning architect you are. The following questions have served many learning architects well as they look to the marketing activities of what they do:

- **Mission/purpose.** What business are we/I in? (Answers might include running courses, providing learning opportunities, providing a database of deliverers, delivering workplace training and coaching to the help desk.)
- **Research.** Who are our stakeholders? Who are our customers? How do I involve them as partners? What factors outside our organization will affect what I offer? What needs do our customers have now, and will they have in the future? What does a SWOT analysis of the learning function reveal?
- **Design of services.** What do we offer? Who is involved in the design of what we offer, and who else should be involved? How do we test?
- **Promotion.** What do we/I use to promote what we do? How is the effectiveness of the promotion measured? What can we/I do to improve the promotion? What skill do we/I have in selling?
- **Delivery.** Where does delivery take place? How appropriate is this?
- **Evaluation.** What measures of success are used? How are the measures quantified and validated? How valuable is the information and to whom?
- **Customer satisfaction.** How is customer satisfaction measured? How do we capture all our customers? What initiatives are in place to maintain and improve customer satisfaction? What can be done to involve customers in the process?

- Learning architect type 1 (corporate) will need to market the services of his or her function inside and outside the organization.
- Learning architect type 2 (tactical) may need to use marketing skills to develop a plan for a management development programme.
- Learning architect type 3 (functional) will need to understand the principles of marketing when assessing an outside provider.

■ Learning architect type 4 (individual) can use marketing skills to promote his or her services to a new department.

Example 6.6: Learning architect type 1 uses the marketing mix to prepare a plan for promoting the services of the learning function outside the organization

Learning architect type 1 is the successful head of a large learning function. He believes there is spare capacity within the department. Rather than have to defend any reduction in the services the function offers, he wants to provide revenue for the organization and full employment for his team. Selling learning initiatives to other organizations will create revenue and provide a more secure future.

The conventional marketing mix includes product, price, place and promotion. Through the addition of people, process and physical evidence, the learning architect was able to give a wider perspective to the planning process. These are particularly relevant for any marketing which involves services rather than products. Marketing facilitation skills may be more difficult as they are less tangible than something like a training video.

The first action the learning architect and his team took was to develop a SWOT analysis (see Figure 6.3).

Strengths	**Weaknesses**
Trained and experienced L&D function	Lack of experience outside own organization
Venue and equipment	Lack of resources for promotion
Administrative support	
Marketing support	
Customer base	
Company culture	
Fits with business plan	
Opportunities	**Threats**
Trade association offering less training	Other training consultancies
New legislation	
Health and safety	
NVQs	
Shift to outsourcing	
Decline in other organization's L&D functions	

Figure 6.3   SWOT analysis

The learning architect wanted to maximize the strengths and opportunities identified. What emerged as the most appropriate strategy for the learning function was to be in the business of providing training and consultancy to companies that had specific needs concerning the current and future opportunities related to legislation, health and safety and NVQs. The seven Ps were applied as follows:

- **Product/service**

    Courses: off the shelf, bespoke, open

Training needs analysis	Consultancy
Assessing NVQs	Assessment centre for NVQs
Technical knowledge	Coaching
Management development	Recruitment and selection

- **Place/delivery**

Customer premises	Organization's own training facilities
Hotel	Conference/training centre
Trade association premises	Chamber of commerce

- **Promotion**

    To: organization's existing customer base; competitors within the industry/sector; allied organizations and suppliers.

    Through: telephone, e-mail, website, cold calling, existing contact network, workshop, seminar tasters, newsletters, trade publications, word of mouth, chamber of commerce events, trade association's conference and meetings, other networking meetings/events.

- **Price**

    Using data from other training providers the price was pitched mid-range for all services.

- **People**

    Existing learning and development team comprising the learning and development manager, three internal trainers, one administrative coordinator.

Use of organization's existing infrastructure for accounting, marketing.

Use of associates or ability to recruit additional team members when demand looks to exceed resources.

- **Physical evidence**

Certificates	Course notes
Invoices	Pens
Presentation material	Business cards

  New logo incorporating organization's existing logo

- **Process**

Policies	Procedures
Values	Ethics

  Contracts (invoicing, cancellation, copyright, credit terms)

The learning architect understood that different elements of the marketing mix would have more importance at different times of the product/service cycle. For a new venture like this it was likely that promotion and price were going to be important. For a more established initiative the process may be more significant.

Having completed the marketing mix the learning architect was able to present the plans to the board. Since he had used the marketing mix in this way, he was confident there was enough flexibility built into the plan to allow for change. He was also aware that the key to success is the constant review and monitoring of results against objectives.

NEGOTIATING

The ability to confer and communicate well with others, in order to come to terms or reach an agreement for both parties, is a skill that learning architects are using frequently. Negotiation may come as a result of identifying where you need to influence. You may have to negotiate with an individual or group in order to achieve your objectives. The ability to keep all parties on side, without compromising the learning objectives, is a skill that marks out the really successful learning architects from the rest. Many of the interpersonal qualities outlined in Chapter 7 help to make the learning architect a successful negotiator. Combining excellent communication skills with an ability to gain rapport while maintaining values and focus is a valuable set of skills to have and maintain.

▌ Learning architect type 1 (corporate) will need to negotiate with the finance director or manager about the budget allocation for the new learning resource centre.

▌ Learning architect type 2 (tactical) may need to negotiate with line managers about the time they will release staff for essential safety training.

▌ Learning architect type 3 (functional) is likely to negotiate with his manager for more allocation of time, resources or reward for extra responsibilities.

▌ Learning architect type 4 (individual) will have to negotiate with department administrators for the use of a quiet room in which to hold a coaching session.

Many researchers have produced models to describe the process of negotiation, and it may be that you have a process that works well. You may be conscious of the process you use, or you may use one without being consciously aware of your behaviour and application of skills. A commonly

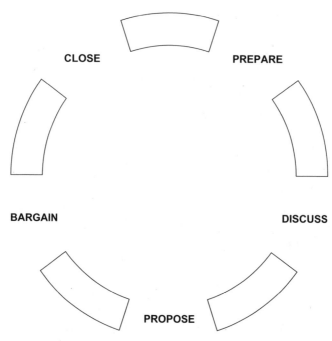

Figure 6.4   Negotiation process

used process involves five stages, and can be applied when negotiating with any of the identified players: your manager, learners and their managers, stakeholders, performers, suppliers and your team. Learning architects use it in one-to-one, group-to-group, face-to-face and remote situations.

When using the model you do not have to follow predetermined steps from start to finish. It is designed to be an open process which is flexible, dynamic and allows for a cyclical process. Those learning architects who use the process successfully move around the stages as appropriate in order to maintain objectives and rapport.

Example 6.7: Learning architect type 2 uses the negotiation process when signing an agreement with a conference centre

The tactical learning architect had selected a new venue that the organization wanted to use for the delivery of training courses, senior managers' meetings, functional presentations, conferences and any other activities requiring conference facilities. The conference centre offered all the facilities that were required by the company, and met all the criteria that had been identified by the learning architect's working party. The only issue that had to be overcome was the cost. The daily rate for delegates offered by the venue was more than the organization wanted to pay.

The learning architect was meeting the conference centre's general manager at the venue. Following the five step process the negotiation went something like this:

- **Preparation.** Before the meeting the learning architect set out the objectives for the meeting: to sign the agreement which would include all the facilities and arrangements required by the organization but at a rate at least 10 per cent lower than the one quoted by the conference centre. As well as writing down the organization's objectives, he gained a sense of what the conference centre manager would have as her objectives. He believed the centre would want to secure the organization's business for as long a period as possible in order to avoid fluctuations in business that led to lay-offs.

- **Discussion.** The learning architect created rapport with the centre manager by having an intention that the meeting would be successful for both parties. This enabled him to display behaviour that was congruent. He stated the organization's position, highlighting the positive aspects and outlining the unacceptable daily rate. He asked open questions of the centre manager in order to understand her position, then summarized what he understood from the discussion. The centre was very keen to have the organization's business, and the daily rate had already been reduced.

I **Propose.** Having established a good environment in which the discussion could proceed without hostility, the learning architect asked for proposals from the centre manager. The manager proposed that if the organization could provide the centre with some more guaranteed business over the period of the agreement, she would be able to reconsider the price. The learning architect proposed to ask some of the organization's suppliers if they could use the centre for some of their activities, at a reduced rate in order to increase the amount of usage under the contract. The rate would have to be at least 10 per cent less than the daily rate proposed.

I **Bargaining.** The centre manager offered to reduce the daily rate by 7.5 per cent in exchange for a guarantee of at least two weeks' worth of extra usage over the period of the year's agreement. The learning architect could not agree to this. He needed the rate to be reduced by 10 per cent, but suggested that in exchange for this he would consider extending the length of the agreement to 16 months. He stated that this was his final offer, and asked the centre manager to consider the proposal.

The centre manager agreed to reduce the daily rate by 10 per cent in exchange for an 18-month agreement.

I **Closing.** The learning architect agreed to the final proposal and summarized to check both parties' understanding.

This is an example of a relatively straightforward negotiation, but one in which we believe both parties gained a sense of a win. The relationship remained positive and neither party felt it had been cheated. It was an agreement gained through good communication and mutual respect.

CHAPTER SUMMARY

I We have identified seven core skills required by a learning architect.
I All learning architects have to manage some or all of the players.
I Not all the skills will be used with all the players at any one time.
I Developing the core skills will enable a learning architect to develop in his or her existing role, and provide guidelines for future role development.
I Learning architects can use the skills as a framework to develop others.

7

Qualities of a learning architect

The purpose of this chapter is to:

▌ identify and share the qualities that make learning architects successful in their roles;
▌ highlight the intensity of each quality required by the four types of learning architect;
▌ suggest ideas for developing the qualities and increasing their intensity;
▌ provide stimulus for the creation of a personal development plan.

One of the many benefits gained from the research we did for this book was the opportunity to meet learning architects and to notice the qualities they shared that made them successful in their role. The qualities we have identified are common to all learning architects of whichever type: corporate, tactical, functional or individual. What differs from type to type is the intensity or depth of the quality required. For example, all learning architects need to be well informed, but it is likely that the corporate learning architect has a need to be more informed about organizational strategy than an individual learning architect working within one function.

We suggest that you use this chapter to:

I   confirm the qualities you already have;
I   identify those qualities you believe you will need to develop for the role you have now;
I   gain an understanding of the intensity of the qualities you need to develop for the role you want to have;
I   develop a personal development plan.

We have listed indicators for each quality, and highlighted the relevance for each type of learning architect using high, medium or low as a measure of intensity (see Table 7.1). Following on from the list are a number of suggestions on how you can increase the intensity of the qualities you already have. The ideas are gathered from our discussions and observation with learning architects, knowledge and experience that we have gathered along our own journey of learning, and the odd thought that may serve you well!

BE WELL INFORMED

Read

I   Read communications distributed internally within your organization: intranet, postings, notice boards, newsletters, minutes of meetings, reports from other functions in the organization. Let the report sponsor know you have read it and offer feedback if wanted.
    Learning architect type 1 (corporate) will have more access to higher order communication as he or she is operating at a senior level. While it will be useful for a learning architect type 4 (individual) to be more informed about the organization as a whole, it could serve the corporate learning architect to be informed about what is happening where the service or product is being delivered.
I   Journals, magazines, e-mail forums from the sector your organization operates in and the world of learning in which you have a specialist role.
I   Newspapers, national and local. A quick scan through the relevant sections in a Sunday paper can keep you up to date with events. Tactical learning architects will increase their credibility if they are able to discuss share movements at a senior manager's meeting. A functional learning architect will appear to be well informed at the staff council if he or she is aware of the local school closure.

Table 7.1 Qualities, indicators and levels

Quality	Indicator	LA1	LA2	LA3	LA4
Well informed	Organizational strategy and plans	H	M	L	L
	Organizational structure and people	H	H	M	M
	Market sector	H	H	M	L
	Current world events	H	H	M	M
	Current and future trends	H	H	M	M
	General business knowledge	H	H	M	M
Understand business of the organization and those close to it	Organization's culture	H	H	M	M
	Your own and other functions	H	H	H	H
	What the organization does	H	H	H	M
	Major influences	H	H	M	M
	Product, service, system	H	H	M	M
	How the above is delivered	H	H	M	M
	Funding	H	H	M	L
	Impact of legislation	H	H	M	M
	Integration of learning	H	H	M	M
	Supply chain	H	H	M	M
Motivated	Energetic	H	H	H	H
	Inner belief	H	H	H	H
	Motivate others	H	H	H	H
	Optimism	H	H	H	H

Table 7.1 Qualities, indicators and levels (Cont.)

Quality	Indicator	LA1	LA2	LA3	LA4
	Inner reserves	H	H	H	H
	Theories of motivation	M	H	M	H
	Self-starter	H	H	M	H
	Balanced life	H	H	H	H
Create a network	Inside organization and function	H	H	M	M
	External to organization and function	H	H	M	M
	Membership of professional association	H	H	L	L
	Official	H	H	M	M
	Unofficial	H	H	H	H
	Like-minded people	H	H	H	H
	Proactive versus reactive	H	H	M	M
	Make connections and connect	H	H	H	H
	Making connections	H	H	H	H
	Broadcast news beyond organization	H	H	M	M
Know what you want	Personal goals and outcomes	H	H	H	H
	Function's goals and outcomes	H	H	L	L
	Strengths and weaknesses	H	H	H	H
	Building a personal architecture	H	H	H	H
	Pragmatic visionary	H	H	M	M
	Role model	H	H	H	H

Table 7.1 Qualities, indicators and levels (Cont.)

Quality	Indicator	LA1	LA2	LA3	LA4
Build trust and rapport	Recognizing a relationship	H	H	H	H
	Building a relationship	H	H	H	H
	Maintaining a relationship	H	H	H	H
	Congruent	H	H	H	H
	Communication	H	H	H	H
	Coach, counsellor, confidant	M	H	H	H
Know how people learn	Theories	M	H	M	M
	Learning styles	M	H	M	H
	Delivery methods	M	H	M	M
	Outcomes	H	H	H	H
	History of development of learning initiatives	M	M	L	M
	Practical experience	M	H	M	H
	Organizational development	H	H	M	M
	Advise others	H	H	H	H
	Holistic approach to learning	H	H	M	H
Recognized as a contributor to the organization	Official recognition through role and benefits	H	H	H	H
	Unofficial recognition through informal sources	M	H	H	H
	Understand power structures	H	H	M	L

Table 7.1 Qualities, indicators and levels (Cont.)

Quality	Indicator	LA1	LA2	LA3	LA4
	Adding value to the organization	H	H	H	H
	Role model	H	H	H	H
	Being in the positive/ winning camp	H	H	H	H
	An expert inside and outside the organization	H	H	M	M
	First call for advice	M	H	M	H
	Accepted	H	H	H	H
Obtain management support	All levels of management	H	H	H	H
	Learners' managers	H	H	H	H
	Authority	H	H	M	M
	Sponsorship	M	H	H	H
	Shared understanding	H	H	H	H
	Understanding and then managing expectations	H	H	H	H
	Identify the art of the possible	M	H	M	M
	'On side'	M	H	M	H
	More than just training results	H	H	H	H
Creative	Entrepreneurial	H	H	M	M
	Quick delivery of solution	H	H	M	M
	Joint risk taker	H	H	M	L
	Create a solution with limited resources	M	H	H	M

Table 7.1 Qualities, indicators and levels (Cont.)

Quality	Indicator	LA1	LA2	LA3	LA4
	Challenges 'we have always…'	H	H	M	M
	Stretches and shifts models and paradigms	H	H	M	H

Listen and watch and ask

Listening is a skill that all of us could improve, and one that we have many opportunities to practise. Take the opportunity to listen to people at meetings and in one-to-one situations.

Being well informed is about being aware of what is going on for other people in their world. Making informed, workable suggestions to provide a solution with a learning initiative relies on your knowing what is really going on.

CASE STUDY

A tactical learning architect had made a significant shift since working with his coach. He realized that his eagerness to appear dynamic in his new role as learning and development manager was producing behaviour that could be interpreted as overpowering. He changed from believing he had to be the first to chip in with a suggestion to just watching and listening. This slowing down enabled him to ask more informed questions of his colleagues and senior managers. Asking 'What do you believe has led to the increase in staff turnover?' rather than suggesting, 'Your managers obviously need some interviewing training' enabled the learning architect to be more informed and accepted in his role.

Ask people about the things that matter to them, and understand the current or common issues facing them. Attend presentations and activities in other departments and functions, be aware and willing to be visible at events that would not usually be seen as the remit of learning or training. Listen for common links or themes across the organization. You can be the conduit for the sharing of information by putting people in touch with each other who seem to share a common purpose or issue.

Engage a mentor

If you need to know more about the workings of your organization and sector, working with a mentor will fast-track your knowledge and experience. The type of advice, opportunities and wise words that a mentor can provide will enable you to be well informed. Aspects of the organization to which it would otherwise be difficult for you to gain access are more easily opened through the connections a mentor can make. Use his or her knowledge and experience of organizational structure, politics and culture.

UNDERSTAND THE BUSINESS OF THE ORGANIZATION AND GET CLOSE TO IT

Understand and work with the culture of the organization

Before getting closer to the business of the organization, learn about the culture. Organizational culture can be thought of as frames of reference that have been built up over time. Imagine a new learning and development manager, a learning architect type 1, joining an organization. She will need to learn the norms of operation in order to communicate and have influence within a framework, to be understood by others.

CASE STUDY

Sue was getting on with her new boss, and although they were both speaking English it seemed that they were talking different languages. Her new boss had worked for his previous company for over 20 years and was unconsciously using the same code in his new one. It was a code for behaviour and communication that would have been understood without question in his old company. In his new organization the unwritten code was slightly different. The codes needed to be acknowledged, learnt and maybe realigned. The frames of reference for decision making, communication channels and requests were different.

A useful reference for understanding an organization's culture is to create a diagram that identifies all the codes and frames of reference. Drawing on the work of Johnson and Scholes (1993) and their cultural web, it is possible to create a cultural web for your own organization. At the centre of the diagram are the beliefs and assumptions that lie at the core of an organization: beliefs such as 'the organization is a market leader', 'we are a traditional company', 'we provide for our employees', and 'the company is innovative'. These beliefs will be protected by the structures and codes that have developed, within and by the organization. Johnson and Scholes identified the following key areas:

- **Control systems.** The measurement and rewards indicate what is important to the organization.
- **Organizational structures.** Formal and informal structures reflect the power bases, indicating who and what is important.
- **Rituals.** 'The way we do things around here.' What happens when someone leaves the organization (cards, gifts, parties, nothing?), assessments, promotion, training and development, expenses.
- **Symbolic.** The language, cars, logos, titles all provide a code for those who know and a symbol for those outside the organization.
- **Power structures.** Where and with whom does the power lie? The most powerful managerial groups in the organization are usually strongly aligned with the core beliefs and values.
- **Routines.** The way members of the organization behave towards each other. Combined with rituals, the routines add to the 'way we do things around here'. They cover attendance at meetings, punctuality, dress code, holiday procedures, reporting styles and presentation.
- **Stories.** Members of the organization relate the history of the organization by recounting events and characters that have happened. These stories help to reinforce the other areas of the web and serve to safeguard the core beliefs. The 'Do you remember when Paul arrived 15 minutes late at the Executive Managers' meeting and John made him look a fool?' type of story reinforces routines, rituals and power bases.

Some useful questions to ask yourself in relation to you and your organization's culture:

- What do I have to do as a learning architect to demonstrate that I really understand the culture of my organization?
- How do the learning and development initiatives I sponsor impact, positively or negatively, on the culture?

- What do I believe needs to change about the culture of my organization to enhance the learning strategy?
- What do I believe needs to change about the learning strategy to enhance the culture of my organization?

Spend time in all parts of the organization

Spend time not just as an observer but as an active player within the function. A television programme shown in the UK in which the boss of an organization went 'back to the floor' produced a great shift in understanding from all parties. More insight into the workings of the organization was gleaned and some useful action was taken.

Learning architect types 3 and 4 are probably spending more time within the organization than the corporate and tactical learning architect.

Do you need to widen your perspective? How much do you know? The following may assist you:

- List the functions of your organization.
- How many of the function that you have listed have you spent time in?
- When was this?
- What plans do you have to revisit or visit?
- What will you gain from the experience?
- What is stopping you?
- Make a plan.

The learning architect who understands how staffing levels are affected by sickness absence on a hospital ward, warehouse or help line will have some idea of the obstacles facing a learning initiative.

Understand where you and your function are positioned in your organization

Misunderstandings occur within organizations when factions arise: operational versus non-operational, head office versus site/field based, professional versus non-professional. Get closer to the business of your organization by spending time with people from other factions. You may be a corporate learning architect based at head office who is viewed by the operational sites as remote and aloof. What impact does this have for your department and the initiatives you are trying to implement? A functional learning architect who is closely aligned to one department may be viewed with suspicion by other departments when he or she tries to arrange training. Learning architects who have been successful in working across functions have:

I Recruited people from other functions to work with them on a secondment or for a permanent role.
I Placed themselves or their staff within other functions for specific projects.
I Supported and championed initiatives that other parts of the organization are running. They have assisted sales departments in launching new promotions, provided support for health and safety events, attended presentations when new procedures are announced to production areas or customer service advisers.

Carry out research within your organization

The research can be on behalf of your own function or for another part of the organization:

I A corporate learning architect provided members of her team for the HR survey into sickness absence.
I A tactical learning architect asked to join the marketing group researching the feasibility of setting up a mystery shopper campaign.
I A functional learning architect helped facilitate staff focus groups in another retail district.
I An individual learning architect worked with the admissions team as they ran a pilot for the new IT system.

KEEP YOUR MOTIVATION

Acknowledge that you may have to find ways of keeping yourself motivated

A learning architect can be a lonely role, and the expectations of others are that you are there to provide initiatives that will motivate them and their teams. Motivation is an elusive commodity, but one that you will need to sustain yourself through the building of the learning architecture. Successful learning architects have an inner belief that providing learning initiatives to solve workplace issues is essential to the survival and growth of an organization. They guide, support and refresh others.

Optimism, combined with pragmatism, is maintained through understanding what contributes to their motivation and energy levels.

Notice what adds to your energy levels and what drains you

Reserves act like a piggy bank of energy and motivation. By depositing reserves in our piggy bank we have enough to sustain us through the leaner times. When we are surrounded by people who drain us, when we are working on something we find less fulfilling, if we have reserves we are sustained. Topping up your personal piggy bank on a regular basis will prevent a long-term motivation drain.

Surround yourself with people who energize you

It may be your team, if you are a corporate learning architect. As a tactical or functional learning architect you may have an informal team of colleagues and managers you draw on for support. In your role as an individual learning architect it could be an informal network of coaches that you have met working in other organizations, people who just make you feel good about yourself.

One tactical learning architect we met gained motivation from catching up with people who had participated in the first management development programme the organization had run: 'Finding out what the group of managers who had gone through the first management development programme were doing now, gave me a real buzz.'

Engage a coach and/or a mentor

Working with a coach and or a mentor has helped many learning architects generate and maintain motivation. Many of us act as coaches and mentors to people inside and outside our organization, and we extol the virtues of this method of support and learning. How many of us gain the benefits from experiencing some coaching or mentoring for ourselves?

Coaching encourages independent thinking, stimulating and challenging us to find new and motivated thinking to meet goals and address issues. Your coach may be someone from inside your organization, but more usually he or she will be someone independent, who has the ability to remain objective and can provide the confidential yet challenging stimulus required to motivate.

A mentor is usually a colleague or someone from within the organization or organization's sector, a respected role model who has considerable knowledge of the organization that you both work in. Solutions and direction can come from the mentor. He or she shares his/her experience with you and will make suggestions about what you might do, or to whom you might speak about an issue. Many learning architects have gained much from the reassurance of a mentor, and have increased the intensity of other qualities through this source of motivation.

Keep healthy

Take care of your physical and mental well-being. Following some of the basic principles of healthy living will provide you with energy:

- Drink at least six to eight glasses of water per day.
- Avoid coffee and carbonated sugar drinks.
- Eat fresh fruit and vegetables daily.
- Limit your intake of alcohol, sweets, chocolate, cakes and biscuits.
- Do not smoke.
- Eat breakfast.
- Try to eat regular meals and not to leave eating too late in the evening.
- Take regular exercise. Twenty minutes walking, each day, will be a start.

Work/life balance

Learning architects of all types are providing initiatives that promote a balanced work and home life for the people in their organization. They include providing facilities for lunchtime exercise sessions, liaising with HR to train managers in how to handle flexible working, and working with their own teams to reduce travelling times and nights away from home. What standards are you setting?

Have interests that motivate and fulfil you, and take the time to pursue them. Learning architects we met have had a rich variety of interests including running, triathlons, cycling, walking, horse riding, golf, motor racing, yoga and working out at a gym. If you have a sense that you are neglecting the non-work aspects of your life, a coach will be able to help you develop a new strategy.

Take a sabbatical

Taking a sabbatical or 'gap time' has become common practice for professionals who have progressed in their career beyond the first few years. Learning architects have negotiated with their employers for time off to pursue travel, voluntary work at home and abroad, or to take up further study. New skills and experiences are gained from implementing learning in a different culture, being a student, teaching in another country, or being part of a team working on an environmental project. If you feel you want to use your skills in a really worthwhile area, perhaps a working adult gap year/sabbatical is the way to proceed. VSO (www.vso.org.uk) is the best known name in the UK, and places more than 750 people a year on all kinds of voluntary work overseas. The average age of volunteers is 38.

Draw motivation from learning

Learning architects are in the business of learning, and many of us gain energy and therefore motivation from learning new things. Aside from the formal, recognized qualifications connected to learning, learning architects are engaged in many and varied learning activities. They are supporting and complementing their lives through learning more about counselling, coaching, voice therapy, drama, neurolinguistic programming, communications, mediation, equality and diversity, marketing, first aid, facilitation, psychology, Reiki, yoga, aromatherapy and many more subjects.

CREATE A NETWORK

Construct a network map

Include people you believe add value to your position as a learning architect. Include people inside and outside your organization. Think about people that you have met through past and present job positions, training courses, periods of study, social events, friends and pastimes.

Attend events

These include those hosted by chamber of commerce, networking organizations, specific initiatives for learning professionals. Offer to represent your organization at a sector or industry-specific event, exhibition or conference.

Apply for a role

Apply for, or ask someone to recommend you for, a role on an advisory or steering group. A learning architect type 1 became chairman of the local learning skills council. A tactical learning architect became a director of the industry's sector skills council. A functional learning architect contributed to the development of NVQs for the relevant sector. Alternatively you might offer to become a governor of a local school.

Offer to present

Consider speaking and making presentations at schools and colleges, learning forums and conferences.

Connect other people

Introduce people to each other at work. Offer suggestions of people it might be helpful for a colleague to speak to. Most people are flattered if you approach them to ask if it would be all right to pass on their details to someone who is looking for advice 'from an expert'. Your role as a learning architect puts you in touch with people from different functions. You are in a unique position to use the opportunities you have to make connections for people.

KNOW WHAT YOU WANT

Create an outcome

The ability to create an outcome for yourself has relevance for anything you want to achieve.

> Outcome – goals or desired states that a person or organization aspires to achieve. (Bandler, 1993)

Few of the learning architects we have spoken with started their career in learning. Popular routes have been through sales, HR and general management. What is common to all is that once they gained a sense of what it was like to be involved with learning, they were hooked. Some started as trainers, sharing the knowledge and experience they had gained from their previous roles. Others took on the role of workplace coach or became mentors for less experienced colleagues. You, like others, may have bypassed any direct learning delivery and moved straight into a managing role, using the management skills developed in other functions and applying them to learning and training.

What is evident from all the successful learning architects we observed was a strong sense of what they wanted for themselves and their learning function for the future. At some point during their career they created an outcome for themselves, and they have worked towards creating that outcome.

Learning architects build architectures for their organizations, and they also develop a personal architecture, a strong sense of where their future is and what it will be like. Holding this outcome enables successful architects to move with confidence into different roles within and outside their organization. You may be using this book to gain a sense of an outcome for your own development. If you are a tactical learning architect you may aspire to become a corporate learning architect with a team of your own and an opportunity to work at a more strategic level. These outcomes may not have been expressed to anyone beyond yourself and your coach or mentor.

An outcome for an architect will be the finished structure. He or she will have a sense of what it will look like, where it will be, what it feels like, who will be using it, the sight, sound and feelings associated with the structure being created. A model that many learning architects find useful for creating an outcome for themselves, and their learners, comes from neurolinguistic programming. It is simply a set of criteria or conditions that something must satisfy in order to produce an effective outcome.

A well-formed outcome is:

I Stated in positive terms: 'I want to be a coach' rather than 'I don't want to be doing this job'.
I Defined and evaluated according to sensory-based evidence. When you describe your goal or outcome you can experience it through your senses. You have a picture, you feel something, you hear sounds, and you may be able to describe a smell or taste.
I Initiated and maintained by the person who describes the goal or outcome. Whose goal is this? If you believe it is yours, can you maintain the desire? Experience demonstrates that when the goal comes from someone else's expectation or suggestion, it is unlikely to materialize. How many unmet goals exist after being set by someone else? An example is the manager who realized, during a goal-setting exercise, that the recurring goal of attending a presentation skills course was initiated by his manager and not himself.
I Made to preserve the positives of the present state. What might you lose as a result of achieving your outcome? An outcome that means you sacrifice the pleasure you receive from spending time with friends and family in your present role may mean your goal will not be sustainable.

If you believe your current salary is a benefit, ask, what does it give you? The answer to the secondary question is more likely to be the benefit (such as holidays, status, recognition) than hard cash.

| Able to happen in the environment in which you exist. Where and when do you want to achieve your outcome? Will it be in your current organization or somewhere else? When you imagine yourself in your outcome, how appropriate is it?

Asking yourself the following questions will help you create a well-formed outcome:

| What do you want? State it in the positive.
| When you have achieved your outcome what will it sound, feel, look, taste, smell like? What evidence will other people have that you have achieved your goal?
| How in control of your outcome are you, to achieve and maintain it?
| How will you keep the benefits of what you have now?
| Where and when do you want your outcome?

CASE STUDY

A tactical learning architect created a well-formed outcome: 'I want to be a learning and development director'. Evidence for the outcome was in the form of a new car, own office, a learning team and recognition from other directors for the work he would be doing. The learning architect described all this in detail. He believed he was in control of his outcome, that he had many of the resources needed to achieve the desired state, and recognized the gaps in his skills, knowledge and ability that could be filled.

The learning architect realized that the benefits of his current state – freedom to choose, motivation, a sense of achievement – could be maintained and enhanced if he achieved his outcome. The outcome was a year away, and would be in another organization. He used the outcome exercise to check out goals for the stages he believed were needed along the way. This gave him goals such as:

■ I want to be successful at networking.
■ I want to have more experience at negotiating.
■ I want another professional qualification.

As you establish outcomes for yourself, use the exercise to check the criteria. The outcome will be achievable if it is well formed. Have a go!

Carry out a SWOT analysis

Using this type of analysis for your own development can be very productive. Identifying strengths, weaknesses, opportunities and threats will enable you to develop a plan for your own development. Becoming aware of your own strengths and opportunities provides a useful reminder of your own successes and worth. Enlist the help of colleagues, coach, mentor and friends to construct your own personal SWOT analysis.

Talk in the positive

Learning architects who have a strong sense of what they want and where they want to be, talk positive. 'The strategy will be influential.' 'When we complete the project ....' 'The board will be interested.' 'We shall achieve.' Successful learning architects have the ability to reframe statements and situations to put them in the positive for themselves and others. The glass half full or half empty reframe is one familiar to most of us. The ability to reframe allows you to have more ways of looking at a situation or problem, to have more choices.

The dull and frustrating meeting chaired by someone with little or no facilitation skills can be thought of as an interesting study of group dynamics. The poor attendance on an appraisal training workshop can be reframed as an opportunity to explore the entire appraisal process within the organization. Reframe to represent an experience in ways that support your personal outcomes or those you have identified for your team, department and organization.

Make your strategy visible to others

If you have created a learning strategy for yourself, your function or your organization, then broadcast its message. It provides something tangible for you to talk about, present to others and refer to. A strategy provides other people with a framework or structure on which to hang their own ideas and passions. Providing a document for discussion provides evidence that you know what you want for the function and where you want to be.

An assistant director of education and learning from an NHS trust published her strategy within a couple of months of her appointment. She explained, 'It allowed me the opportunity to discuss learning issues with the board and inform them that I had an idea of where learning should be for the trust.'

BUILD TRUST AND RAPPORT

Listen

However well we believe we listen, it is always useful to take a skill check to gain a sense of how much more listening we can do. Take into account both the quantity and quality of listening. A successful learning architect commented:

> I don't believe I always offer any advice or a suggestion when people ask for my opinion, but what I know I do is listen. Providing someone with the space to talk and having them know that what they say remains with me has enabled me to gain trust within my organization.

Listen to as many people as you have the opportunity to. Find out essential information from stakeholders both internal and external. Listen to feedback in order to flex your plans to respond to the needs of the organization in order to provide successful learning initiatives. How many people did you listen to yesterday? That means listen, as distinct from talking to or with.

> The quality of your attention determines the quality of other people's thinking. (Kline 1999)

Giving someone your attention requires you to slow down, park your own beliefs and assumptions and 'be with' the person in the present as he or she talks. Any temptation to interrupt, finish a sentence or relate your own story is avoided. A recurring complaint from people working in organizations, at all levels, is that they do not feel listened to. Improving the quality of your listening provides the following benefits:

I People tell you more.
I You gain rapport more quickly.
I People remember you, as you make them feel valued.
I Communication is quicker.
I It improves your communication skills.
I You gain a sense of what is really happening in an organization.
I You are able to join up information from different parts of the organization.

▌ It enables people to develop ideas for themselves by giving then space to think.

▌ You are able to model a coaching environment for your organization.

Ask questions

Do this to involve other people. We know you are aware of the importance of asking open questions that require the respondent to give you more than a yes or no answer. Open questions run in tandem with good listening, and enable you to establish rapport through engaging someone in a conversation, finding out what common ground you share, gaining a sense of what is important to the other person, and asking for his or her input.

Learning to ask what, who, where, when, how provides the foundation skill for coaching.

Beware of losing rapport by asking a 'Why?' question. Many people believe asking a 'Why?' question is a short cut to getting a direct answer. Asking a 'Why?' question can also be a short cut to losing rapport. If you are not aware of the effect of asking or receiving a 'Why?' question, ask a colleague, friend or coach to ask you some questions beginning with 'Why?' The usual reaction is that the receiver of the question reports feeling attacked, has to justify his or her beliefs, is put on the spot, and feels defensive and uncomfortable. He or she has a sense that there is something else behind the question: another motive, a hidden agenda.

Be sensitive

Be sensitive to what people in the organization value, and where and who their loyalties are with. It is likely that you are going to propose changes, especially if you are a corporate or tactical learning architect. If you are new to a role you will be making changes too. Through listening and questions you will gain a sense of what is valued. Understanding the culture of the organization will assist you with this.

A functional learning architect made the mistake of bringing in a new provider of manual handling training over a popular trainer. Participants were resistant to the training, and therefore health and safety was compromised.

A learning architect type 4, a workplace trainer and coach did not pick up comments about the coaching taking place in an open office, and experienced resistance to coaching sessions.

A corporate learning architect reorganized the working space of his new team without being aware of the unofficial status symbols that had developed within the office.

All the above actions were appropriate and in the best interests of the organization, but caused negative outcomes for learning. A little more asking and listening, and being aware of other people's needs and values, might have avoided resistance.

Deliver and do what you say you are going to do

This seems a simple principle, but much trust is lost by not following up or getting back to people. You may not be able to provide the instant training solution requested by a line manager or the IT resources required for the new e-learning package. However, you can keep people informed, offer suggestions and involve them in the process, and provide updates.

Be supportive of colleagues in your organization

Ask the marketing manager how you and your function can support him or her for the next presentation to the board. Then ask him or her how things went after the event. This helps build trust and rapport. Knowing that you can be relied upon to be supportive and give answers when asked, helps build trust.

Maintain confidentiality

This must be done within the boundaries of what is legal. Once you have broken a confidence your credibility is gone and any attempt to build trust and rapport will be difficult.

If you believe you are being told something that should be passed on, discuss your concerns with the teller. Work with him or her to agree the best approach for you both.

A learning architect type 4 worked with individuals who often shared issues that they were not comfortable discussing with their line manager. One example was a case where an employee felt she was being bullied by another member of staff. While acknowledging the need for confidentiality, the learning architect worked with the employee to help her gain the confidence to speak with the bully. If the situation had not been resolved the learning architect would have felt an obligation to let the line manager know. This would have needed to be with the agreement of the employee.

Use language that engages other people

A learning architect told us she used the word 'partnership' when talking to other functions in her organization. Learn to use the words and language of the people you are talking to. It is part of getting close to the business and understanding it.

The learning and training world has its own language too. How much jargon are you using? Talking to line managers about a TNA, competencies or skill sets will not help you to gain rapport. Phrase your explanations in language that others will understand.

Take an interest in other people

The advice of Dale Carnegie may serve us well in this area. He suggested smiling, remembering a person's name and using it, being a good listener and following up points that a person makes. Find out what others are interested in, and make others feel important by recognizing what they do.

KNOW HOW PEOPLE LEARN

Learn about learning theory

Learning about the theory, structure and history of learning will serve all learning architects in the roles they play. We are aware that the level and depth of knowledge will vary. A corporate learning architect who has been given the responsibility for learning on the board may not need to know the ins and outs of learning theory. He or she will need to be aware of which people in the team do know about it. A tactical learning architect may well have come from a background of delivering training, and have a good understanding of what the structures to learning are about. Functional and individual learning architects will probably have gained their experience of the function of learning from their own experiences and the thoughts of others.

Most learning architects we spoke to have some understanding of how people learn from learning and have set about learning about learning themselves, usually in a formal directed way. If you want to learn about learning, the most popular, recognized learning undertaken by learning architects is the Certificate in Training and Development. Some learning architects studied years ago when the qualification was offered in the UK by the Institute of Training and Development. Now it comes with the CIPD (Chartered Institute of Personnel and Development) badge and is called the Certificate in Training Practice:

> The CIPD Certificate in Training Practice is an ideal programme for those who require a means of professional recognition in the field of learning and development.
>
> (CIPD, 2004c)

The content covers: the training cycle, identifying training needs, training design, assessment and evaluation, different strategies and methods for providing training and learning. This qualification, or one similar, will provide you with the underpinning knowledge on which to base discussions, proposals and decisions about training and learning in your organization.

There are also plenty of shorter courses, one-day workshops and articles in learning magazines that can give you a grounding in some of the theory and structures of learning.

Develop your knowledge and skills

The choice of how much you learn in order to provide the service your role demands is up to you. Learning architects have taken the following training to develop further their interest and knowledge about learning: diploma in training management, Dale Carnegie, NLP practitioner, master practitioner, trainer training, MSc in human resource development, consultancy skills for trainers, MBA, emotional intelligence, PGC, equality and diversity, counselling, project management, workplace mediation, psychometric testing, and coaching.

Deliver some training

If you have arrived at the place you are now without having been a trainer, then have a go at delivering a learning initiative. Many of you will know what it is like to be in the training role, and will have an understanding of the link between training and learning. Gaining perspective from the role of a trainer helps us understand the link between learning, the environment, the behaviour of participants, skills and capabilities of learners, what beliefs prevent or enable them to learn, and who they are.

Does their identity help or hinder individual learners? You may encounter managers who believe they are too senior in an organization to learn anything new, junior staff who are intimidated, professionals who believe their role is to further the cause of their profession and not to learn about 'unrelated' subjects. Gaining an understanding of these perspectives will help all types of learning architects when they are building the learning architecture.

Build a learning culture

Successful learning architects understand that learning is not just about delivering courses. The move towards self-directed, self-managed, self-aware learning in the workplace comes from initiatives that support individuals learning from their everyday activities. Work shadowing, job swaps, projects, sabbaticals, cross-functional teamworking, peer coaching and buddying are just some of the interventions that can encourage learning. The challenge for the learning architect is to lay the foundations so that individuals do not feel abandoned, dumped on or short-changed when they do not receive training in a more traditional format.

BE RECOGNIZED AS A CONTRIBUTOR TO THE ORGANIZATION

Measure your contribution

Assess your contribution to the organization in relation to its key performance indicators. How does your organization measure its success: profit, turnover, sales, loyalty of customers, waiting times, share price, clinical excellence? What contribution do you make personally to those indicators or measures? What contribution do the learning interventions you instigate and manage make to the business of the organization?

Be known for something

What do you have a reputation for or as in your organization? You might be seen as:

I The functional learning architect who always knows who to contact about most things.
I The corporate learning architect who brings in a project on time, every time.
I The tactical learning architect who delivers inspirational training sessions.
I The individual learning architect who helps people to make changes in their working lives.

It is helpful to have a blueprint for your own reputation by creating a well-formed outcome using the process outlined in this chapter.

The learning architects who contributed to this book wanted to be known for being creative and innovative, raising the profile of learning and development, a good leader, and a 'bringer together' of departments.

Be known as a giver

Successful learning architects appear to put more into the organization than they immediately get back in return. Giving can be frustrating when no immediate returns are evident. Trust that the time, effort and money you give will be recognized. Taking a mentor role or coaching someone, offering to provide time and other resources for other functions will pay dividends in the long run.

Provide a good service

Who are your customers and how do you ensure that they receive the outcomes that they expected? Carrying out and analysing any evaluation highlights the need to establish learning outcomes that are aligned to the needs of the organization. Measuring how well those outcomes have been met and then providing feedback to relevant parties is essential.

How can you be recognized as a contributor to the organization if people do not know that it was you and your initiatives that improved morale, reduced staff turnover, improved customer satisfaction ratings, increased sales? Broadcast the results of training and learning initiatives through:

- one-to-one follow-up/feedback sessions with line managers;
- presentations at meetings and conferences;
- newsletters;
- intranet broadcasts and postings;
- notice boards in corridors, canteens, restaurants.

One of the contributors to this book has created a reputation for the learning and education department's noticeboard. The colourful, attractive notices and features on the board have become a talking point in the organization. Staff make a point of reading the notices on the board, encouraged by the learning architect's 'What do you think about the notice board this week?' Forthcoming courses, outcomes from recent and past events, general information and fun items are all on the board. The notice board is always up to date and professionally presented. This could have been presented electronically if the culture and structure of the organization lent itself to this style.

Share information

Share information that you collect with colleagues in your own and other functions. Some learning architects have the opportunity to get outside the organization more than other colleagues. Share information from a conference you attended, a working party you are a member of, publications that you read, forums you belong to. This sharing can be in the form of a regular bulletin which is produced electronically or paper-based. Take the opportunity to share information informally too.

Be recognized as a contributor to a market sector

Many learning architects become recognized as contributors to their organization through being recognized as contributors to the sector in which their organization operates. They contribute by being members of learning skills councils, representatives on regional and national boards for learning and development. They contribute to trade associations and industry-specific forums, developing new standards in learning and development for occupational and vocational learning such as NVQs and apprenticeships. Corporate and tactical learning architects have been asked for input on codes of conduct and practice for sector specific processes.

Raise the profile of the whole organization

Learning architects who enter themselves, their team or organization for awards gain recognition for winning and for being nominated. Learning architects who have entered National Training Awards have found this an excellent route to gain a number of benefits: a reason to ask for management support, providing a vehicle to showcase the work of the learning and development function, a subject to talk with and present to senior management, and obtaining buy-in from learners. The kudos from a nomination and possibly a win will help the future development of any learning architect.

In the UK the National Training Awards are run by UK Skills on behalf of the Department for Education and Skills. In 2004 61 per cent of the finalists were from small to medium-sized enterprises (SMEs). Linking up with the person or function responsible for PR and marketing, to promote the entry, will gain recognition for you and the learning function.

OBTAIN MANAGEMENT SUPPORT

Understand the importance of management support

Life for the learning architect who does not have management support will be frustrating. Successful learning architects who have managed to build a robust architecture for their organizations have done it with support. Interventions that have been imposed or forced through may have brought short-lived rewards, but the relationships needed for long-term development may well have been damaged.

Managers will understand the need for their people and themselves to have skills, knowledge and experience that will enable them to meet targets or performance indicators. What they may not be able to do is to provide the resources in terms of time, energy, people or money to allow that to happen. The thought of releasing two people from an already over-stretched department for a day to learn about interviewing is a stretch too far for some managers.

A learning architect who fails to gain management support through working with and understanding a manager's reality will, in time, become the enemy. A learning architect who has management support will have a shared understanding with management, easy communication, open discussion and well-thought-through input from managers about learning for their people.

Understand the beliefs of managers

It is important to understand the beliefs managers hold with regard to learning, training and development. Managers' beliefs will be based on their own past experience and the experience of people they listen to. If the beliefs are negative they may well have come from a memory of learning at school, a poor training event they attended, or previous training and learning professionals who failed to build a relationship. You can gain an understanding of the limiting beliefs that managers have about learning by listening and then ask questions to explore.

A functional learning architect learnt to engage production managers, who were resistant to training events for their staff, through rapport-building conversations, finding common ground and asking them about their personal experiences of learning and training and those of their team and organization. Like the functional learning architect, you too will be showing interest and gaining a sense of what may be blocking managers.

There are a number of questions you could ask in response to the comment, 'We tried a mentoring scheme a couple of years ago and it didn't work then':

▌ I'm pleased you have had experience of mentoring. It's always good to talk with someone who has experienced it for real. What do you believe stopped the scheme from being successful?
▌ What do you believe the mentoring scheme was established to achieve?
▌ What suggestions do you have for making a scheme work next time?
▌ How would you describe mentoring?
▌ How would you change your involvement in the scheme?

Careful questioning will enable you to discover whether the resistance is to mentoring in general, or to the process of mentoring as it was experienced. Mangers who believe they will be left in a worse position, with fewer resources, will resist anything that gets in the way of the 'work'.

Develop champions

Having a sponsor or champion at a senior level may be more appropriate for learning architects type 2, 3 and 4. The corporate learning architect is probably working at a senior level, but he or she too may need the support of those senior to him or her, or seek support for external stakeholders. Having a sponsor or a champion in senior management who can present the case for learning at strategic level is a key requirement in the building of many learning architectures.

If you are a corporate learning architect who operates at a strategic level, who else do you recognize as a champion? For other learning architects, who is your champion? What are the qualities that enable him or her to represent your function at a level in the organization that can effect change? Your champion may be from HR, operations, sales or marketing. He or she is likely to be resilient, and have credibility and recognition from others that he/she is competent and delivers in his/her own sphere. The champion must have the ability to interpret and then present your plans and proposals.

A champion who is deemed operational can often shift the belief of others about the place of learning and development within an organization. A learning architect type 4 was grateful for the input of the operations director at the production meeting when the topic of workplace training was discussed. The operations director was able to explain to line managers the benefits they would gain from their staff being able to process the work more quickly.

Understand what is important to managers

Understanding what is important to managers at any one time is crucial to gaining their support. Be aware of the demands and pressures they face in their functions. Learning architects who work with managers to create solutions to problems that are real for the managers are learning architects who integrate with the organization.

Be flexible

Be flexible enough in your beliefs to acknowledge that a learning or training intervention may not be the most appropriate solution. A manager who asked a tactical learning architect to provide some time management training for the sales team appeared frustrated when the learning architect did not immediately say 'Yes'. The learning architect explained that there might be a method that would provide more effective outcomes, and he would like to carry out a needs analysis. He came to believe, based on the needs analysis, that the sales team were resisting the recent changes to their sales areas. Sales had dropped as a result of an unofficial 'go slow'. The learning architect suggested that the manager hold a team meeting to discuss the changes, and offered to facilitate the meeting, if required. The meeting proved to be a success, and only limited training was required for managing time, which was delivered through one-to-one coaching.

Managers will usually support proposals if they believe that suggestions are based on business benefits and not 'training for training's sake'.

Admit it when you are wrong

You should be able to admit it when a learning initiative that you have instigated has not produced the desired outcomes. Meeting with managers to ask for their input and ideas for 'what to do differently next time' will gain credibility and support. A little humility will gain support for the future.

Involve managers

Learning architects who involve managers in the design and implementation of initiatives at an early stage gain valuable input, support and the possibility of learning architects for the future. Looking for opportunities to involve other functions at any stage helps to integrate the organization.

A tactical learning architect invited all the operations managers to form part of the team designing the new customer care programme. Two of the managers were keen to be involved and played a key role in driving the project through. Their support of the project was critical when it came to rolling out the delivery to all staff at all operational plants.

BE CREATIVE

Create and design

Much of the work done by learning architects is in the design of learning initiatives. You may or may not deliver them yourself, but you will probably provide input to the provider or player who will be delivering. 'Design' implies the use of the resources and elements available to you and that you are aware of. 'Create' can include design, but also includes the unknown, the unproven, elements from other sources than the ones usually employed.

The use of radical resources for a learning initiative may not be appropriate for the organization. Sending everyone on a trapeze course may be a step too far, but including it in an individual development plan for a manager may be appropriate.

Be an entrepreneur

There is much talk in management development about managers becoming more entrepreneurial, in the sense of creating opportunities for themselves and developing their own business within an organization. For learning architects, having more of an entrepreneurial spirit is about: looking for opportunities, taking on an enterprise, being a catalyst, having ideas and challenging the status quo.

▌ A corporate learning architect may propose that the learning function links with the sales function to provide increased revenue through joint ventures.

▌ A tactical learning architect may suggest and take on the operation of the new staff incentive scheme.

▌ A functional learning architect might change his/her reaction from dismissing any idea to considering a new idea.

▌ An individual learning architect could propose a 'learn at lunch programme' for employees in their head office site.

Be creative with delivery of learning

Tighter budgets, less funding for training courses, and a move to more self-directed learning mean that learning architects are looking for ways to create initiatives that cost less but deliver more. The chapter on delivering learning will give you some ideas on how to present learning in a different format. A traditional week's residential training course could be replaced by a series of facilitated workshops and one-to-one coaching. A two-day teambuilding course could be replaced by a volunteer project where managers work on a real project to build a playground, redevelop a garden or something similar.

Develop your creative ability

All of us have the potential to be creative, but many of us have been working in structures that have inhibited our creative ability. When was the last time you did something that you believed was creative? What is stopping you?

If the opportunity to express your creative talents is not apparent in your working world, change something in the time you have outside work. Learning architects are exercising their creative muscles by joining in with their children's play activities, belonging to a singing group, attending art classes, cooking, writing personal journals, articles or novels, and learning to play musical instruments.

CHAPTER SUMMARY

▌ There are a number of qualities shared by all types of learning architects.

▌ The level of intensity for each quality depends on the role of the learning architect.

▌ Developing and maintaining the qualities helps a learning architect to build a robust learning architecture.

▌ Identifying the qualities can assist with the creation of a personal development plan.

8

Delivering learning

The purpose of this chapter is to provide guidance on:

I the major methods of delivering learning;
I deciding whether to use internal or external players to provide the learning initiative;
I how to select and manage an external player.

E-mail
From: Tom, Distribution Manager
To: Bob, Service Manager
I want to run some appraisal training for my supervisors in the next week or two, can you find someone to provide this?
While on the subject of training the new starters in the warehouse will need manual handling training. Do you know what we did last time? I read somewhere that you can get hold of a video that shows people what to do.
Regards
Tom

Bob suddenly realized what 'having responsibility for training' meant: e-mail from other managers who seemed to think he had all the time in the world to arrange training for them. He had enough to do with running his own department. How was he supposed to know what happened last time?

This is an example of correspondence that any of the identified learning architect types may have to deal with. In this case it would seem that Bob fits the category of learning architect type 3, the functional learning architect. Bob has little or no knowledge of learning theory, or how best to provide solutions to the training and learning issues he is being presented with, and very little time in which to deal with them.

While those of you who fit more comfortably into types 1 and 2, corporate and tactical, may be more experienced in dealing with the issues faced by Bob, all of us can be mindful of the pressures posed by an organization that is having to respond to change and is looking for quick solutions.

The stage at which this chapter is most useful is when a decision to provide a learning initiative has been agreed. How the decision to 'push the button' for a learning event is made, and by whom, is explored in an earlier chapter. At this stage of the process you have the agreement that learning has to take place in the organization, and you now need to know *what* is the most appropriate method of delivery, *who* is the most appropriate provider and *how* it will be delivered.

METHODS OF DELIVERY

One of the most important roles fulfilled by the learning architect is the choice of which one, or which grouping, of learning methods is most applicable to fulfil a particular identified learning need. There are a wide variety of learning methodologies, many of the most important of which are described in this chapter. The choice of which method to use to deliver the training or learning initiative will impact on the organization's move to creating a learning environment, in which learners learn to use whatever opportunities are available to increase their capacity to learn and therefore become more flexible and adaptive to change. Being aware of some of the major methods of delivery that can affect this shift from directed training towards self-managed learning will help.

We are aware that many of you will be very familiar with the methods of delivery available, and you may well have pioneered some yourselves. We suggest that the following descriptions serve as a reminder for those of you who are more experienced learning practitioners, and as a useful insight for those who have other priorities but need to have easy access to what methods are available.

The functional learning architect described in the paragraphs above has a particularly challenging role when it is necessary to choose learning methods. A functional learning architect often has none of the appropriate background and experience, and may well be advised to seek the assistance of an external learning consultant, although it is important to ensure that the external consultant is not simply guiding you towards a choice most financially beneficial to their learning approach.

The path to a most appropriate decision includes:

▌ having clear learning objectives;
▌ understanding what is available in terms of methods of delivery, sourced internally or externally;
▌ understanding what methodologies are most appropriate when considering the learning architecture that is in place (see Chapter 5);
▌ recognizing the considerations for time and cost with each possible sourcing method in comparison to the budget available for the required learning, the timescales required, and the priorities involving this learning implementation and others.

A learning architect type 3 who immediately reaches for the external providers' directory when asked to provide a training initiative may want to consider that there may be another method of delivery available, and the resources may be in-house.

CASE STUDY

Phil had been asked by the manager of another department to find some project management training for one of his team. Instead of calling the local chamber of commerce and asking if they did a course, Phil decided to organize a workshop to which he invited those people he believed had run successful projects, a good facilitator, the manager of a project that was about to start, and learners who would benefit. Phil arranged for the learners to shadow some of the more experienced managers, and asked the learners to form a group to support each other.

The initiative provided the outcome that was required, in that the team members could run a small project for themselves. The other benefits came from the learning achieved by sharing skills and knowledge, and the relationships developed across functions.

Phil's first efforts may appear a bit rough and ready to the skilled learning professional, but they show a willingness to move the organization from very structure-directed training towards more self-discovery learning methods.

CASE STUDY

Across a national food supermarket group, annual performance reviews/appraisals had been completed for the regional managers. Managers within the human resources department had reviewed the learning requirements, and were now discussing plans for training with the learning and development manager and the operations director.

There was a clear demand for financial training for the regional managers. The operations director firmly agreed that the need existed. She had observed that most of the regional managers were lacking in confidence when it came to preparing budgets, and that this resulted from a lack of knowledge in understanding financial data: typically, how to read a balance sheet, to determine cash flow and profit/loss, and how these applied to the workplace.

The human resources manager suggested that the learning and development manager seek out an external course on which the regional managers could be sent. She had knowledge of a highly prestigious training organization, which was known to be expensive, although she thought its brand would be motivational for the regional managers who would attend.

Since joining the organization a year ago, the learning and development manager had been adding value to any learning initiative. This had been achieved through proposing methods of delivering learning that would do more than deliver skills and knowledge. The identified delivery methods were chosen to add another dimension to the organization through the additional learning experienced by learners. The financial training offered an ideal opportunity for an initiative that would offer more than a course, however prestigious. The learning and development manager suggested that a programme be built where:

I the regional managers spend time with managers who had demonstrated the relevant level of experience, knowledge and skills in finance for business (not necessarily finance managers and accountants);

I the coach/mentor managers would come from the organization's suppliers and customers;

I regional managers spend time with at least two coach/mentor managers with different styles and marketplace experiences;

I the operations director used her knowledge of suppliers and customers to give an initial list of contacts for the learning and development manager to call regarding the project;

I once agreed, regional managers would select their coach/mentor and, taking ownership for their personal development, arrange for the visits;

I a list of learning outcomes would be created and used by all involved in the project to provide a measure for success and learning;

I the learning and development manager acted as a sponsor, guide and coordinator for the project;

I regional managers were supplied with a computer-based package that outlined basic financial terms and provided activities for checking understanding.

The identified major benefits of providing the learning in this way were:

I the organization moved away from directed training towards more self-managed experiential learning;

I the organization moved towards its stated ambition of having more vertical integration through the chain supplier, provider and customer;

I regional managers broadened several facets of their experience, leading to an all-round increase in knowledge and skills;

I the organization increased involvement and ownership in the learning process;

I there would be an increased supplier and customer knowledge of the organization, leading to better working relationships;

- although the whole programme would almost certainly take longer than a one-off training course, the ongoing relationships would provide learning networks that would last above and beyond a 'one off';
- the programme was less costly and more cost-effective than the initial outlay for a training course;
- regional managers would have ownership of the learning;
- the programme provided high levels of flexibility for the regional managers in scheduling their time away from the organization to visit and study;
- there would be an increased profile of the organization with suppliers and customers as a 'learning organization', and an opportunity to create a network for all involved parties;
- there was an opportunity to discuss reciprocal learning programmes with suppliers and customers, again building relationships and profile.

Each initiative will require some evaluation of the most appropriate method of delivery, and will depend on such criteria as time, expertise and willingness. If the aim is to build an architecture that will flex with the organization, the willingness of the learning architect to flex too is significant in pursuit of that aim.

We have grouped the main methods of delivery under headings that demonstrate where they lie on the training to learning continuum: see Table 8.1. Some of the methods can be used within other methods of delivery. A business game or case study may be used within a planned training course, and a coach may provide a demonstration of listening when coaching a client.

You may want to ask yourself:

- What methods of delivery have been used by your organization over the past six months?
- Where in the continuum do the majority lie?
- What can you do to influence a shift?

Table 8.1 Methods of delivery

Directed/training	$\longrightarrow$	Self-discovery/learning
Planned formal training	Workshop	Coaching
Lecture	E-learning	Work shadowing/job swap
Demonstration	Open/distance learning programme	Secondment
		Mentoring
Lesson	Tutorial	Action learning set
	Seminar	Sabbatical/voluntary work
		Working parties
		Projects
		Business games
		Case studies
		Role play
		Encounter groups

Main methods of delivery

Planned formal training

This is a structured programme of training normally provided off the job in an establishment, centre or training room designed or designated specifically for training. The training may be delivered in-house by the organization's own trainers or by external providers. Alternatively the training may be delivered in a location external to the organization. The training may be run exclusively for the organization, or participants may join an open course where staff from several organizations are attending. The venue will be staffed and equipped for this purpose. The formal training may include some informal elements such as case studies and discussion groups within the more formal programme structure of lesson, lecture and demonstration.

Typical applications are:

▌ a week-long management development programme at an outside training centre;

I a language course for new salespeople joining the international division, run in-house over six months;

I English as a second language course held over a 10-week period at the local college.

Lesson

This is a form of instruction incorporating a number of instructional techniques designed to ensure a group of learners reach specified behavioural objectives. Demonstration combined with question and answer is a common technique. Typical applications are:

I manual handling training;

I use of fire extinguisher.

Lecture

This is a straight talk or exposition, possibly using visual aids, but without group participation. There may be some questions allowed at the end. Typical applications are:

I launch of a new product or service;

I a report on the financial status of an organization.

Demonstration

An instructor or expert uses sensory-based aids to replicate a task to learners. The demonstration uses all or some of sight, hearing, touch, taste and smell to enable the learners to gain a sense of what they will have to do for themselves. Typical applications are:

I using new equipment;

I selling a product;

I lifting a patient;

I restraining a child.

Workshop

This is a topic-related meeting for which the outcome is learning. It may be facilitated, and either subject experts or people with the skills and knowledge to be taught attend in order to share tools and techniques. The group usually works through a topic or issue using methods and models such as brainstorming, SWOT analysis, case studies, business simulations and role plays. The event is interactive, with a high degree of group participation. The degree of structure and framework will depend on the resources and constraints such as time, cost, level of expertise and complexity of the topic.

Typical applications are:

I   account management;
I   handling conflict;
I   marketing strategy.

E-learning/computer-aided learning

This involves the use of the computer as a teaching medium or a learning resource. Learners use the internet, intranet or specifically designed packages, usually on their own without the guidance of a trainer. Some e-learning does involve a tutor being present virtually, through real-time connections. Used as a teaching medium, the computer's program controls the presentation of material to the learner. Speed, complexity and difficulty levels can vary as the learner responds to instruction, so the program adapts to the individual.

Used as a learning resource the computer act as a tool for the learner, providing resources of information, modelling, problem solving and simulations. The computer used in this way is not teaching but being used as a medium for learning.

Typical applications are:

I   legal training such as data protection and employment law;
I   computer packages or operating systems;
I   accounting packages;
I   administration procedures.

Open/distance learning

This term is used for any form of learning in which the trainer and learners are not in the same place. The usual format for this type of learning method is a course undertaken by learners for some form of certification. Subjects that are popular in this delivery method are management, learning and personal development. Many managers study for certificates, diplomas and MBAs through distance learning. Many courses consist of a combination of self-managed reading and research, workshops and tutor support. The sophistication of information technology in the form of computers and telephone means that complex learning can take place virtually in real time.

Virtual classrooms can be created through the internet, on telephone bridge lines and video conferencing.

Typical applications are:

I management development qualifications;
I learning and development qualifications;
I Open University degrees;
I coaching qualifications.

Tutorial

This is a semi-structured meeting between a learner and a tutor. A tutor is someone who gives knowledge and guidance to individuals or small groups of learners/trainees. A tutorial is most likely to occur in distance/open learning when there is a guided programme of study and learners need to gain feedback on their assignments.

Mentoring can be closely aligned to the role of a tutor, and this is explored later in the chapter.

Typical applications are:

I management development programmes;
I Open University degrees.

Seminar

This is usually a short course or conference at which experts share insights and experience about a subject or theme. A seminar will probably combine lecture-style presentations with participative methods such as group discussion, syndicate groups and case studies. Typical applications are:

I new developments in learning and development;
I proposed changes in taxation;
I forthcoming changes to legislation in environmental controls.

Coaching

Coaching as a method of delivering learning has come of age in the past few years, and it is a subject we discuss in more detail in another chapter. The popularity of coaching as a method of increasing learning is not surprising. It is a method that sits very clearly on the self-discovery/learning end of the continuum.

A coach seeks to act as a guide for the learner to discover new learning based on past experience and future opportunities. The coach's skilful use of questions, excellent listening and ability to get out of the way of the learner and not be the expert enable the learner to learn. This is the role that learning architects type 4 predominantly play in organizations

Since many organizations now report that they are using coaching as a learning method and that their managers are trained to coach, you may find it useful to examine what is going on in your organization in relation to coaching.

The introduction of a coaching culture to any organization raises the same issues as any other change programme. The same processes of identification, evaluation and planning will have to take place. Just announcing that 'we are an organization with a culture of coaching' will not be enough.

- Identify the culture, indicators of power and sources of influence within your organization (outlined in other chapters in this book) as they relate to coaching.
- Explore what beliefs are held about coaching by all stakeholders.
- Link coaching to the business strategy.
- Obtain commitment and a sponsor at the top of your organization. This must be someone who really understands what coaching is from having experienced it.
- Develop options for delivery of the programme.
- Define what resources you have available and design a cost versus benefit analysis for each of your options.
- Once the programme has been agreed:
  - communicate;
  - select coaches.
- Integrate coaching into as many activities as possible: training, performance measures, appraisals, induction and so on.
- Evaluate.

Selecting external and internal coaches and coach training providers

Most learning architects, when selecting external coaches, follow the same selection process as for other players: word of mouth recommendations, experience of existing coaching relationships and a recognized track record, are the preferred sources. Table 8.2 highlights a set of criteria that will prove helpful when selecting external, internal and coach training providers. Not all the criteria will be relevant, but they will serve as a useful starting point if you are evaluating several candidates. Ticks indicate key considerations, question marks indicate other points you may want to consider.

It is likely that you will be selecting internal coaches based on the skills, knowledge and attitude potential candidates display. You will use your own methods of assessing and evaluating, but the core skills list will provide a framework for initial selection.

Table 8.2 Checklists: selecting coaches and coach training providers

Criteria	External	Internal	Coach training provider
Fit with and knowledge of organization	√		√
Knowledge of industry/ sector	?	?	?
Professional experience	√	?	√
Coaching qualification	?	?	√
Personal style	√	√	√
Location and mobility	?	?	?
Able to adapt to volume up/ down	√	√	√
References	√	?	√
Continuous personal/ professional development	√	√	√
Membership of coaching body with ethical standards/code of practice	?	?	√
Coaching experience and success	√	?	√
Evaluation	√	√	√
Fees	√		√

Table 8.2 Checklists: selecting coaches and coach training providers (contd.)

Criteria	External	Internal	Coach training provider
Level of coaching: executive, middle management	√	√	√
Model/framework used	√	?	√
Confidentiality	√	√	√
Advanced listening skills	√	√	√
Ability to ask questions that shift, develop and stretch	√	√	√
Able to gain rapport	√	√	√
Credibility	√	√	√
Able to 'get out of the way' and park limiting beliefs and prejudices	√	√	√
Has a belief in the potential of other people	√	√	√
Comfortable with and within him/herself	√	√	√

Typical applications for coaching are:

▌ changes in job role;
▌ interpersonal skills development;
▌ presentation skills;
▌ motivation.

Work shadow/job swap or rotation

This involves swapping jobs with another person, shadowing him or her, or carrying out a planned series of jobs in different functions. The learner works with different teams and for different objectives. The change in perspective and development of new beliefs created by gaining a sense of someone else's job is one of the most powerful learning methods available.

How many times have we heard someone come back to their place of work, having spent time with another function, and declare, 'Now I know why this doesn't happen,' or 'No wonder they get so cross with us'? It is a relatively easy to arrange and low-cost method which gets sidelined as a result of inter-functional divides or insufficient staff resources to let someone move temporarily elsewhere in the organization.

Many organizations make job rotation part of an induction programme. This is an excellent idea but often it comes too early in an individual's career with an organization for him or her to appreciate any new perspective.

Job swapping can be combined with project work or coaching to gain maximum benefit from the experience. Typical applications for job swaps are:

- problem solving on a help desk;
- quality control on a production line;
- customer service in a call centre.

Secondment

Secondment usually implies being attached to another organization, as opposed to a job swap within an organization. However, in large organizations secondments to different functions, often in different parts of the world, can be equivalent to being with a different organization.

Being attached to another organization can provide individuals with new knowledge, experiences and beliefs, enabling them to practise and develop their existing skills and knowledge in another environment, free of any limiting beliefs and constraints. Combining this form of learning with coaching, mentoring and project work will increase the learning experience and enhance the outcomes. Typical applications are:

- graduate development;
- project management;
- knowledge of supply chain;
- customer service.

Mentoring

Mentoring, like coaching, is a method of delivering learning that relies on the skills of the mentor. A mentor should be a wise and responsible tutor: an experienced person, who advises, guides, teaches, inspires, challenges, corrects and serves as a role model. He or she is usually someone in the organization or market sector who has 'been there and done it'. Successful mentoring initiatives usually work when both parties have an opportunity to select each other. Typical applications are:

I graduate development;
I new job role;
I studying for a professional qualification, such as an accountancy, medical or legal qualification.

Action learning

Professor Reg Revans is credited with the invention of action learning. His assumptions were that people learn only when they want to, and that a major barrier to learning can be the mental attitude or beliefs formed by previous experience. The desire to learn emerges strongly when learners are faced with difficulties they would like to overcome. The environment in which a learner has the best opportunity to learn is one in which:

I learners can help each other to recognize their own past personal experiences and their current beliefs;
I learners feel secure;
I learners recognize the need for change and perceive the effects of their actions on real issues.

An action learning set is a group of learners who come together to provide mutual support and encouragement, share a wide range of experiences, offer different perspectives on issues, and test out ideas and presentations. It will usually have a set advisor who establishes contact, provides opportunities for action, resources the set and provides maintenance and development in the early stages of the set.

Learning through the means of an action learning set will provide learners with a new concept, a chance to 'do', a group environment, exposure to different experience, work with real issues and problems, the opportunity to self-manage with their own ground rules, the opportunity to network, and to work in an environment that is risk free and confidential.

A set relies on the input, motivation and support of each member to enable learning to take place. This method can support other methods of learning delivery. Typical applications are:

I personal development;
I study for a professional qualification;
I interpersonal skills development.

Sabbatical/voluntary work

Offering a sabbatical or gap time to individuals who have progressed in their career beyond the first few years has become common practice for many organizations. The image of students taking a gap year pre- or post-study is changing as the average age of 'gappers' increases. Successful employees with no dependants who hold a belief that they will return to a career in some organization are typical 'gappers'. Learners have negotiated with their employers for time off to pursue travel, do voluntary work at home and abroad, or take up further study.

New skills and experiences are gained from learning in a different culture, being a student, teaching in another country, or being part of a team working on an environmental project. Employees return to their organizations with new beliefs, perspectives, motivation, and an ability to carry out their job role with new skills and knowledge. They will probably make valuable mentors or coaches, and may want to develop their career in the organization in a different function.

The fear that employees will not return and the upheaval caused by finding and then training a temporary replacement makes some organizations reluctant to allow sabbaticals. In practice, if not offered a sabbatical, the employee may resign with no intention of returning, leaving the organization with the same and more issues.

For voluntary work, VSO (www.vso.org.uk) is the best known name in the UK. It places more than 750 people a year on all kinds of voluntary work overseas. The average age of a volunteer is 38.

Typical applications in which sabbaticals have a role are:

▮ career development;
▮ motivation;
▮ project management;
▮ personal development.

Working parties

Individuals from different functions come together to work as a group, usually, to solve and/or implement organization-wide issues. Learners are encouraged to think beyond their own areas of expertise and experience. They learn about problem solving, project management and interpersonal skill development. The opportunity to increase cross-functional cooperation is also a good source of learning in an organization that is moving towards providing a learning environment. Typical applications are:

I project management;
I interpersonal skills;
I career development;
I organizational development.

Projects

Projects enable learners to work on limited-life endeavours which help link theory and method to practical work-based activity. Learners have an opportunity to: develop relationships with other parts of their organization, increase their profile and credibility, put into practice theories learnt from other methods of delivery, and develop skills in research and presentation. Learners usually have the support of a coach, mentor or tutor, and may work in a group as part of a working party. Typical applications are:

I professional qualifications such as learning and development, management, health and safety;
I induction programmes;
I graduate and management development.

Business games, simulations, case studies and role play

These methods of delivery can be 'stand alone' or can be delivered as part of another method. Wherever they are used they encourage the move towards a learning environment, as they are methods that encourage self-discovery and participation if offered as a group activity.

Business games and exercises offer learners an opportunity to work in groups as a management team of an imaginary organization or function. They have to solve issues, make proposals, evaluate decisions and improve performance based on structured information outlined during the game. Learning takes place through the activity and from the feedback provided at the end of the game.

Case studies are similar to business games but can be used for individual learners. The usual format of a case study involves real or fictional situations or events which the learners have to analyse, consider, identify issues, make proposals and offer solutions. Case studies are often compared with what happened in real life, enhancing the learning experience.

Role plays or skill rehearsals are activities where learners are presented with a situation which they explore by playing out various roles using the skills they have learnt. This method of delivery often strikes fear into the minds of learners, as they worry about performing and their performance in front of others, rather than practising newly acquired skills. Learning may be impaired if role playing is not handled in a sensitive manner. It may be appropriate to use another method of learning such as case study, projects or job swap.

Typical applications for games and role play are:

▌ interviewing;
▌ marketing;
▌ graduate development.

Your choice of which method of delivery will depend on such criteria as the culture of the organization, cost, speed of delivery, available resources, constraints, penalties and the overall learning strategy of the organization (if there is one).

We, like many of you, are mindful of current fads and flavours in methods of delivery. Keeping in mind the outcomes for the learning always helps, and prevents many of us being seduced by a method that may sound appealing but in reality does not deliver the desired outcomes.

We made a conscious decision not to highlight the pros and cons of each delivery method. We hold a belief that each method has merit when it is used in a context that is appropriate and is supported by the organization, perhaps in conjunction with other methods of delivery. For example, e-learning offers much in terms of flexibility, ongoing cost reduction, the opportunity for self-managed learning and minimal trainer input. Many organizations have embraced and are successfully using e-learning to deliver training. They often find that the initial costs escalate. In order to ensure the effective transfer of learning back to the workplace, technical coaches are required to support the learners.

Action learning sets may not produce the outcomes originally outlined because a workshop was required at the beginning of the initiative to inform all those who were going to be involved, and this did not take place.

Some learners have struggled to complete distance learning programmes because the lack of interaction from fellow learners inhibited their opportunity to learn.

We know that you will have examples of your own, and as you reflect on those experiences, you will become mindful of the effects of the choice of method for delivering learning.

INTERNAL OR EXTERNAL PLAYERS?

For some learning architects the choice of whether to use an internal or external player to provide the learning is limited. A learning architect type 1 is likely to have more access to internal resources than a learning architect type 3, who may only be able to call on someone to provide a brief induction for a new starter. The decision may be clear-cut: there can be no option but to seek external providers.

If some choice exists, it may be useful to compare internal with external provision. The following questions may serve as a useful framework for making a decision:

▌ What do we want? What are the outcomes, what will be different after the learning event?

▌ How willing is the organization to undertake the initiative? What impetus does it need from an outside resource?

▌ What is the timescale? What are the constraints? What are the penalties for not bringing the learning to delivery by a certain date? What time is available to train trainers to deliver the learning?

▌ How much money is in the budget? What are the consequences of 'doing the learning on the cheap'?

▌ What expertise is available? What skills, knowledge and beliefs do we have in the organization to deliver the learning to achieve the outcomes we require?

▌ What is the credibility rating of the internal providers? What will the learners believe about themselves and their learning if training is provided in-house?

▌ What experience does the organization have of providing learning initiatives in-house? What experience can it draw on from the past?

CASE STUDY

Jo was head of learning and development for a medium-sized distribution company, a type 2 learning architect who had no department reporting directly to her. She had developed a network of workplace trainers and assessors, who reported directly to their line managers. The workplace trainers had their own jobs to do, but were instrumental in training and assessing NVQs for the organization.

A visit from a health and safety inspector highlighted the need for manual handling training for staff in the new warehouse. The senior management board tasked Jo with arranging the necessary training. It had to be completed in time for the inspector's return in a month, not only for the sake of compliance but for the health and safety of the staff.

Jo used the questions as a method of making a decision whether to use internal or external resources to deliver the learning. The desired outcomes were clear: all relevant staff should know how to lift objects safely, and this should be part of an induction programme for all new staff. The willingness to undertake the initiative was high. An outside influence had provided the impetus.

The timescale was defined, in that the learning had to be completed in a month's time and there would be penalties if the training had not been completed, in terms of staff welfare and the operation of the organization.

The cost of the training had been agreed in principle by the senior management board. As was usual for Jo, when tasked with arranging unplanned training initiatives, the message was 'Get the training done but watch the costs'. Jo sensed that the prospect of having the warehouse operation compromised, or the costs that would be incurred if staff were injured, had focused certain managers' minds!

Internal expertise and resources were available in that there were workplace trainers with training skills, but they did not have skill and knowledge in manual handling. The workplace trainers were competent in training one to one, not to groups. The training had to be completed in a short timeframe, and for this reason the delivery would have to be to small groups. There was not enough time to train one or all of the trainers in manual handling and group training, so the initial training would have to be from an external player.

The credibility of the workplace trainers was good. While they did not have the explicit skills in manual handling training at that time, if they were to gain those skills for the future, the transfer of the learning to the workforce would be successful.

Her experience of providing in-house initiatives was positive, and without the tight timescale Jo's preference would have been to use the workplace trainers to deliver as much of this workplace training as possible. Jo was aware that the production timescales were tight and line managers were under pressure. Any loss of production hours would have a significant effect, so she was mindful about demands placed on workplace trainers that would take them away from their main production roles.

Jo decided that she would seek an external provider to deliver manual handling training to essential staff in groups within the month. In order to provide a sustainable source of in-house training for the future, she would also arrange for the workplace trainers to be trained to deliver manual handling training. She realized that there was a further training requirement for the workplace trainers, in their ability to deliver training to small groups. Jo would be able to provide a learning initiative for this purpose herself, and in a timeframe that would suit the production schedules of the organization.

The question now, for Jo, was which external trainer to use.

Selecting and managing an external player

Your knowledge of external players may well depend on the type of learning architect you are and the use you have to make of external providers. Learning architects of type 1, with a large learning and development function, may have less knowledge of external providers than types 2 and 3, who nearly always have to rely on external providers.

The most popular 'finding strategy' used by people we questioned when researching for this book was word of mouth. This is not an unusual occurrence when most of us prefer to have some comfort in our initial selection of a product or service through drawing on the experience of those we trust.

It is often useful to have a clear sense of what you want from the provider before you start your search. This is rather like looking for a house. If you know you want a three-bedroom house with two bathrooms within an hour's drive of work, in a rural location on a bus route near to shops and schools for a certain budget, estate agents have an opportunity to provide you with properties that match your requirements. It may be that the provider can suggest alternatives that may match your needs more specifically. It may also be able to provide details of interventions of which you were not aware.

When making the search specific, the following sources may be useful:

| **Word of mouth.** This is by far the most popular source, and usually successful. Use any networks and contacts you have to ask for a recommendation. Good providers usually stay in business because they provide a service that people talk about and are happy to refer. They will also have a network of providers that they can refer you to for areas of learning and development that they do not provide. Internet-based trainer forums are a good source of 'Does anyone know… ?'

I **Local chambers of commerce** usually provide training services themselves through contracted trainers, but also have a members' directory, which is usually categorized by subject. It could be useful to ask the chamber if you can speak to an organization that has used the providers you are considering. Many chambers run seminars and events, often free or for a nominal fee, which are presented by learning and training providers. This is an opportunity for you to get a taster of who they are and how they perform.

I **Trade associations, government and advisory organizations** are also sources of advice, especially for specialist training such as health and safety, employment issues and legislation.

I **The internet** is another source, using the usual search mechanisms. Popular sites such as www.trainerbase.co.uk in the UK provide a useful resource.

I **Direct marketing** is more often used by the larger, mass market seminar providers, but material you receive in this way can be a good resource if you ensure you evaluate it effectively.

I **Network meetings** are yet another option. We discuss the role of networking in other contexts throughout the book, and a good place to meet training providers in person is at one of the many network forums that exist. You can choose from breakfast, lunch, after-work or dinner meetings, where you will find many companies and individuals who are keen to make contact with organizations in an informal way. Many meetings provide a forum for individuals to make a short presentation, or there may be a more formal and longer presentation. We are aware that network meetings are not everyone's first choice of meeting potential providers, but they are popular, and many successful business relationships are formed as a result.

CASE STUDY

Gill was delighted that she had the green light to proceed with the personal development programme for the organization's management team. She wasted no time in speaking with a number of external providers that she believed would be able to deliver the outcomes desired, and the final decision on who to appoint lay with her.

The two main contenders for the assignment were very different. One was a national company with a large team of trainers and coaches, the other a very experienced trainer and coach who worked for herself. Both seemed to have a very good grasp of the culture of

> Gill's organization, had excellent references, and she liked the personalities who had come to see her. One organization was more expensive but it was still within budget. How was she to decide?

As an experienced learning architect you may well be aware of the differences that exist in the structures of external training providers. The three structures that are most popular are:

- a training company that employs its own staff;
- a training company that uses associates (learning providers who work for themselves but contract to work under the company's banner) to deliver its programmes;
- an individual provider who works for him or herself as a sole trader or private limited company.

There are benefits to using each type of provider, and in order for you to make the most informed purchasing decision it may serve you well to find out the structure of your proposed provider. Points to consider when choosing a larger organization over a small one are:

- It will have worked with more and larger organizations.
- It may have an account manager to liaise with you.
- It can provide replacement 'deliverers' in the event of sickness and staff leaving.
- It is often a known name.
- It will have a large resource of 'deliverers'.
- There is more administrative back-up.
- It has time and resources to spend on marketing and selling.
- It should offer a range of standard and bespoke programmes.
- It is often more expensive as it has larger overheads to fund.
- The deliverer is more distant from the client and process in the early stages, and there is often less input by the deliverer into the needs analysis.
- Materials can be off the shelf.
- It may be less flexible to requests and changes by the client.
- There is a reduced relationship with the person doing the delivery.
- Contracts are common with larger organizations.
- A rapport with the person selling the programme is no guarantee of a rapport with the person delivering it.

▌ It can be time-consuming to meet and assess all the providers' personnel who will be involved in the project.

We have been purchasers of learning programmes for organizations, we are providers who have worked as associates for other companies, and we are regularly engaged directly by clients as individual providers of training, learning and coaching. We believe that our experiences may offer you some insight to help you with the task of selecting and managing an external provider. We have used our own and other learning architects' beliefs to create some 'ask yourself' questions that will help with the selection process:

▌ What other organization has this provider worked with? Working with larger household names and brands may appear to be impressive, but is not always an indication of the quality of the provider's work.
▌ How well does this provider know my organization? The provider may not need to know your organization personally, but it may be useful for you to know what experience he or she has had in a similar sector. Remember that the ability of the provider to gain rapport and assess the culture, values and processes of your organization may be more significant.
▌ What action will the provider take to get to know our needs?
▌ What time will the provider spend with us before delivering, and will it charge for this?
▌ Will I have to sign a contract?

Not all providers have contracts or agreements, but if they do, they serve as a framework for both parties to know what to expect from each other. A fear shared by most providers is cancellation. Most providers of any service are not happy to spend time and effort in preparing for a piece of work, and perhaps refuse other work because of the commitment, only to be faced with a cancellation. If an agreement is not signed, it is good practice to discuss and agree the consequences of a cancellation, by either party, before the event, to retain a good working relationship through trust and commitment.

Other things to consider when creating a contract are:

▌ Commercial sensitivity (for both parties).
▌ Copyright and intellectual property. The provider usually wants copyright of its product and services, but if you are working on a joint project you may want to sort out what belongs to which party.

▌ Expenses. Establish in advance what you will be charged for over and above the agreed rate. Expenses are likely to include travelling (mileage, rail, air tickets), accommodation and subsistence, hire of equipment and facilities, and written material. Some or all of the preparation time may be charged too.

▌ Satisfaction. What will happen if the players do not provide the service to the agreed standards? As standards are often subjective it is advisable to discuss outcomes in detail before commencing.

▌ Illness. Will the provider provide a substitute or postpone?

▌ Invoicing. Agree terms: who, what and when. Liaise with whoever is dealing with purchase orders and payment to ensure all goes smoothly.

▌ Cancellation. Agree terms for cancellation by either party.

▌ Insurance and liability. What cover does the provider have? Who is covered in the case of accidents? What precautions do both parties need to take? This is very relevant for outdoor activities.

▌ What happens if we have to change something or cancel? A formal contract may cover this. If not, agree the procedures beforehand.

▌ Who exactly will provide the learning? Meet the player before embarking on the project. The person who is selling the initiative may not be the person who will be delivering the event.

▌ How do I know if it is value for money? Identify what you are evaluating. Value for money is subjective, and your value may be different from the finance director and the players' sense of value.

▌ Who will I speak to about the programme on a day-to-day basis? Larger organizations will have administration back-up, whereas sole players will probably be the main contact for everything.

▌ Who provides insurance and who is liable if there is an accident? The provider will probably have insurance, but do check. If activities are going to be outdoors or involve people doing things they would not normally do, a double check with your own and the provider's insurance companies is a good idea.

▌ Who will provide the facilities? If an external provider is providing an event for your organization exclusively, it is usual practice for the organization, not the provider, to cover the cost of the venue and facilities. You may have facilities at your premises; if not, you will have to source them elsewhere, in a hotel or similar establishment. Agree with the provider who is going to organize the facilities, and be mindful of what equipment may need to be hired. A learning event without refreshments can be a disaster, so please agree with the provider who is to do what and what is covered in the fee. If you are sending delegates to an open event, not exclusively for your organization, the usual practice is that the venue and facilities will have been organized by the provider. You will need to check whether accommodation is included in the cost.

I Confidentiality. The provider will hear and read things that could be confidential. How will you know he or she will not tell other people? Confidentiality is something that most reputable providers have high on their list of values. Any breach of confidentiality is not good practice and could lead to them jeopardizing future work with new, existing or future clients they could gain through referrals. Putting a clause in a contract or asking the provider to sign a confidentiality clause will provide you with security if you require it.

What an external player expects

Beyond the terms of a formal or informal contract or agreement, external players have expectations about the organizations they are working with. Typical expectations are that they will:

I receive feedback above and beyond the 'happy/reaction sheets' at the end of an event;
I have regular meetings with the sponsor;
I be kept informed of changes to procedures and processes that may affect what they are delivering;
I be informed of changes in personnel that may affect the learning event,
I be mindful of confidentiality;
I be told if their services are no longer required and the reasons for this;
I be paid under the terms of the invoice;
I feel part of the organization in order to provide a service which reflects the needs and culture of the organization;
I be offered the opportunity to explain what else they can offer.

Licensing trainers

An option for learning architects who want to combine the use of external and internal resources for delivering training is offered by licensing. Providers license an organization's internal trainers to deliver and use the products and services developed by the external provider. Licensing is an option for all types of learning architect. It may suit learning architect type 1 who has a team of trainers but wants consistency across different countries. A learning architect type 2 may become a licensed trainer using a provider's tool him or herself, along with other staff he or she chooses to nominate as trainers. A learning architect type 3 may be in a similar situation to type 2, or may choose to license external trainers to act as associates for the organization with the specific product. A learning architect type 4 will certainly be one of the trainers who is licensed.

Organizations are most likely to use licensing to accommodate all or some of the following needs:

▎ lack of internal resource or expertise in developing training/learning resources and materials;
▎ lack of time to develop a learning event;
▎ consistent product, service, delivery across all deliverers;
▎ up-to-date resources;
▎ regular updates;
▎ ability to deliver a tried and tested product;
▎ trainers that need training;
▎ a professional package;
▎ accreditation or certification for a legal requirement such as food hygiene or financial services;
▎ recognized outside the organization;
▎ back-up and support from experienced practitioners and deliverers;
▎ a global programme requiring multi-language delivery.

Licensing agreements and the procedure by which trainers are licensed vary, but typically an external provider who offers licensing will provide:

▎ materials and training which has been developed and tested in a wider market;
▎ training for the organization's trainer(s) in the use and presentation of the materials;
▎ training for the organization's trainer(s) in training delivery;
▎ ongoing support for trainers;
▎ ongoing refresher training for trainers;
▎ use of material for the method of training/learning being employed;
▎ regular updates on changes to the training material;
▎ accreditation or certification for trainers and learners.

The fees charged by companies who license their products and services vary, along with what they will charge for. Organizations can expect to pay for all or a combination of the following:

▎ fees for trainers who attend a training course to learn how to deliver the product and materials associated with it;
▎ a licensing fee for trainers;

▌ annual renewal of the licensing fee for each trainer or the organization as a whole, which may involve a refresher course;

▌ a charge for the resources, materials, packs that are used by trainers for delegates;

▌ fees for the accreditation or certification of delegates who complete the training/programme;

▌ charges for updates.

CHAPTER SUMMARY

▌ There are many methods of delivering learning.

▌ The choice of method can achieve more for the organization than the immediate learning outcomes.

▌ Several criteria exist that can influence the decision of whether to provide the method of delivery using internal or external resources.

▌ Several criteria can be explored when making the decision which external provider to use.

▌ Maintaining a successful working relationship with your external provider relies on understanding the needs of all stakeholders.

9

Current learning issues

The purpose of this chapter is to:

I share the thoughts and questions that are being asked by learning architects about current learning issues;
I highlight topics that are occupying the minds of many learning architects;
I provide a forum for further thought and debate.

We have had the opportunity to meet many learning architects who are working in different roles in various organizations. We noticed that there were some common themes and topics being expressed by learning architects as we discussed their work with them. We offer these topics for you to explore and add your own thoughts. We have no definitive answers. We wonder if there are any answers to some of the issues, but hope that if we share the interests and concerns of other learning professionals, you too will gain some learning.

The topics are: coaching, diversity, health and safety, the skills shortage, engagement and e-learning.

COACHING

Coaching appears to have come of age as a method of learning and development. Many of you will insist that coaching has always been around and available. Many of you will say that you have been coaching for years. 'I believe I have been coaching but it wasn't called that then' is a comment often heard amongst learning architects.

A measure of the growth, interest and popularity of coaching is evident from the number of articles in the specialist and popular press, conferences dedicated to coaching, television programmes and features, and the number of people who call themselves coaches. The inaugural conference of the Association of Coaching in the UK attracted over 300 delegates, the majority of whom had 'coach' in their title. The focus was very much business-related, which marked a shift from the 'new age' feel that coaching had a few years ago.

Many beliefs are shared about the reasons for the emergence of coaching at this point in history as a profession; a discrete method; a phenomenon. Some have a positive frame and others are more negative, sometimes cynical. We are sure that you will have your own beliefs to add to the ones we have identified.

Reasons for the emergence of coaching

▌ Sir John Whitmore's explanation for the emergence of coaching in its current form comes from what he calls a 'crisis of meaning' for individuals in organizations. This often affects the successful managers who have achieved their targets, climbed the career ladder, achieved monetary reward, collected the badges of status with cars, offices, staff, international travel. These managers have fulfilled the expectations of their early goals and now they are 'there' are finding life is not providing the satisfaction they believed. They are often searching for something else, for who they are or who they really want to be. Coaching appears to provide them with a mechanism or way of rebalancing, a means of finding a sense of meaning for where they have been in their careers and who and what they want for the future.

▌ Coaching is a career that many who have had their 'crisis of meaning' take up. The role of a coach fulfils the need for independence, an opportunity to share experience, skills and knowledge, to create a role for oneself without the expectations of the corporate world, and a chance to continually 'develop oneself'.

▌ Coaching has replaced the more traditional support frameworks such as those provided by religion or family, which have declined over recent decades. The loss of the support, guidance, friendship, channels for communication and role models provided by extended families and religious communities has left a gap for many individuals. The support, guidance, objectivity, confidentiality and role modelling provided by a coach fulfil the need for many people.

▮ Successful marketing has rebranded an already existing service. Coaching may not be anything new, but skilled promotion, packaging and positioning have created a demand. Whether the demand is real, perceived or over-inflated, a profession has developed to provide a service.

▮ Flatter organizations have removed the layers of management and support services that were in place to fulfil the needs and requirements of employees. Managers do not seem to have the time and energy to listen, develop and support their employees. No one is there to provide support for the managers either. The gap left is being filled by coaches.

▮ The increased use of technology for communication, and in particular e-mail, has meant that people talk to each other less. The interaction with another human being, which can be a key driver for satisfaction at work, has been lost. The opportunity for a conversation, to be listened to, to hear yourself speak, to interact with someone who has an interest in you is compelling. A coach can provide this. The person receiving coaching may not be consciously aware that his or her need is being fulfilled in this way, but he or she will have a sense of feeling good, of something being complete again.

▮ Many executives collect badges of status and power. It may be the make and value of the car, the size and design of an office, number and composition of staff, membership of airline lounges or clubs. A coach can become one of the badges of achievement and power, an indication of an executive's status and worth to an organization.

▮ Coaching as a profession has been the recipient of many individuals' redundancy packages. For some people coaching fulfils all the requirements they want from a new career: they fulfil their own expectations and achieve their outcomes. For some, the sometimes over-hyped statistics of earning potential and flexible lifestyle that coaching can provide do not match with reality. As organizations continue to make employees redundant and individuals seek to use the opportunity to do something new, one of the new things will be coaching.

▮ There is a demand from employees, supported by government intervention and legislation, for a more accommodating workplace. The growth in family-friendly policies and calls for work/life balance have prompted more responsible organizations to move beyond the minimum legislation. The fundamental skills of coaching, asking questions and listening, have been encouraged in the workplace through training and a shift in culture. This has increased the demand for in-house and external coaches and the provision of training for coaching.

I The United States embraced coaching in its rebranded form a few years before the UK and other parts of the world. Some of the early coach training providers were US companies. The reasons for the emergence of coaching in the United States are probably the same as the ones outlined here. The impetus for other countries to embrace it was probably influenced by the US move. The United States has a tradition and an acceptance of individuals engaging a specialist to help them with issues.

I Demand for coaching has grown with the emergence, or re-emergence as some would say, of more alternative ways of looking after oneself both physically and mentally. The market for aromatherapy, hypnotherapy, Reiki, acupuncture, yoga, holistic, sports massage and other body works, and for personal trainers, continues to grow. There are several possible reasons for the demand and acceptance that individuals need to pay some attention to their inner and outer selves. Some would cite the increased pace at which people lead their lives. The speed and availability of communication technology has increased expectations of providers and consumers alike. There is a shift to finding relief from pressure in recharging the mind and body.

I With the demand for coaching comes the demand for training to be a coach or learn coaching skills. Coach training providers – schools, colleges, academies, universities – are growing in numbers and providing more and varied qualifications. Certificates, diplomas, degrees and more are all available for varying rates and through different methods for delivery: intensive courses, distance learning, modular weekends, telephone and internet-based methods are on offer. Coaching can be viewed as an industry, and with an increase in availability of coach training schools, the supply of coaches will drive demand.

I Research carried out for the CIPD research report _Helping people learn_ (2004) indicates that there is strong support for the following statements:

- Individuals need advice and support if they are to take more responsibility for their own learning.
- Line managers should play a significant role in helping their teams to learn and develop.
- Employees need to take more responsibility for their own learning and development.

If this shift from training to learning is happening then it is not surprising that the demand for managers to take on the role of coach and develop coaching skills is increasing. If individuals are taking more responsibility for their own learning and development, they may seek that development through using the services of a coach.

We have explored the use of coaching as a style and a skill of managing, and the benefits of having a coach, in other chapters. It is likely in your role as a learning architect that you will also be involved in implementing coaching in your own organization, and selecting external and internal coaches.

Implementing a coaching programme in an organization

The CIPD 2004 *Training and Development Survey* indicates that nearly 80 per cent of UK respondents were using coaching as a part of their learning and development activities. 'Using coaching' can range from a large-scale corporate investment in an extensive pool of external coaches, made available to all management, to a couple of coaching skills workshops offered to first-line managers as part of their training programme.

Like many other learning architects, you may believe that introducing coaching in any form will benefit an organization. Your evaluation of the mechanisms available to effect change in the organization, combined with budgetary and other resource factors, may have led you to adopt a specific strategy. This may be to use external coaches, internal coaches or a combination of the two; or to train employees to coach. The introduction of a coaching culture to any organization raises the same issues as any other change programme. The same processes of identification, evaluation and planning will have to take place. Just announcing that 'We are an organization with a culture of coaching' will not be enough.

For those of you embarking on the process of implementing a coaching programme the following tips will be of help:

▮ Identify the culture, indicators of power and sources of influence (outlined in other chapters in this book) within your organization as they relate to coaching.
▮ Explore what beliefs are held about coaching by all stakeholders.
▮ Link coaching to the business strategy.
▮ Obtain commitment and a sponsor at the top of your organization. This should be someone who really understands what coaching is from having experienced it.

▌ Develop options for delivery of the programme.

▌ Define what resources you have available and design a cost versus benefit analysis for each of your options.

▌ Once the programme has been agreed:

- communicate;
- select coaches.

▌ Integrate coaching into as many activities as possible: training, performance measures, appraisals, induction.

▌ Evaluate.

DIVERSITY

In your role as a learning architect it is likely that you will have been involved in helping yourself and/or your organization to embrace the benefits of encouraging diversity in the workplace. You may have been developing and delivering programmes for employees, or establishing strategic policies for your own and other organizations. An understanding of the wider implications of diversity will be required for the learning architect who has responsibilities as: a manager of people, a role model within the organization, a guardian, provider and distributor of learning material, and an employer.

Many beliefs exist about what is meant by diversity. If the purpose of this book is to enable the learning architect to build and maintain changing architectures, then an awareness of the meaning of diversity in a global sense will probably serve us well.

The United Nations states:

> Diversity management should thus be viewed as an inclusive concept, encompassing a broader focus than employment equity would suggest. It requires one to look at the mindset and culture of an organization and the different perspectives people bring to an organization on account of their ethnicity, social background, professional values, styles, disabilities and other differences.
>
> (United Nations, 2000)

While it may be the role of HR in many organizations to create policies that embrace diversity, we imagine that it will be your role, directly or indirectly, to help turn these policies into tangible and measurable action through learning initiatives. The increase in the number of laws relating to equality and discrimination could be viewed as a sad reflection on society, in that it is unable to embrace diversity without the necessary checks and penalties.

Before we outline some of the laws relating specifically to equality and discrimination that you need to be aware of, it may be timely for you to ask yourself a few questions in relation to your own thoughts on diversity. The following questions come from the work of Phil Clements and John Jones in *The Diversity Training Handbook* (2002). A more comprehensive set of questions can be found in their 'Diversity health check':

▌ If someone asked you 'What are your prejudices?' what would you say? What would you say you were doing to manage them?
▌ What diversities do you recognize in the organization you work for?
▌ When you discuss diversity issues with people, what issues make you feel defensive?
▌ How do you promote diversity in your interactions with others?

Following the United Nations description of diversity it is our personal belief that diversity is more than a set of rules and regulations, but as we have indicated, laws do exist. In your role as a champion of learning it will serve you well to be aware of the current legislation that may affect you, as you and your team goes about delivering the business of learning. The ones listed below relate to UK law:

▌ disability discrimination;
▌ equal pay;
▌ fixed-term contracts;
▌ rehabilitation of offenders;
▌ part-time employees;
▌ race discrimination;
▌ religion and belief;
▌ sex discrimination;
▌ sexual orientation;
▌ trade union membership;
▌ age discrimination (legislation to be introduced in 2006).

Learning architects have concerns about how learning professionals can integrate diversity in learning initiatives rather than have diversity seen as a 'bolt on'. If learners believe they only know about diversity if they have been on a diversity course, organizations are missing out on providing learning opportunities in every learning intervention.

Anyone involved in providing a learning intervention, whether it is a classroom-style training session or a facilitated meeting, needs to be 'diversity aware'. The following suggestions serve as a good checklist:

▍ Demonstrate the business benefits of a diverse organization to anyone who may be reluctant to integrate or change to accommodate diversity in a learning initiative. Issues include the cost of not being diverse when recruiting, and the benefit gained from the knowledge and experience of having a diverse organization in terms of age and culture.

▍ Find out as much information as possible about the needs of individuals before a learning event in order to prevent anything occurring which may impact on the potential for learning:

- Consider accessibility to the building, room, facilities, equipment, furniture.
- Consider any need for assistance with hearing, perhaps with the use of hearing loops.
- Consider dietary requirements.
- Consider the impact of religious observances such as fasting and prayer breaks.
- Allow for visual impairments in choosing the size of visual materials: print, colour, detail. Bear in mind the option to use audio.
- Consider timing and location, and try to ensure these are conducive to learners with dependants and those who have more difficulty with access to travel.
- Consider the impact of dyslexia.
- Take into account any requirement for left and right-handed materials, or workbooks.
- Allow for regular breaks, and be mindful of the need for comfort and relief from stressful physical positions.

▍ Evaluate the learning interventions in terms of diversity. What sector of the organization is taking up learning opportunities? What reaction do people have to the events? Review your evaluation methods and include feedback on diversity.

▍ Be aware of videos/DVD, role plays and case studies that may have stereotypes and include inappropriate language, smoking or discriminatory actions.

▍ Ensure performers vary their learning style to suit all types of learners. Consider whether they draw on Honey and Mumford's (1982) learning styles to appeal to pragmatists, activists, theorists and reflectors.

Provide interventions that appeal to all the senses, particularly auditory, visual and kinesthetic.

I Review your e-learning provision and materials. How accessible are they for learners with disabilities in terms of such things as access and what is presented on the screen? A review of typeface, colour and ease of navigation around a website or learning package may prove beneficial. There are specialist agencies who can provide you with guidance.

I Ensure that learning providers do not cause offence with their own language or style of humour. Performers need to know how to handle inappropriate comments made by learners which could cause offence and be discriminatory. If they are handled correctly an opportunity for learning is created, and the message about diversity is integrated into the learning event.

HEALTH AND SAFETY

Learning architects are involved in health and safety in their roles as managers of people, as sources for the provision of health and safety training and as employees of an organization. 'Most of my training budget has already been allocated for health and safety training. I know it is a legal requirement and important but what about the other stuff?' This is the cry from many of those who are trying to squeeze the most out of an ever shrinking training budget. Understanding the legal requirements may not help you with the budget, but it will help gain a new perspective or understanding. Under the Health and Safety at Work Act (HASAWA) 1974 a learning architect will probably have the following duties.

As an employer

A learning architect in a managerial role has the duty, so far as is reasonably practicable, to ensure the health, safety and welfare at work of his or her employees. This may be more relevant for the corporate learning architect who is responsible for a team, but all types of learning architect will be responsible as they liaise with learners and their managers, their own managers, and performers who work directly for the organization.

As an employer of persons other than the organization's own employees

A learning architect needs to be mindful of the risks to health and safety to which performers, suppliers and stakeholders may be exposed when involved in any learning initiative.

As an employee

Most learning architects are employees, and while at work should take reasonable care of the health and safety of themselves and of other persons who may be affected by their acts or omissions at work. They should cooperate with their employers to carry out any duty or requirement imposed under any of the relevant statutory provisions.

'No person shall intentionally or recklessly interfere with or misuse anything provided in the interests of health, safety or welfare in pursuance of any of the relevant statutory provisions.' This includes, for example, covering a fire exit sign in a training room or lifting boxes that exceed the guidance weight for manual handling. Section 2 of HASAWA places a duty on employers 'to provide such information, instruction, training and supervision as is necessary to ensure, so far as is reasonably practicable, the health and safety at work of their employees'.

Many of us have been in possession of a training budget, which we believe to be under-funded for the type of initiatives we wish to provide for the organization, and have had to spend a large part of it on health and safety training. Somehow health and safety training does not have the same cachet or lure as some other initiatives that excite learning architects. Understanding the requirements of health and safety in terms of training may assist us in our making the shift towards embracing this type of statutory training.

Every employer shall, in entrusting tasks to their employees, take into account their capabilities with regard to ergonomic considerations, physical and mental limitations of people and the potential for human error.

Every employer shall ensure that their employees are provided with adequate health and safety training:

- on their being recruited into the employer's undertaking;
- on their being exposed to new or increased risks because of:
  - being transferred or given a change of responsibility;
  - introduction of new work equipment into or a change to work equipment already in use;

- introduction of a new system of work or change to a system of work already in use.

Training shall:

❚ be adapted to take account of new or changed risks;
❚ take place during working hours.

Training design and delivery

Jeremy Stranks makes some valid points in *A Manager's Guide to Health and Safety at Work* (2003) for those learning architects who have accountability, responsibility and authority for the design and delivery of health and safety training. In order for health and safety training activities to be successful and effective at conveying the appropriate messages to staff, the following points will be useful to bear in mind:

❚ Develop a list of topics to be covered: for example, manual handling, fire evacuation, and personal protective equipment. Specific programmes can then be formulated.
❚ Sessions often work better when they are bite-sized, that is, around 30–45 minutes long.
❚ Visual aids such as flip charts, video and posters are effective.
❚ Topics, as far as possible, should be relevant to the group or individuals.
❚ Participation needs to be encouraged to gain a sense of the understanding at the time of training. The learning from health and safety training needs to be effective. There is often no chance for a practice in a safety situation. The fire equipment has to be operated correctly, first time.
❚ As with most training the language used should be understood, and translation needs to be offered. The use of technical, scientific or legal terms without a thorough explanation is to be avoided.
❚ The environment and delivery should be conducive to learning. A too formal classroom environment can be counter-productive for many learners. Training providers need to balance informality with ensuring the seriousness of the subject is relayed.

SKILLS SHORTAGE

An acute lack of skilled workers is jeopardizing the competitiveness of UK businesses in every sector of the economy, from engineering and construction to healthcare and IT. Skills shortages and gaps are also apparent at all levels of employment, from shop floor workers to senior management. Many people lack even the basics such as literacy and numeracy – a situation that is costing UK employers £10bn a year. These were the findings of the National Employers Skills Survey – the largest research of its kind – that was carried out by the Learning Skills Council (LSC) IN 2003.

(IOD/LSC, 2004)

The core message of *Skills: Transforming business,* from which that quote is taken, is that businesses need to acknowledge skills shortage or gaps, and adopt a systematic approach to upskilling their workforce. A retort from many learning architects is that they believe their organizations have been let down by the education system, and surely it is the job of schools, colleges and universities to provide learners with the basic skills. A belief held by many is that the skills shortage or gap has probably been caused by a combination of: education not providing what employers want, and organizations not providing basic and ongoing training to ensure their staff have the skills required for the future.

The demise some decades ago of training boards, through which organizations had mandatory levies placed on them in order to provide training, may have contributed to the lack of investment. Skills-based training in the form of apprenticeships has all but disappeared in many UK organizations. Witness the lack of technicians in the motor industry, as many organizations scrapped or downsized their apprenticeship schemes. This has led to their seeking skilled technicians from other countries in order to fill the gap.

The cry from many organizations that have cut their training provision for core workplace skills is that if they train employees they will only leave to join competitors. Companies argue that they will not waste money on training when they can recruit from a competitor by offering more benefits. The result, a few years on, is that there is an acute shortage for all organizations, and for some trades the pool of skilled workers is becoming smaller and smaller. The topic of engaging employees so that they do not leave to go to a competitor is explored later in the chapter.

With an increasing ethnically diverse workforce, where English is often not a first language, new challenges are facing organizations. They have had to adapt the main language of communication, or provide language education for those staff who have a need to communicate in a language other than their own. It would seem a tall order for learning architects to take on the task of changing a trend that has been gathering momentum for many years, but what you can do is to become instrumental in trying to shift the trend with the assistance of other stakeholders. Learning architects of all types need to become aware of the role they can play, through being instrumental in creating a strategy for their own organization or by influencing what is provided by education through becoming involved with the provider.

What to do within your own organization

Skills audit

Understanding the skills shortage or gap in your own organization would seem a sensible place to start. A skills audit will help an organization to:

▌ identify existing skills;
▌ identify what further skills are needed to carry out existing strategy;
▌ plan, develop and improve the skills and knowledge needed for the future.

The ability of the different types of learning architect to carry out a skills audit will vary. The corporate learning architect will have the in-house resources and in-depth knowledge of the corporate and learning strategy to carry out a thorough skills audit. This should be part of the ongoing role of the learning function, one of the integral responsibilities of the function. The tactical learning architect will probably be close to the corporate strategy, and will have made efforts to align any learning strategy with it. He or she is unlikely to have the resources internally to carry out a skills audit, and may have to carry out the audit personally or bring in consultants.

Learning architects type 3 are unlikely to have the skills or resources to carry out an audit. The issues typically facing a functional learning architect may well be caused, in the main, by a skills shortage and gaps. There is a demand from other managers for quick-fix training, coupled with an inability to find any time for staff to train because of staff shortages. All these symptoms point to a skills shortage or gap. The learning architect type 3 has to make managers aware of the problem, and suggest having a skills audit carried out.

A learning architect type 4 will be very aware of any skills shortage or gap, as he or she is probably providing learning and training for employees who have a skills gap. Large gaps in organizations are being plugged by the efforts of individual learning architects who are formally or informally providing workplace training and learning in the form of coaching. The learning architect type 4 could be instrumental in being part of a team that carries out a skills audit, a suggestion he or she may want to make to the relevant person.

The issue for all learning architects is whether the organization has a sense of where and what it wants to be in the future, and whether those ambitions have been documented in the form of a strategy. This is a recurring theme for many learning professionals who are trying to build an architecture. If it is not known what the organization needs for the future, how will it know if it has a skills shortage or gap, real or potential?

Develop a skills strategy

A skills strategy has to be aligned to the business strategy, and will be constructed along the lines developed elsewhere in the book. A skills shortage that required a strategy for future organizational success is that of IT in the National Health Service. It is a 'hot topic' for learning architects within the National Health Service, who face the challenge of ensuring the majority of employees are deemed competent to use the new technology that comes with the introduction of electronic records for all employees and patients. The decision to use one standard, across the Health Service, as the measure of competence requires a huge resource to be used in training and then evaluating skills. One tactical learning architect said, 'The implementation of this one initiative will use up the entire training budget and will require a full-time trainer, the use of local colleges and online packages.'

The need for IT skills is not something unique to the National Health Service. In research carried out by e-skills UK, the sector skills council for the IT industry found:

I nine out of ten jobs require IT skills;
I seventy-five per cent of British companies claim that employee time is wasted through lack of computing skills;
I under-trained users are six times more likely to require IT support than adequately trained users.

Upskilling existing employees

A question asked by many learning architects is where their organization can get help and assistance with basic skills training, and what funding is available. Some of the bodies and initiatives offering assistance to learning architects present at the network meeting were:

I **The Learning Skills Council**, which has the challenging role of investing public money in vocational education and training to deliver the skills employers and individuals need, for those who are over 16 years of age. It delivers this through the following initiatives, some of which are only available in certain geographic areas.

- Apprenticeships. Apprentices learn through a combination of on and off-job education and training. Apprenticeships are currently available in 80 sectors.
- Employer training pilots (ETPs). These help employees by offering employees entitlement to a minimum amount of paid time off during working time, and financial support for employers to compensate them. ETPs offer basic numeracy and literacy training as well as opportunities to study for NVQ level 2.
- Employer skills offer. The primary objective of this scheme is to engage with and support employers that have not previously invested in workforce development. Employers can access the scheme through brokers such as a business link advisor.

▌ **The Union Learning Fund** supports partnership projects to develop work-based learning opportunities for employees. The fund has helped train over 10,000 union learning representatives, who advise union members about training and educational development. The representatives have helped many members develop new skills and update existing ones, particularly basic literacy, numeracy and IT skills. A learning architect type 4 may well be functioning in this role.

▌ **Get On Campaign.** This is a Department for Education and Skills initiative that focuses on adults who are in the workplace but have language, literacy or numeracy needs.

▌ **Sector skills councils** are employer-led and actively involve trade unions, professional bodies and other stakeholders in the sector to address its skill and productivity needs. Many learning architects of all types have become involved in sector skills councils, whereby they can gain influence for their own organization, the sector and themselves.

▌ **Investors in People** is a tried and tested framework that assists organizations to provide consistent identification, implementation and evaluation of learning and development needs.

▌ **Learndirect business** provides online learning solutions for organizations.

What to do outside your organization

Business leaders are often in the press complaining that schools, colleges and universities do not provide the relevant skills for the employees of today, and the skills they do instil are lacking in quality and application.

A direct way of addressing this is for learning architects to not only involve themselves with local education providers, but encourage senior management to do so too. The benefits for an organization that has a manager who takes a role as a governor or some other advisory capacity are that they:

I will be better placed to influence the overall direction of course development;
I are able to make courses more relevant to the immediate needs of the organization;
I discover what funding might be available;
I find out where the most appropriate courses are;
I attract potential new employees;
I raise the profile of the organization within the community;
I network with other managers;
I increase knowledge and understanding of learning strategy at different levels, locally and nationally.

Other learning architects have become members of their local learning skills council, where they have an opportunity to be involved in more strategic decisions about funding and the allocation of resources arising from government initiatives.

The UK is not the only country facing a skills shortage; some states in Australia are also suffering an acute shortage of skilled workers, particularly in the building and construction industry. An interesting project is being pioneered in Queensland by a state high school. In response to the national skills shortages the school's industrial technology staff redesigned their construction and engineering courses to provide a seamless progression of students through to industry. This is an example of a learning architect from education working closely with learning architects in organizations to provide an industry with exactly what it wants in terms of trainees and their relevant skills.

The school's learning architect designed a programme in conjunction with companies from construction and building, whereby students participate in real-life work situations, designed and supported by industry. Traditional apprenticeships were not working. Young people faced enormous difficulties gaining access to real-life work experiences in the building and construction industries because of the transitory nature of work sites and access to transport. This, combined with the fact that they are thrown in at the 'deep end' with no real knowledge of what is required of them, usually makes them lose interest and give up. The school has created a factory which offers a transition experience where students participate in real-life learning experiences while still in a familiar environment.

In the construction class students make frames and trusses for local builders, and in engineering they make box trailers to order which are sold to the public. They also make bracketry for one of the main industry sponsors. The philosophy is that the students are coming to work, not school. They learn their way around the workplace, using real tools and working in teams instead of carrying out individual projects. Students make the transition to full-time working in the sponsoring organization, by spending increasingly more time in the organization.

The head of department, the learning architect with the vision, says, 'This is a model that can be adapted anywhere. Anywhere you have got a school that has an industry connection, you can use this template, and it does not matter if you are talking automotive or bricklaying. The teachers bring the students, industry brings the support.'

ENGAGEMENT

The topic of skills shortage and gaps leads to the subject of engagement. The link between engaged employees and their commitment to not only staying with an organization but being more productive has been demonstrated through a number of research projects carried out over recent years.

The shortage of employees with relevant skills, and the need to retain staff who have the skills and/or learning capabilities for the organization, mean that many employers are turning their attention on what to do to retain this valuable resource. An audit published by the CIPD (Guest and Conway 2004) identified three distinct groups of employees in terms of attitudes to their employment and career:

I traditionalists, highly committed to their organization and highly motivated;

I disengaged, not driven by work and lacking strong commitment to their organization;

I independent, primarily interested in their own career prospects and with no allegiance to any one organization.

While it is important to keep the traditionalist motivated and committed, the primary focus for managers is how to gain buy-in from the other two groups in order to engage them. Research has discovered that engagement involves more than just offering financial incentives, and is about employees feeling valued and involved. While HR functions have a significant role to play in harnessing all the benefits that can engage the disengaged and independents, learning architects have a contribution to make through the learning initiatives they provide.

If employees need to feel valued and involved, a learning event, if correctly planned and delivered, will add to their sense of value and involvement. Learning architects should be aware, in their move towards self-managed learning from more directed training, that employees may not feel so involved and valued. The invitation to attend a training course is very often perceived by an employee as recognition of achievement, that someone has noticed them. The rituals that go with training courses, such as social events, overnight accommodation at a hotel or training venue, and the opportunity to meet participants from their own and other organizations, adds significantly to the feeling of value and involvement. Learning architects have to add engagement to their checklist when designing and evaluating a learning event.

E-LEARNING

E-learning has come a long way since it arrived on the learning scene with some significance at the turn of the century. Most learning architects will have had some experience of e-learning. These range from being an interested or sceptical participant on early learning programmes through to being the champion of major e-learning initiatives within an organization.

The learning architects we encountered seemed keen to share their experiences of implementing e-learning in terms of: 'mistakes to avoid in the future' or 'how to do it better next time'. You may well be a learning architect who has learnt through your mistakes and has a well formed strategy for implementing, sustaining and developing e-learning within an organization. For those of you who are less well travelled in the e-learning world we share some of the hints, tips and suggestions that our contributors were keen to tell us.

The e-learning strategy should be part of the overall learning strategy and designed to support the business objectives of the organization

This is a reminder for any learning architect designing any learning intervention. Somehow we need a stronger reminder when e-learning is involved. It is as if we forget the core principles of what learning and training are there to achieve. Perhaps the excitement of a new medium can sometimes get in the way and the means becomes the end.

Remember that e-learning is about learning, not process

It is easy for the principles of learning to diminish or disappear as the technical processes come into play. The 'e' in e-learning means that the mode has a background in IT, and for the less than IT savvy learning architect there is a temptation to be swept along by the technology and forget that the 'e' is the method, not the outcome.

Learning programmes need to connect with a learning management system (LMS) in a manner that provides meaningful information

The information you receive from the LMS needs to provide you with more information than the number of users who have logged on. As one learning architect commented, 'It is no good getting all excited that you have had 200 learners to the site if they only made it to the second screen'. Questions, tasks and feedback activities need to be built in to encourage the learners through the programme, and to enable to learning site managers to know that the learning has been completed. One learning architect had an induction programme designed so that parts of the programme have no action keys, ensuring that learners do not skip through activities.

The justification for e-learning needs to be more than cost reduction

Many organizations are lured away from more traditional methods of delivering learning and training because of what appear to be immediate cost savings: not having to pay for internal and external trainers, venues to hold training, accommodation, travel costs and time away from the business often makes e-learning seem a viable option. Learning architects need to dig deeper than the initial cost savings, look at return on investment, and employ the evaluation methods they would usually use for more traditional methods of delivery (see Chapter 5).

E-learning needs to be driven by the opportunities it provides for the organization

Many e-learning programmes are driven by the technology, and are viewed as a technology decision and solution, and not in terms of what they will deliver for the organization.

Put learners first

Some e-learning initiatives fail to meet expectations because the organization has failed to take the learners' perceptions into account. How accessible is the hardware? How easy is it to use? How much time will it take? Have the learners used anything like it before? What peer pressure is there going to be? Have adequate time and support resources been allocated? What is the environment like? What limiting beliefs might learners have? What incentive is there to learn? How relevant is the learning for the learners' situation? These are all issues that need to be taken into account when designing any learning programme, but even more thought needs to be given when changing a whole method of delivery.

The initiative requires management buy-in and support

This applies to any programme, but the success of e-learning seems to need management support to a greater degree. If managers have not embraced the new method of delivery and there is no evidence that they are using the technology, there will be little impetus for learners to 'have a go'.

The remote nature of the learning means that managers are required to support learners in a way they may not have done when using more traditional classroom-style learning. The learner is isolated, and the immediate support and feedback provided by a trainer in the classroom or workplace may need to be replaced by the line manager. This may be a function that learning architect type 4 is providing.

Bridge the transition from instructor-led training

The new method of delivering learning through e-learning may be a step too far for many individuals, and some organizations have recognized this by creating a transition. A mixture of traditional instructor-led learning and training with some e-learning helps learners to make the shift. This is an initiative that may have given rise to the term 'blended learning'.

Market e-learning

Engage the marketing function if you have one, or create a cross-functional team to spread the word about e-learning. Learning architects have: developed roadshows to deliver the message and provide taster sessions to learners, spread the good news stories and success through the usual available methods of communication, and provided incentives for learners in terms of certificates, prizes, team and individual challenges.

Test

Failing to adequately test e-learning in an organization can lead to some unwanted outcomes. Develop a pilot which includes all types of learners, and test the usability of the product, the system, the learning unit and regression. The temptation to go live with an initiative because of deadlines should be resisted if the pilot does not provide the outcomes that indicate a successful launch into the rest of the organization.

CHAPTER SUMMARY

▌ The popular issues occupying the thoughts of learning architects are: coaching, diversity, health and safety, the skills shortage, engagement and e-learning.

▌ Legislation and best practice require learning architects to be aware of and congruent with the requirements of their organization and society in general.

▌ The demand for learning to be delivered effectively and quickly with fewer resources requires learning architects to be 'up to speed' with what must be learnt and how to deliver that learning.

▌ A learning architect who can contribute to popular debate on current issues increases his or her own reputation as a contributor to their organization and the world of learning.

▌ Issues that are current for today may well be replaced by new topics in the future.

▌ Learning architects can learn from the experiences of others in the present and past, and through modelling excellent learning, use their own learning for the future.

▌ There appear to be no easy answers and short-cuts to some issues, but the debate is always interesting.

References

Bandler, Richard (1993) *Time for Change*, Meta Publications, California

CIPD (2004a) *Helping people learn*, research report, Chartered Institute for Personnel and Development, London

CIPD (2004b) *Training and Development Survey*, CIPD, London

CIPD (2004c) Information from CIPD website, www.cipd.org.uk

Clements, Phil and Jones, John (2002) *The Diversity Training Handbook*, Kogan Page, London

Dilts, Robert (1991) *Tools for Dreamers*, Meta Publications, California

Dilts, Robert (1998) *Modelling with NLP*, Meta Publications, California

Friedman, Thomas L (2000) *The Lexus and the Olive Tree*, Anchor Books, London

Guest, D and Conway, N (2004) *Employee Well-Being and the Psychological Contract*, research report, CIPD, London

Honey, P and Mumford, A (1982) *Manual of Learning Styles*, Peter Honey Publications, Maidenhead

Institute of Directors and Learning and Skills Council (2004) *Skills: Transforming Business*, IOD and LSC, London

Johnson, Gerry and Scholes, Kevan (1993) *Exploring Corporate Strategy*, Prentice Hall, London

Kline, Nancy (1999) *Time To Think*, Ward Lock, London

Starr, Julie (2003) *The Coaching Manual*, Pearson Education, London

Stranks, J (2003) *A Manager's Guide to Health and Safety at Work*, Kogan Page, London

FURTHER READING

Coach the Coach (2004, 2005) Fenman, Cambridge

Covey, Stephen R (1998) *Seven Habits of Highly Effective People*, Simon & Schuster, London

Dilts, Robert (1990) *Changing Belief Systems with NLP*, Meta Publications, California

Handy, Charles (1994) *The Empty Raincoat*, Hutchinson, London

Hunsaker, Philip (2001) *Training in Management Skills*, Pearson, Canada

Kanter, Rosabeth M (1989) *When Giants Learn to Dance*, Simon & Schuster, London

Katzenbach, J and Smith, D (1993) *The Wisdom of Teams*, Harvard University Press, Cambridge, Mass.

Lambert, Tom (1996) *The Power of Influence*, Nicholas Brearley, London

Mayo, Andrew (1998) *Creating a Training and Development Strategy*, CIPD, London

McCain, Donald (2005) *Evaluation Basics*, ASTD Press, Alexandria

Peltier, Bruce (2001) *The Psychology of Executive Coaching*, Brunner-Routledge, New York

Peters, Tom (1992) *Liberation Management*, Macmillan, London

Peters, Tom (1997) *The Circle of Innovation*, Hodder and Stoughton, London

Phillips, Jack (2004) *Making Training Evaluation Work*, ASTD Press, Alexandria

Singh, R P (2002) *Management of Training Programmes*, Anmol, New Delhi

Thorne, Kaye and Mackey, David (1996) *Everything You Ever Wanted to Know about Training*, Kogan Page, London

United Nations (2000) *United Nations Expert Group on Managing Diversity in the Civil Service* [online] www.un.org

Waitley, Denis E (1984) *The Psychology of Winning*, Berkley, New York

Waitley, Denis E (1984) *Seeds of Greatness*, Pocket Books, New York

Weafer, Seán (2004) Building powerful rapport, *Coach the Coach*, issue 2.

Index